This Book Comes With a Website

Nolo's award-winning website has a page dedicated just to this book, where you can:

DOWNLOAD FORMS – All the forms and worksheets in the book are accessible online

KEEP UP TO DATE – When there are important changes to the information in this book, we'll post updates

READ BLOGS – Get the latest info from Nolo authors' blogs

LISTEN TO PODCASTS – Listen to authors discuss timely issues on topics that interest you

WATCH VIDEOS – Get a quick introduction to a legal topic with our short videos

You'll find the link in the appendix.

And that's not all.
Nolo.com contains thousands of articles on everyday legal and business issues, plus a plain-English law dictionary, all written by Nolo experts and available for free. You'll also find more useful **books, software, online services,** and **downloadable forms.**

Get forms and more at
www.nolo.com

15th Edition

How to Form Your Own California Corporation

Attorney Anthony Mancuso

FIFTEENTH Edition	FEBRUARY 2013
Editor	DIANA FITZPATRICK
Cover Design	SUSAN PUTNEY
Book Design	TERRI HEARSH
Proofreader	ROBERT WELLS
Index	BAYSIDE INDEXING SERVICE
Printing	BANG PRINTING

Mancuso, Anthony.
How to form your own California corporation / Anthony Mancuso. -- 15th ed.
p. cm.
Summary: "Learn about: - different types of California corporations and how they work - filing articles of incorporation - corporate taxes"-- Provided by publisher.
ISBN 978-1-4133-1827-2 (pbk.) -- ISBN 978-1-4133-1828-9 (epub ebook)
1. Close corporations--California. 2. Incorporation--California. I. Title.
KFC357.C55M36 2013
346.794'0668--dc23
2012038384

Please note

We believe accurate, plain-English legal information should help you solve many of your own legal problems. But this text is not a substitute for personalized advice from a knowledgeable lawyer. If you want the help of a trained professional—and we'll always point out situations in which we think that's a good idea—consult an attorney licensed to practice in your state.

Acknowledgments

Special thanks to Diana Fitzpatrick, my editor. Also thanks to the production and design staff and all the other hardworking people at Nolo for their help in making it all happen.

About the Author

Anthony Mancuso is a corporations and limited liability company expert. He graduated from Hastings College of the Law in San Francisco, is an active member of the California State Bar, writes books and software in the fields of corporate and LLC law, and has studied advanced business taxation at Golden Gate University in San Francisco. He also has been a consultant for Silicon Valley EDA (Electronic Design Automation) and other technology companies, most recently working on a C++ open-source integrated circuit database project team.

Tony is the author of many Nolo books on forming and operating corporations, profit and nonprofit, and limited liability companies. Among his books are *Incorporate Your Business, How to Form a Nonprofit Corporation, Form Your Own Limited Liability Company, Your Limited Liability Company: An Operating Manual, LLC or Corporation?* and *The Corporate Records Handbook*. His books have shown over a quarter of a million businesses and organizations how to form and operate a corporation or LLC.

Tony has lectured at Boalt Hall (Berkeley Law, University of California) and at Stanford Law School. He taught Saturday Morning Law School business formation and operation courses for several years at Nolo's offices in Berkeley. He has also scripted and narrated several audio tapes and podcasts covering LLCs and corporate formations and other legal areas for Nolo as well as The Company Corporation. He writes articles for and hosts the Nolo blog, *LLC and Corporation Small Talk*. He has given many recorded and live radio and TV presentations and interviews over the years covering business, securities, and tax law issues. His law and tax articles and interviews have appeared in *The Wall Street Journal* and *TheStreet.com*.

Tony is a licensed helicopter pilot and has performed for years as a guitarist in various musical idioms. Currently, he works at Google.org in Mountain View, California.

Table of Contents

Your Incorporation Companion

Corporations are not only for the big financial players—they are an excellent way to organize and run a small business. They provide a number of built-in layers to help you organize, manage, and run your business, and they can help you attract talent and equity so your business can succeed.

More importantly, corporations provide legal liability protection so that you—as the owner of your business—are shielded from the debts, obligations, and lawsuits of your business. In today's volatile business world, this type of protection is more needed than ever. You don't want to be personally exposed in the event your business gets in trouble and can't pay bills as they become due. Forming a corporation can give you the peace of mind you need to keep going with your business in these turbulent economic times.

Don't be daunted by the seeming complexity of corporate law and taxation. Once you get a handle on the basics, you can understand and accomplish most of the routine decisions and paperwork necessary to start and run your own corporation.

To help you decide whether a corporation is right for you, we provide information that explains the laws and tax requirements that apply to privately held corporations, including:

- the legal and tax laws and procedures that apply to forming and running a California corporation, and
- how to approach and handle securities law issues and formalities at the state and federal level.

If you decide to incorporate in California, this book shows you how to:

- prepare articles of incorporation, bylaws, initial board minutes, and state securities exemption forms to organize your California corporation, and
- what you will need to do after you incorporate.

The material in this book respects your intelligence and business smarts. It highlights areas of complexity and potential customization as you proceed along your incorporation path. It not only gives you the basics, but also scratches below the surface to expose potential areas of tax and legal complexity that may require the help of a legal or tax adviser. To help you clear any of these special hurdles, we explain our approach to finding a legal or tax coach—namely, an expert who will work with you to get the job done efficiently and at a lower cost.

If you are thinking about incorporating in California and want to learn more about the legal and tax rules that are attached to doing business as a corporation, the beginning chapters will help you. If you end up deciding to form your own California corporation, the later chapters will show you the way.

Get Forms, Updates, and More Online

You can download any of the forms in this book at:
www.nolo.com/back-of-book/CCOR.html.
If there are important changes to the information in this book, we'll post updates there. And you can find other useful information there too, including author blogs, podcasts, and videos.

CHAPTER

1

Choosing the Right Legal Structure for Your Business

To help you make sure that forming a California corporation is the best legal and tax choice for your business, this chapter compares the California corporation to other small business legal structures. Our discussion is based upon recent tax and legal rule changes, and—most significantly—the rise in use of the limited liability company. This relatively new business structure shares some of the traditional legal and tax qualities of the corporation, while at the same time offering some of the less formal attributes of a partnership. The corporation continues, however, to stand apart from all other business forms because of its built-in organizational structure and unique access to investment sources and capital markets. It also continues to uniquely answer to a need felt by many business owners for the formality of the corporate form, a quality not shared by the other business structures.

The Different Ways of Doing Business

There are several legal structures or forms you can use to operate a business, including a sole proprietorship, partnership, limited liability company, or corporation. Two of these structures have important variants: The partnership form has spawned the limited partnership and the registered limited liability partnership. And the corporation can be recognized, for tax purposes, as either the standard C corporation or an S corporation. In a standard C corporation, the corporation and its owners are treated as separate taxpaying entities, whereas in an S corporation, business income is passed through the corporate entity and the owners are taxed on their individual tax returns.

Often, business owners start with the simplest legal form, the sole proprietorship, then move on to a more complicated business structure as their business grows. Other businesspeople pick the legal structure they like best from the start, and let their business grow into it. Either way, choosing the legal structure for your business is an important decision you must make when starting a business. The analysis that follows, which includes examples of businesses that might sensibly choose each type of business structure, should help you make a good decision.

RESOURCE

Nolo can help you find the right lawyer. If you decide you need some legal assistance at any point, Nolo's Lawyer Directory offers comprehensive profiles of the lawyers who advertise, including each attorney's education, background, areas of expertise, fees, and practice philosophy. It also states whether the lawyer is willing to review documents or coach clients who are doing their own legal work. You can find Nolo's Lawyer Directory at www.nolo.com/lawyers.

Sole Proprietorship

A sole proprietorship is the legal name for a one-owner business. It is the easiest business entity to establish. Just hang out your shingle or "Open for Business" sign, and you have established a sole proprietorship. Sure, there are other legal steps you may wish to take—such as registering a fictitious business name different from your own individual name by filing a "dba statement" with the county clerk—but these steps are not necessary to establish your business legally.

Personal liability for business debts, liabilities, and taxes. In this simplest form of small business legal structures, the owner, who usually runs the business, is personally liable for its debts, taxes, and other liabilities. Also, if the owner hires employees, he or she is personally responsible for claims made against these employees acting within the course and scope of their employment.

Simple tax treatment. All business profits (and losses) are reported on the owner's personal income tax return each year (using Schedule C, *Profit or Loss From Business,* filed with the owner's 1040 federal income tax return). And this remains true even if a portion of this money is invested back in the business—that is, even if the owner doesn't pocket business profits for personal use.

Legal life same as owner's. On the death of its owner, a sole proprietorship simply ends. The assets of the business normally pass under the terms of the deceased owner's will or trust, or by intestate succession (under the state's inheritance statutes) if there is no formal estate plan.

CAUTION

Don't let business assets get stuck in probate. The court process necessary to probate a will can take more than a year. In the meantime, it may be difficult for the inheritors to operate or sell the business or its assets. Often, the best way to avoid having a probate court involved in business operations is for the owner to transfer the assets of the business into a living trust during his or her lifetime; this permits business assets to be transferred to inheritors promptly on the death of the business owner, free of probate. For detailed information on estate planning, including whether or not it makes sense to create a living trust, see *Plan Your Estate,* by Denis Clifford (Nolo).

Sole proprietorships in action. Many one-owner or spouse-owned businesses start small with very little advance planning or procedural red tape. Celia Wong is a good example—Celia is a graphic artist with a full-time salaried job for a local book publishing company. In her spare time she takes on extra work using her home computer to produce audio cassette and CD jacket cover art for musicians. These jobs are usually commissioned on a handshake or phone call. Without thinking much about it, Celia has started her own sole proprietorship business. Celia should include a Schedule C in her yearly federal 1040 individual tax return, showing the net profits (profits minus expenses) or losses of her sole proprietorship. Celia is responsible for paying income taxes on profits, plus self-employment (Social Security) taxes based on her sole proprietorship income (IRS Form SE is used to compute self-employment taxes; Celia attaches it to her 1040 income tax return).

If Celia has any business debts (she usually owes money on a charge account at a local art supply house), or a disgruntled client successfully sues her in small claims court for failing to deliver prepaid art work, Celia is personally liable to pay this money. In other words, she can't simply fold up Wong Designs and walk away from her debts claiming that they are the legal responsibility of her business only.

CAUTION

Put some profits aside to buy business insurance. Once Celia begins to make enough money, she should consider taking out a commercial liability insurance policy to cover legal claims against her business. While insurance normally won't protect you from business mistakes (like performing incomplete or late work or failing to pay bills), it can cover many risks including slip-and-fall lawsuits, damage to your or a client's property, or fire, theft, and other casualties that might occur in a home-based business.

Running the business as an informal sole proprietorship serves Celia's needs for the present. Assuming her small business succeeds, she will eventually need to put it on a more formal footing by establishing a separate business checking account, possibly coming

Businesses Co-Owned by Spouses

Spouses in all states who work together and share profits and losses in an unincorporated business can elect to be taxed as a "qualified joint venture." This designation means they get treated as sole proprietors for tax purposes. To qualify, the couple must be the only owners of the unincorporated business and they must both "materially participate" in the business. The spouses must also file a joint Form 1040 with two separate Schedule Cs showing each spouse's share of the profits. Each spouse includes a self-employment tax schedule (Schedule SE) to pay self-employment tax on their share of the profits. If the couple qualifies for this exception, each spouse gets Social Security credit for his or her share of earnings in the business.

What if a couple jointly own their business as an LLC? In this case, the spouses will normally be treated as partners and must file a partnership tax return for the LLC. However, if the couple lives in one of the nine community property states (Arizona, California, Idaho, Louisiana, Nevada, New Mexico, Texas, Washington, and Wisconsin), then they have the option of treating their business as a sole proprietorship. They do this by filing an IRS Form 1040 Schedule C for the business, listing one of the spouses as the owner. There is no requirement that both spouses materially participate in the business, so this election is easier than the qualified joint venture status described above.

Only the listed spouse pays income and self-employment taxes on the reported Schedule C net profits. This means only the listed Schedule C owner-spouse will receive Social Security account earning credits for the Form SE taxes paid with the 1040 return. For this reason, some eligible spouses will decide not to make this Schedule C filing and will continue to file a partnership tax return for their jointly owned spousal LLC. Also, the IRS treats the filing of a Schedule C for a jointly owned spousal LLC as the conversion of a partnership to a sole proprietorship, which can have tax consequences.

Finally, if one spouse manages the business and the other helps out as an employee or volunteer worker (but does not contribute to running the business), the managing spouse can claim ownership and treat the business as a sole proprietorship.

For more information on spousal businesses, see "Forming a Partnership" in IRS Publication 541 and "Husband and Wife Business" and other information on the IRS website at www.irs.gov. In all cases, be sure to check with your tax adviser before deciding on the best way to own, file, and pay taxes for, a spousal business.

up with a fancier name and registering it as a dba with the county clerk. If she hires employees, she will need to obtain a federal Employer Identification Number (EIN) from the IRS. She may also feel ready to renovate her house to separate her office space from her living quarters (this can also help make the portion of the mortgage or rent paid for the office deductible as a business expense on her Schedule C).

Celia can do all of this and still keep her sole proprietorship legal status. Unless her business grows significantly or she takes on work that puts her at a much higher risk of being sued—and therefore being held personally liable for business debts—it makes sense for her to continue to operate her business as a sole proprietorship.

RESOURCE

A great source of practical information on how to start and operate a small sole proprietorship is *Small Time Operator,* by Bernard Kamoroff (Bell Springs Press). Also, see *Tax Savvy for Small Business,* by Frederick W. Daily (Nolo), a small business guide to taxes, which includes a full discussion of setting up and deducting the expenses of a home-based business.

Partnership

A partnership is simply an enterprise in which two or more co-owners agree to share in the profits of a business activity. No written partnership agreement is necessary. If two people go into business together, and do not incorporate or form a limited liability company, they automatically establish a legal partnership. Partnerships are governed by each state's partnership law. But since all states have adopted a version of the Uniform Partnership Act, laws are very similar throughout the United States. Mostly, these laws contain basic rules that provide for an equal division of profits and losses among partners and establish the partners' legal relationship with one another. These rules are not mandatory in most cases, and you can (and should) spell out your own rules for dividing profits and losses and operating your partnership in a written partnership agreement. If you don't prepare your own partnership agreement, all provisions of California's partnership law apply to your partnership.

A general partnership has the following characteristics:

Each partner has personal liability. Like the owner of a sole proprietorship, each partner is personally liable for the debts and taxes of the partnership. In other words, if the partnership assets and insurance are insufficient to satisfy a creditor's claim or legal judgment, the partners' personal assets can be attached and sold to pay the debt.

The act or signature of each partner can bind the partnership. Each partner is an agent for the partnership and can individually hire employees, borrow money, sign contracts, and perform any act necessary to the operation of the business. All partners are personally liable for these debts and obligations. This rule makes it essential that the partners trust each other to act in the best interests of the partnership and each of the other partners.

Partners report and pay individual income taxes on profits. A partnership files a yearly IRS Form 1065, *U.S. Partnership Return of Income*, which includes a schedule showing the allocation of profits, losses, and other tax items to all partners (Schedule K). The partnership must mail individual schedules (Schedule K-1s) to each partner at the end of each year, showing the items of income, loss, credits, and deductions allocated to each partner. When a partner files an individual income tax return, she reports her allocated share of partnership profits (taken from the partner's Schedule

K-1), and pays individual income taxes on these profits. As with the sole proprietorship, partners owe tax on business profits even if they are plowed back into the business.

Partnerships Can Choose to Be Taxed as Corporations

Unincorporated co-owned businesses, including partnerships and limited liability companies (discussed below), can choose to be taxed as corporations by filing IRS Form 8832, *Entity Classification Election*. Most smaller partnerships will not wish to make this election, preferring instead to have profits divided among the partners and then taxed on their individual tax returns. But this is not always true. For example, some partnerships—especially those that want to reinvest profits in expanding the business—may prefer to keep profits in the business, and have them taxed to the business at the lower initial corporate tax rates. Your tax adviser can tell you if this tax strategy makes sense for your business. (See Chapter 7.)

Partnership dissolves when a partner leaves. Legally, when a partner ceases to be associated with carrying on the business of the partnership (when he or she withdraws or dies), the partnership is dissolved. However, a properly written partnership agreement provides in advance for these eventualities, and allows for the continuation of the partnership by permitting the remaining partners to buy out the interest of the departing or deceased partner. Of course, if one person in a two-partner business leaves or dies, the partnership is legally dissolved—you need at least two people to have a partnership.

CAUTION

Watch out for a partnership tax termination. A partnership terminates for tax purposes if 50% or more of the interest in the partnership's capital and profits are sold or exchanged within a 12-month period. Under these circumstances, the partnership might continue legally under the terms of the partnership agreement, but would terminate for tax purposes. Upon the deemed termination of partnership, each partner could owe significant income taxes. (I.R.C. § 708(b).)

RESOURCE

For a much more thorough look at the legal and tax characteristics of partnerships, and for a clause-by-clause approach to preparing a partnership agreement, see *Form a Partnership*, by Ralph Warner and Denis Clifford (Nolo).

Partnerships in action. George and Tamatha are good friends who have been working together in a rented warehouse space where they share a kiln used to make blown glass pieces. They recently collaborated on the design and production of a batch of hand-blown halogen light fixtures, which immediately become popular with local lighting vendors. Believing that they can streamline the production of these custom pieces, they plan to solicit and fill larger orders with retailers, and look into wholesale distribution. They shake hands on their new venture, which they name "Halo Light Sculptures." Although they obtain a business license and file a dba statement with the county clerk showing that they are working together as "Halo Light Sculptures," they don't bother to write up a partnership agreement. Their only agreement is a verbal one to equally share in the work of making the glass pieces and splitting expenses and any profits that result.

California Limited Partnerships

Most smaller partnerships are general partnerships—this means that all owners agree to manage the partnership together, and each partner is personally liable for debts of the partnership. However, there are two other fairly common types of partnerships: limited partnerships and registered limited liability partnerships (RLLPs). Each of these is quite different from a general partnership.

The Limited Partnership. The limited partnership structure is used when one or more of the partners are passive investors (called "limited partners") and another partner (called a "general partner") runs the partnership. A certificate of limited partnership is filed with the secretary of state to form a limited partnership, and a filing fee must be paid. The advantage of a limited partnership is that, unlike a general partnership where all partners are personally liable for business debts and liabilities, a limited partner is allowed to invest in a partnership without the risk of incurring personal liability for the debts of the business. If the business fails, all that the limited partner can lose is his or her capital investment—the amount of money or the property paid for an interest in the business. However, in exchange for this big advantage, the limited partner normally is not allowed to participate in the management or control of the partnership. To do so means losing limited liability status and being held personally liable for partnership debts, claims, and other obligations.

Typically, a limited partnership has a number of limited partner investors and one general partner (there can be more, but there must be at least one) who is responsible for partnership management and is personally liable for its debts and other liabilities.

The Registered Limited Liability Partnership. The registered limited liability partnership (RLLP) is a special legal structure designed for persons who form a partnership in California to perform the licensed professional services of attorneys, accountants, or architects. (Architects can form a California RLLP until January 1, 2019.) An RLLP is formed by filing a registration of limited liability partnership form with the California Secretary of State.

The point of an RLLP is to relieve professional partners from personal liability for debts, contracts, and claims against the partnership, including claims against a nonparticipating partner for professional malpractice by another partner. However, a professional in an RLLP remains personally liable for his or her own professional malpractice.

> **EXAMPLE:** Martha and Veronica have a two-person accounting partnership, registered as an RLLP. Each has her own clients. If Martha loses a malpractice lawsuit, and Veronica did not participate in providing services to that client, Veronica should not be held personally liable for the judgment. If Martha's malpractice insurance and partnership assets are not sufficient to pay the judgment, Martha's personal assets, but not Veronica's, are subject to seizure to satisfy the unrecovered judgment. If they had an accounting general partnership practice that was not registered as an RLLP, both Martha and Veronica could be held personally liable for either CPA's individual malpractice.

Many professionals cannot form an LLC in California. They can obtain similar legal liability protection by forming a California professional corporation. Ask your state licensing board for additional information.

Why You Need a Written Partnership Agreement

Although it's possible to start a partnership with a verbal agreement—or even with no stated agreement at all—there are drawbacks to taking this casual approach. The most obvious problem is that a verbal agreement can be remembered and interpreted differently by different partners. And having no stated agreement at all almost always means trouble. Also, if you don't write out how you want your partnership to be operated, you lose a great deal of flexibility. Instead of being able to make your own rules in a number of key areas—for example, how partnership profits and losses are divided among the partners—California state partnership law will automatically come into play. These state-based rules may not be to your liking (for example, state law generally calls for an equal division of profits and losses regardless of partners' capital contributions).

Another reason why you should prepare and sign a written partnership agreement is to avoid disputes over what happens when a partner wants to leave the business. Here are just a few of the difficult questions that can arise if a partner wants to leave the partnership:

- If the remaining partners want to buy the departing partner out, how will the interest be valued?
- If you agree on value, how will the departing partner be paid—in a lump sum or installments? If in installments, how big will the down payment be; how many years will it take for the balance to be paid; and how much interest will be charged?
- What happens if none of the remaining partners wants to buy the departing partner's interest? Will your partnership dissolve? If so, can some of the partners form a new partnership to continue the partnership business? Who gets to use the dissolved partnership's name and client or customer list?

California law does not necessarily provide helpful answers to these questions, which means that if you don't have a written partnership agreement, you may face a long legal battle with a partner who decides to call it quits. To avoid these and other problems, a basic partnership agreement should, at a minimum, spell out how much interest each partner has in the partnership, how profits and losses will be split up between or among the partners, and how any buyout or transfer of a partner's interest will be valued and handled. The aftermath of the dissolution of the partnership also should be considered, and rules set out for a continuance of the partnership's business by ex-partners if desired.

This type of informal arrangement can make sense for the very early days of a co-owned business, where the owners, like George and Tamatha, wish to split work, expenses, profits, and losses equally. However, for the reasons mentioned earlier, from the moment the business looks like it has long-term potential, the partners should prepare and sign a written partnership agreement. Furthermore, if either partner is worried about personal liability for business debts or the possibility of lawsuits by purchasers of the fixtures, then forming a limited liability company or a corporation probably would be a better business choice.

The Limited Liability Company

The limited liability company (LLC) has become popular with many small business owners, in part because it was custom-designed by state legislatures to overcome particular limitations of each of the other business forms, including the corporation. Essentially, the LLC is a legal ownership structure that allows owners to pay business taxes on their individual income tax returns like partners (or, for a one-person LLC, like a sole proprietorship), but also gives the owners the legal protection of personal limited liability for business debts and judgments as if they had formed a corporation. Or, put another way, with an LLC you can simultaneously achieve the twin goals of one-level taxation of business profits and limited personal liability for business debts.

CAUTION

Licensed professionals can't form an LLC in California. Only businesses that render services under nonprofessional, occupational licenses can form an LLC in California. Professionals who must form a professional corporation if they incorporate (doctors, architects, lawyers, pharmacists, and so on) are the same group of professionals who can't form an LLC in the state. There may be others, however, who fall into this group. If you provide any type of licensed service that might be considered a professional service, contact your state licensing board and ask if you are allowed to form an LLC in California before getting started on the process.

Here are some of the most important LLC characteristics:

Limited liability. The owners (members) of an LLC are not personally responsible for the LLC's debts and other liabilities. Specifically, members are not personally liable for any debt, obligation, or liability of the LLC, whether that liability or obligation comes from a contract dispute, tort (injury to other persons or damage to their property), or any other type of claim. This type of sweeping personal legal liability protection is the same as that enjoyed by shareholders of a California corporation. In short, the LLC and the corporation offer the same level of limited personal liability protection.

Pass-through taxation. Federal tax law normally treats an LLC like a partnership, unless the LLC elects to be taxed as a corporation (by filing IRS Form 8832). The California Franchise Tax Board treats a California LLC for state income tax purposes as it is treated for federal income tax purposes. An LLC with an annual gross income of $250,000 or more must pay an additional annual fee, based upon a graduated fee schedule that is subject to adjustment from year to year.

If an LLC is treated as a partnership at the federal and state levels, it files a standard partnership tax return (IRS Form 1065, Schedules K and K-1) with the IRS (and Form 568 with the state). The LLC members (owners) pay taxes on their share of LLC profits on their individual federal and state income tax returns. An LLC that elects corporate tax treatment files federal and state corporate income tax returns.

Ownership requirements. You can form an LLC with only one owner (member). Members need not be residents of California, or even the United States for that matter. Other business entities, such as a corporation or another LLC, can be LLC owners.

Management flexibility. LLCs are normally managed by all the owners (members)—this is known as member-management. But state law also allows for management by one or more specially appointed managers (who may be members or nonmembers). Not surprisingly, this arrangement is known as manager-management. In other words, an LLC can appoint one or more of its members, one of its CEOs, or even a person contracted from outside the LLC, to manage its affairs. This setup makes sense if one person wishes to assume full-time control of the LLC while the other owners act as passive investors in the enterprise.

Formation requirements. Like a corporation, LLCs require paperwork to get going. Articles of organization must be filed with the California Secretary of State. And if the LLC is to maintain a business presence in another state, such as a branch office, it also must file registration or qualification papers with the other state's secretary of state or department of state. California's LLC formation fee is $70. California LLCs, like California corporations and limited partnerships, must pay an annual minimum $800 tax to the Franchise Tax Board. There is an additional LLC annual fee, with a tiered rate structure, for LLCs with annual gross incomes of $250,000 or more. The additional fee may be anywhere from $900 to $11,790.

CAUTION

Add in the cost of goods sold when computing annual gross income. A California LLC engaged in an active trade or business must include its cost of goods sold. (Typically, the cost of goods sold is subtracted from gross income.) This means that even unprofitable LLCs can be subject to the annual LLC fee. Ask your tax advisor for more information.

Like a partnership, an LLC should prepare an operating agreement to spell out how

The Series LLC—A Rising Star on the Business Entity Horizon

A new type of LLC is taking shape under state LLC laws: the series LLC. States are still in the process of developing their series LLC statutes and it will take time for them to coordinate the laws, fees, and tax treatments. Once this happens, however, and the courts settle some of the legal nuances of series LLCs, the series LLC may indeed become the next big new thing in business entity formations.

Although not yet allowed under California law, several states including Delaware, Illinois, Iowa, Nevada, Oklahoma, Tennessee, Texas, Utah, and Wisconsin have adopted a series LLC formation statute.

The main characteristic and advantage of the series LLC is that it allows you to set up one or more series of assets within a single LLC. The business and assets of each series can be managed and operated separately—for example, each series can have separate owners and managers, a separate operating agreement that specifies a separate division of profits and losses associated with the series, and other separate formation and operation characteristics. And, under some state statutes, there is also a separation of legal liability between each series within an LLC.

Before you jump on the series LLC bandwagon, however, there are certain things you should keep in mind. For one, a state that does not have a series LLC statute may not respect the characteristics of a series LLC formed in another state. And, because these entities are so new, there are other uncertainties. For example, it is not clear that a federal bankruptcy court will respect the separateness of each series within an LLC.

Finally, forming a series LLC may seem like a good way to avoid paying a lot of formation and annual fees for multiple LLC entities. However, some states may not be willing to forgo these filing fees so easily. In California, for example, the Franchise Tax Board assesses an $800 franchise tax payment, plus an annual added gross receipts fee of up to $12,000 per year, on each LLC formed or operated within the state. It has stated that it will treat each series in many out-of-state LLCs as separate LLCs. (See FTB Form 568 and FTB Publication 689 for further information on California's treatment of out-of-state series LLCs, available at the FTB's website at www.ftb.ca.gov.)

the LLC will be owned, how profits and losses will be divided, how departing or deceased members will be bought out, and other essential ownership details. However, preparation of an LLC operating agreement is not legally required. If it is not prepared, the default provisions of California's LLC Act will apply to the operation of the LLC. Because LLC owners will want to control exactly how profits and losses are apportioned among the members rather than following the default rules set out in the LLC Act, preparing an LLC operating agreement is a practical necessity.

RESOURCE

See Nolo's *Form Your LLC Online* to create your LLC online, or see *Form Your Own Limited Liability Company,* by Anthony Mancuso (Nolo). This book contains instructions on how to form a California LLC, prepare an operating agreement (member- and manager-managed agreements are included), and handle all other LLC formation formalities.

LLCs in action. Under the name "Aunt Jessica's Floral Arrangements," Barry and Sam jointly own and run a flower shop that specializes in unique flower arrangements (the name stems from the fact that Barry used to work for his aunt Jessica, who taught him the ropes of floral bouquet design). Lately, business has been particularly rosy, and the two men plan to sign a long-term contract with a flower importer to supply them with larger quantities of seasonal flowers. Once they receive the additional flowers, they will be able to create more floral pieces and wholesale them to a wider market. Both men are aware that they will encounter more risks as their business grows. Accordingly, they decide to protect their personal assets from business risks by converting their partnership to an LLC. They could accomplish the same result by incorporating, but they prefer the simplicity of paying taxes on their business income on their individual income tax returns (rather than reporting profits and paying business taxes on a separate corporate income tax return). They also realize that they can convert their LLC to a corporation later to obtain the advantage of lower corporate tax rates on money kept in the flower business or, even more simply, make an IRS election to have their LLC taxed as a corporation without changing its legal structure.

Do-Good LLCs and Corporations—The Latest in LLC Entities

A number of states allow for the formation of hybrid entities (LLCs and/or corporations) that can exist to make a profit and do good. For example, some states authorize the formation of a "low-profit LLC" (also called an "L3C") that can be formed for an educational or charitable purpose but also can make a profit. States initially created this special type of hybrid entity to allow foundations to more easily distribute funds to a qualified social-purpose organization, although the IRS has not yet formally approved L3Cs for this purpose. L3Cs are not allowed in California at present.

Closer to home, California allows the formation of "flexible purpose corporations" and "benefit corporations," which can be formed to do good works as well as to make money. The advantage of these new California entities is that they can allow the principals to spend time and money trying to do good without having to worry about stakeholders being upset (and suing them) for not spending all their time trying to turn a profit.

All of the above hybrid entities are sometimes loosely referred to as "B corporations." However, this term really refers to a certification that a socially responsive corporation, LLC, or other entity can seek, not to a separate type of corporation or other distinct legal entity (see www.bcorporation.net for more information).

The Corporation

Now let's look at the basic attributes of the corporation, the type of business organization this book shows you how to organize.

A corporation is a statutory creature, created and regulated by state law. In short, if you want the privilege—as the courts call it—of turning your business enterprise into a California corporation, you must follow the requirements of the California Corporations Code.

What sets the corporation apart from all other types of businesses is that it is a legal entity separate from any of the people who own, control, manage, or operate it. The state corporation and federal and state tax laws view the corporation as a legal person—it can enter into contracts, incur debts, and pay taxes separately from its owners.

Limited Personal Liability

Like the owners (members) of an LLC, the owners (shareholders) of a corporation are not personally liable for the corporation's business debts, claims, or other liabilities. This means that a person who invests in a corporation (a shareholder) normally only stands to lose the amount of money or the value of the property which he or she has paid for its stock. As a result, if the corporation does not succeed and cannot pay its debts or other financial obligations, creditors cannot seize or sell the corporate investor's home, car, or other personal assets.

> EXAMPLE: Rackafrax Dry Cleaners, Inc., a California corporation, has several bad years in a row. When it finally files for bankruptcy it owes $50,000 to a number of suppliers and $80,000 as a result of a lawsuit for uninsured losses stemming from a fire. Stock in Rackafrax is owned by Harry Rack, Edith Frax, and John Quincy Taft. Their personal assets cannot be taken to pay the money Rackafrax owes.

During hard economic times, the limited liability protection you receive with a corporation can be crucial. It provides a layer of protection between the owners of the business and the business itself. If the business starts to fall behind in paying its bills, the only resource creditors have is against the business itself. Often this means the creditors will be motivated to work with the owners so that the business can continue and pay its bills. And, if the business does fail, the owners won't be held personally for its debts.

If you are running an unincorporated business, such as a sole proprietorship or partnership, consider converting to a corporation (or LLC). This could help you and your business survive downturns in the economy. After you incorporate, send a written notice to each creditor informing them that your business is now a corporation and that any future invoices, bills, and other statements should be made out in the name of the corporation. Be sure and re-sign any outstanding obligations in the name of your corporation and have the creditor acknowledge the new instrument. Also, ask them to send you any paperwork necessary to change your current accounts over to the name of your corporation. (See Chapter 6 for instructions on preparing a notice to creditors.)

Exceptions to the Rule of Personal Limited Liability Protection

In some situations, corporate directors, officers, and shareholders of a corporation can be held responsible for debts owed by their corporation. Here are a few of the most common exceptions to the rule of limited personal liability (these exceptions also apply to other limited liability business structures, such as the LLC):

Personal guarantees. When a bank or other lender makes a loan to a small corporation, particularly a newly formed one, it often requires that the people who own the corporation agree to repay it from their personal assets should the

When Your Creditors Can Go After Your LLC Interest

The LLC's limited liability shield protects the personal assets of LLC owners from lawsuits that arise from LLC business operations and claims, with a few exceptions. However, this protection doesn't always work the other way—that is, an LLC owner's interest in LLC assets is not necessarily protected from creditors seeking to satisfy personal debts or lawsuit judgments against the owner.

In most states, including California, a personal creditor of an LLC owner can seize the owner's interest in the LLC. Because an interest in an LLC is the personal property of each LLC owner, personal creditors are typically allowed to obtain a "charging order" against the owner's interest in a business, such as a partnership interest, an LLC interest, or stock in a corporation. Essentially, a charging order is a lien against the owner's business interest, which allows the creditor to receive profit payments that would otherwise go to the owner.

> EXAMPLE: Sam defaults on a personal bank loan unrelated to his LLC business, and the bank obtains a charging order against Sam's LLC membership interest. This order allows the bank to be paid any profits that would otherwise be distributed to Sam under the terms of the LLC's operating agreement.

A charging order may not do a creditor much good if an LLC does not regularly distribute profits to members. In that case, the creditor may be able to ask a state court to foreclose on (become the owner of) the LLCs member's interest. If state law allows this (California Corporations Code Section 17302 does) and the court agrees, the creditor can become the new legal owner of the owner's LLC interest. However, under most state laws, including California's, a creditor who forecloses on an LLC interest does not become a full voting member of the LLC. Instead, the foreclosing creditor becomes a "transferee" or "assignee" who is entitled to all economic rights associated with the interest, such as a share of the profits paid out on the interest and the value of the interest when the business is sold or liquidated. Typically, an assignee or transferee cannot manage or vote in the LLC, nor assume other membership rights granted to full members under the LLC operating agreement. Again, if the LLC does not pay out profits regularly and there is little chance of the business being sold or liquidated, these economic rights might not mean much to a creditor.

Potential problems for one-owner LLCs: Even though the California Corporations Code says that foreclosing on an LLC member's interest is the sole remedy available to the creditor of an LLC owner, in exceptional cases (such as fraud by an LLC member), state and federal bankruptcy courts may figure out a way to allow a person who buys a foreclosed interest in a single-member LLC to become a full member of that LLC with voting rights. After all, with a single-member LLC, there are no other members' rights to protect from the creditor. If this happened, the creditor might be in a position to force the sale of the LLC. We won't discuss how this might happen—this area of law is complex and fast moving. If you are worried about the effects of a charging order against your LLC, please consult a knowledgeable California business lawyer to learn about the latest rules and court decisions in this area.

corporation default on the loan. Shareholders may even have to pledge equity in a house or other personal assets as security for repayment of the debt. Of course, shareholders can just say no—but if they do, their corporation may not qualify for the loan.

Federal and state taxes. If a corporation fails to pay income, payroll, or other taxes, the IRS and the California Franchise Tax Board are likely to attempt to recover the unpaid taxes from responsible employees—a category that often includes the principal directors, officers, and shareholders of a small corporation.

Unlawful or unauthorized transactions. If you use the corporation as a device to defraud third parties, or if you deliberately make a decision (or fail to make one) that results in physical harm to others or their property (such as failing to maintain premises or a work site properly, manufacturing unsafe products, or causing environmental pollution), a court may pierce the corporate veil and hold the shareholders of a small corporation individually liable for damages (monetary losses) caused to others.

Fortunately, most of the problem areas where you might be held personally liable for corporate obligations can be avoided by following a few commonsense rules (rules you'll probably adhere to anyway). First, don't do anything that is dishonest or illegal. Second, make sure your corporation does the same, by having it obtain necessary permits, licenses, or clearances for its business operations. Third, pay employee wages and withhold and pay corporate income and payroll taxes on time. Fourth, don't personally obligate yourself to repay corporate debts or obligations unless you fully understand and accept the consequences.

Corporate Tax Treatment

Let's now look at a few of the most important tax characteristics of the corporation. We'll start with the dual level of taxation built into the corporate business structure.

Dual Taxation and Income Splitting

The corporation is a taxpayer, with its own income tax rates and tax returns separate from the tax rates and tax returns of its owners. This separate layer of taxation allows corporate profits to be kept in the business and taxed at the initial corporate tax rates, which are generally lower than the marginal (top) tax rates of the corporation's owners. The result of this type of business income splitting between the corporation and its owners can result in an overall tax savings for the owners (compared to pass-through taxation of all business profits to the owners, which is the standard tax treatment of sole proprietorships, partnerships, and LLCs).

> EXAMPLE: Jeff and Sally own and work for their own two-person corporation, Hair Looms, Inc., a mail order synthetic wig supply business that is starting to enjoy popularity with overseas purchasers. To keep pace with the surge in orders, they need to expand by reinvesting a portion of their profits back in the business. Since Hair Looms is incorporated, only the portion of the profits paid to Jeff and Sally as salary is reported and taxed to them on their individual tax returns—let's assume their marginal (top) tax rate is over 30%. By contrast, the first $50,000 in profits left in the business for expansion is reported on Hair Looms' corporate income tax return and taxed at the lowest corporate tax rate of only 15%. The next $25,000 is taxed at 25%.

TIP

Corporate tax rates max out at 34% for most corporations. Even though corporate tax rates can go up to 39%, all corporate net income below $10 million is subject to an effective flat tax rate of 34%. (See Chapter 4.)

How Small Corporations Avoid Double Taxation of Corporate Profits

What about the old bugaboo of corporate double taxation? Most people have heard that corporate income is taxed twice: once at the corporate level and again when it is paid out to shareholders in the form of dividends. In theory, the Internal Revenue Code says that most corporations are treated this way (except S corporations, whose profits automatically pass to shareholders each year—see below). In practice, however, double taxation seldom occurs in the context of the small business corporation. The reason is simple: Employee-owners don't pay themselves dividends, which are taxed at the corporate rate when earned and at the shareholder level when paid to them. Instead, the shareholders, who usually work for their corporation, pay themselves salaries and bonuses, which are deducted from the profits of the corporate business as ordinary and necessary business expenses. The result is that profits paid out in salary and other forms of employee compensation to the owner-employees of a small corporation are taxed only once, at the individual level. In other words, as long as you work for your corporation, even in a part-time or consulting capacity, you can pay out business profits to yourself as reasonable compensation. Your corporation won't have to pay taxes on these profits.

Furthermore, because most individuals now pay a 15% tax rate on dividends, the double tax associated with dividends is not as severe as it once was. And, dividends are not subject to Social Security tax, so business owners may realize a small tax savings by choosing to have part of their corporate salaries paid out to them as dividends.

TIP

LLCs and partnerships can elect corporate tax treatment. Dual taxation and income splitting are no longer unique to corporations. Partnerships and LLCs can elect to be taxed as corporations if they wish to keep money in the business and have it taxed at corporate rates. (See "Partnerships Can Choose to Be Taxed as Corporations," above.)

Corporations Can Elect Pass-Through Taxation of Profits

Just as partnerships and LLCs have the ability to request corporate tax treatment, corporations can change their tax treatment to the type of pass-through taxation that normally applies to partnerships and LLCs. A corporation accomplishes this by making an S corporation tax election with the IRS.

TIP

When just starting out, form an LLC instead. An LLC, like an S corporation, gives its owners pass-through taxation of business profits plus limited personal liability for business debts. It also is more flexible than an S corporation for technical reasons (see "LLCs and Partnerships Have Technical Tax Advantages Over S Corporations," below). Therefore, it usually makes more sense to form an LLC when you are just starting to organize your business.

If you are already doing business as a corporation, switching over to S corporation tax status—by making an S corporation tax election—makes sense if you wish to keep your corporation intact but want pass-through treatment of profits and losses to save tax dollars. This might be true, for example, for a corporation that no longer wishes to keep profits in the business, but can't pay all of them out to shareholders as salaries (if some shareholders don't work for the corporation or if the payout of all profits as salaries would render them excessive and subject to IRS attack, for example). It also may be true if a corporation begins to lose money and the owners want to deduct these losses on their individual income tax returns to offset other income (a number of technical hurdles must be overcome for this pass-through of losses in an S corporation to work—see "LLCs and Partnerships Have Technical Tax Advantages Over S Corporations," below, for more information).

LLCs and Partnerships Have Technical Tax Advantages Over S Corporations

LLC owners and partners can split profits disproportionately to their ownership interests in the business (these are called special allocations of profits and losses under the tax code); S corporation shareholders can't. Also, the amount of corporate losses that may be passed through to S corporation shareholders is limited to the total of each shareholder's basis in his or her stock, plus amounts loaned personally by each shareholder to the corporation. (The basis is the amount paid for stock plus and minus adjustments during the life of the corporation.) Losses allocated to a shareholder that exceed these limits can be carried forward and deducted in future tax years if the shareholder then qualifies to deduct the losses. In contrast, LLC owners and partners may be able to personally deduct more business losses on their tax returns in a given year than S corporation shareholders. The reason is that both LLC members and partners get to count their pro rata share of all money borrowed by the business, not just loans personally made by the member or partner, in computing how much of any loss allocated to them by the business they can deduct in a given year on their individual income tax returns. Ask your tax advisor for more information.

The only other way an existing corporation can get the limited liability protection and pass-through tax treatment of the S corporation is to dissolve, then reorganize as an LLC. This can be costly from a legal and tax perspective and a lot more trouble than simply electing S corporation tax status.

U.S. corporations with 100 or fewer shareholders who are U.S. citizens or residents can elect federal S corporation tax treatment by filing IRS Form 2553. Once an S corporation election is made with the IRS, the corporation is automatically treated as a California S corporation. It can opt out of S corporation treatment by filing FTB Form 3560 with the California Franchise Tax Board. An S corporation has all its profits, losses, credits, and deductions passed through to its shareholders, who report these items on their individual tax returns. In effect, this allows the corporation to sidestep federal corporate income taxes on business profits, passing the profits (and the taxes that go with them) along to the shareholders. Each S corporation shareholder is allocated a portion of the corporation's profits and losses according to her percentage of stock ownership in the corporation (a 50% shareholder reports and pays individual income taxes on 50% of the corporation's annual profits, for example).

These profits are allocated to the shareholders whether the profits are actually paid to them or kept in the corporation.

> EXAMPLE: Fred's Furniture and Appliance was incorporated during a period of fast business growth, when Fred brought in two relatives as investors and moved his business to a larger storefront in an upscale neighborhood. He chose the corporate form to limit his and the investors' personal liability and to accommodate his investors by issuing them shares in his

business. With the business growing fast, the investors wanted to see some return of profits. Fred elects S corporation tax treatment. Net profits of the business pass through to the S shareholders directly and are taxed on their individual income tax returns. This meets the investors' needs and avoids the double tax that would have been paid if profits were distributed to the investors as dividends. This also helps Fred, since he can keep his corporate salary reasonably low and still get money out of his corporation. Also, S corporation profits allocated to shareholders, unlike salaries, are not subject to self-employment taxes. (See Chapter 4.) This means Fred ends up with more after-tax money in his pocket.

Tax Consequences of Corporate Dissolution

You should consider an additional tax aspect of forming a corporation before deciding to incorporate—the tax consequences of ending the corporation when it is dissolved or sold. The general rule is that when a corporation is sold or dissolved, both the corporation and its shareholders have to pay tax on appreciated

Does It Make Sense to Incorporate Out of State?

You have no doubt heard about the possibility of incorporating in another state, most likely Delaware, where initial and ongoing fees are lower and regulations may be less restrictive than in California. Does this make sense? For large, publicly held corporations looking for the most lenient statutes and courts to help them fend off corporate raiders, perhaps yes. But for a small, privately held corporation pursuing an active California business, our answer is generally no—it is usually a very poor idea to incorporate out of state.

The big reason is that you probably will have to qualify to do business in California even if you don't incorporate here, and this process takes about as much time and costs as much money as filing incorporation papers in California in the first place. You'll also need to appoint a corporate agent to receive official corporate notices in the state where you incorporate—another expensive pain in the neck.

Incorporating in another state with a lower corporate income tax isn't likely to save you any money. If your business makes money from operations in California, even if it is incorporated in another state, you still must pay California taxes on this income.

EXAMPLE: Best Greeting Card, Inc., plans to open a Jenner, California, facility to design and market holiday greeting cards throughout the country. If it incorporates in Delaware, it must qualify to do business in California and pay California corporate income tax on its California operations. It also must hire a registered agent to act on its behalf in Delaware. It decides to incorporate in California instead.

Unless you plan to open up a business with offices and operations in more than one state and, therefore, have a real reason to shop for the best corporate domiciles, you generally should incorporate in your home state—California.

To see how aggressively California interprets "doing business in California," see the examples under this heading in FTB Publication 3556, available on the Franchise Tax Board's website at www.ftb.gov. For an even more telling example of the risks you take forming an out-of-state corporation to engage in business in California, see FTB Publication 689, *Don't Gamble With Your Taxes: Incorporating in Nevada*, also available on the FTB website.

corporate assets. However, there are ways to minimize this double tax, if you plan in advance. The primary strategy is to arrange for a sale of stock (not assets) when the corporation is sold. (Best of all is a tax-free sale of stock/assets as part of a tax-free reorganization that is a merger with an acquiring corporation.) Check with your tax adviser on the eventual tax ramifications of dissolving your corporation right from the start. One of the most important preincorporation services your tax adviser can provide is to make sure that the future dissolution or sale of your corporation will not result in an unexpectedly hefty tax bill for your corporation and its owners.

Owners Who Work in the Business Are Treated as Employees

A potential benefit of the corporate structure is that business owners who also work in the business become employees. This means that you, in your role as an employee, become eligible for tax-deductible corporate fringe benefits, some of which you would not qualify for as a sole proprietor, partner, or an LLC member.

For example, Henry incorporates his California sole proprietorship, "Big Sur Shoes, Inc." He now works as a full-time corporate employee and is entitled to tax-deductible corporate perks, such as reimbursement for medical expenses and $50,000 worth of group term life insurance paid for by his business. If he gave himself these perks in his unincorporated business, his business could deduct them as ordinary and necessary business expenses, but he would have to report them as income and pay income taxes on them. Corporation employees also receive special tax benefits if they are issued qualified incentive stock options, restricted stock, and other forms of equity-sharing participation interests unique to corporations. (See Chapter 4 for more on corporate fringe and equity benefits.)

Built-In Organizational Structure

Perhaps the most unique benefit of forming a corporation is the ability to divide management, executive decision making, and ownership into separate areas of corporate activity. This separation is achieved automatically because of the separate legal roles which reside in the corporate form: the roles of directors (managers), executives (officers), and owners (shareholders). Unlike partnerships and LLCs, the corporate structure comes ready-made with a built-in separation of these three roles, each with its own legal authority, rules, and ability to participate in corporate income and profits.

EXAMPLE 1: Myra, Danielle, and Rocco form their own three-person corporation, Skate City, Incorporated, a skate and bike shop in Venice Beach, Los Angeles. Storefront access to the Venice Beach rollerblade, skating, and bike path makes it popular with local rollerbladers and bicyclists. Needing more cash, the three approach relatives for investment capital. Rocco's brother, Tony, and Danielle's sister, Collette, chip in $10,000 each in return for shares in the business. Myra's Aunt Kate lends the corporation $25,000 in return for an interest-only promissory note, with the principal amount to be repaid at the end of five years. Here's how the management, executive, and financial structure of the corporation breaks down:

Board of Directors. The management team, which meets once each quarter to analyze and project financial performance and review store operations, consists of the three founders, Myra, Danielle, and Rocco, and one of the other three investors. The investor board position is a one-year rotating seat. This year Tony has the investor board seat; next year, Collette; the third year, Aunt Kate. This pattern repeats every three years. Directors have one vote apiece, regardless of share ownership—this means the founders can always outvote the investor vote on the board, but this also guarantees that each of the investors will have an opportunity to hear board discussions and give input on major management decisions.

Executive team. The officers or executive team charged with overseeing day-to-day business; supervising employees; keeping track of ordering, inventory, and sales activities; and generally putting into practice the goals set by the board are Myra (president) and Danielle (vice president). Rocco fills the remaining officer positions of secretary/treasurer of the corporation, but this is a part-time administrative task only. Rocco's real vocation—or avocation—is blading along the beach and training to be a professional, touring rollerblader with his own corporate sponsor (maybe Skate City if profits continue to roll in).

Participation in profits. Corporate net profits are used to stock inventory, pay rent on the storefront, and pay all the other usual and customary expenses of doing business. The two full-time executives, Myra and Danielle, get a corporate salary, plus a year-end bonus when profits are good. Rocco gets a small stipend (hourly pay) for his part-time work. Otherwise, he and the two investor shareholders are simply sitting on their shares. Skate City is not in a position yet to pay dividends—all excess profits of the corporation are used to continue expanding the store's product lines and add a new service facility at the back of the store. Even if dividends are never paid, all three know that their stock will be worth a good deal if the business is successful. They can cash in their shares when the business sells or when they decide to sell their shares back to the corporation (or, who knows, if Skate City goes public someday). Aunt Kate, the most conservative of the investment group, will look to ongoing interest payments as her share in corporate profits, getting her capital back when the principal amount of her loan is repaid.

As you can see from this example, the mechanisms to put this custom-tailored management, executive, and investment structure into place are built into the Skate City corporation. To erect it, all that is needed is to fill in a few blanks on standard incorporation forms, including stock certificates, and prepare a standard promissory note. To duplicate this structure as a partnership or LLC would require a specially drafted partnership or LLC operating agreement with custom language and plenty of review by the founders and investment group (and, no doubt, their lawyers). The corporate form is designed to handle this division of management, day-to-day responsibilities, and investment with little extra time, trouble, or expense.

There is a flip side to this division of corporate positions and participation in profits. Some businesspeople—particularly those who run a business by themselves or who prefer to run a co-owned business informally—feel that the extra levels of corporate operation and paperwork are a nuisance. That's why incorporating may be a bit of an overload for small start-up companies—they may be better and more comfortably served by the less formal business structures of the sole proprietorship or partnership, or, if limited legal liability is an overriding concern, by the LLC legal structure.

But for many business owners, the ability to separate out corporate management and oversight from day-to-day executive decisions, plus the ability to treat people who invest in the business strictly in their capacities as co-owners and not as active day-to-day participants, makes the corporate model extremely attractive. The fact that there are legal differences among directors, officers, and shareholders becomes particularly attractive as a business grows and people from outside the initial circle of incorporators become involved in the business (as investors, lenders, or even public shareholders).

EXAMPLE 2: Leila runs a lunch counter business that provides her both a decent income and an escape from the cubicled office environment in which she was once unhappily ensconced. Business has been slow, but Leila has a new idea to give the business more appeal, as well as make it more fun for her. She changes the decor to reflect a tropical motif, installs a salt water aquarium facing the lunch counter, adds coral reef (metal halide) lighting and light-reflective wall paneling, and renames the business the "The Tide Pool." The standard lunch counter fare is augmented with a special bouillabaisse soup entrée and a selection of organic salads and fruit juice drinks, and a seafood and sushi dinner menu is added to cater to the after-work crowd. Leila has her hands full, doing most of the remodeling work herself and preparing the expanded menu each day.

The new operation enjoys great success, and a newspaper in the nearby capital city features the Tide Pool in an article on trendy eating spots, giving it a rave review. Patronage increases and Leila hires a cook and three waiters to help her.

A local entrepreneur, Sally, who represents an investment group, asks Leila if she would be interested in franchising other Tide Pools throughout the country. Sally says an investment group would help develop a franchise plan, plus fund the new operation. Leila would be asked to travel to help set up franchise operations for the first year, and would have a managerial role and substantial stake in the new venture.

Leila likes the idea—sure, she'll have to get back into the working world, but on her own terms, and as a consultant and business owner. Besides, she's feeling overworked running the Tide Pool by herself, and it would be a relief to have the new venture take over the business. The investment group wants a managerial role in the franchise operation, plus a comprehensive set of financial controls. Leila and the investment group agree to incorporate the new venture as "Tide Pool Franchising, Inc." The corporate business structure is a good fit. Leila will assume a managerial role as a director of the new company, along with Sally and a member of the venture capital firm. The new firm hires two seasoned small businesspeople, one as president and one as treasurer, to run the new franchise operation. Business begins with the original Tide Pool as the first franchise, and Leila gets started working for a good salary, plus commission, setting up other franchise locations.

If the new venture makes a go of it, Leila and the investment group can either sell their shares back to the corporation at a healthy profit or, if growth is substantial and consistent, take the company public in a few years, selling their stock in the corporation at a sizable profit once a market has been established for the corporation's publicly held shares.

Raising Money—Corporate Access to Private, Venture, and Public Capital

Corporations offer a terrific structure for raising money from friends, family, and business associates. There is something special about stock ownership, even in a small business, that attracts others. The corporate structure is designed to accommodate various capital interests—for example, you can issue common voting shares to the initial owner-employees, set up a special nonvoting class of shares to distribute to key employees as an incentive to remain loyal to the business, and issue yet another preferred class of stock (one that gives investors a preference if dividends are declared or the corporation is sold) to venture capitalists willing to help fund future expansion of your corporation.

Incorporated businesses also have an easier time obtaining loans from banks and other capital investment firms (assuming a corporation's balance sheet and cash flow statements look good). That's partially due to the increased structural formality of the corporation (discussed above). In addition, loans can be made part of a package where the bank or investment company obtains special rights to choose one or more board members, or has special voting prerogatives in matters of corporate governance or finance. For example, a lender may require veto power over expenditures exceeding a specified amount. The range of capital arrangements possible, even for a small corporation, is almost limitless, which helps the corporation attract outside investment.

TIP

Employees often prefer to work for corporations. Key employees are more likely to work for a business that offers them a chance to profit if future growth is strong through the issuance of stock options and stock bonuses—financial incentives that only the corporate form can provide.

Perpetual Existence

A corporation is, in some senses, immortal. Unlike a sole proprietorship, partnership, or an LLC, which can terminate upon the death or withdrawal of the owner or owners, a corporation has an independent legal existence that continues despite changeovers in management or ownership. Of course, like any business, a corporation can be terminated by the mutual consent of the owners for personal or economic reasons and, in some cases, involuntarily, as in corporate bankruptcy proceedings. Nonetheless, the fact that a corporation does not depend for its legal existence on the life or continual ownership interest of a particular individual does influence creditors, employees, and others to participate in the operations of the business. This is particularly true as the business grows.

Downsides of Incorporating

Just about everything, including the advantage of incorporating, comes at a price. And, of course, the answer to the question "How much does it cost?" is an important factor to weigh when considering whether to incorporate your business. For starters, a corporation, unlike a sole proprietorship or general partnership, requires the filing of formation papers—articles of incorporation—with the California Secretary of State. The filing cost is $100. Corporations must pay an annual franchise tax (as explained in Chapter 4). Ongoing paperwork is generally not burdensome, but you will have to hold and document annual meetings of shareholders and directors and keep minutes of important corporate meetings. Creating this paper trail is a good way to show the IRS, in case of an audit (or the courts, in case of a lawsuit which tries to hold shareholders personally liable), that you have, in fact, respected the corporate form and are entitled to claim (hide behind) its insulating layer of limited personal liability.

RESOURCE

You can take care of ongoing corporate paperwork at minimal expense by using *The Corporate Records Handbook*, by Anthony Mancuso (Nolo). This book contains minute forms to hold corporate meetings and helps corporations cope with the tax, business, legal, and financial decisions and transactions that commonly arise during the life of the business.

The other main disadvantage of incorporating has traditionally been the $1,000 to $2,000 (or more) you could expect to pay an attorney for creating the initial paperwork. This book, together with a little effort on your part, should significantly reduce, if not eliminate, this cost.

Corporations in action. Sal Sr. and his son, Sal Jr., co-own and run Sal's Mimeo and Copy Center, a family business run for over 30 years as a partnership with a minimum of legal paperwork. In fact, before Sal Jr. joined the partnership firm, Sal Sr. ran the business as a sole proprietorship. Sal Sr. is retiring, letting Sal Jr., a business school grad, take over operational control.

Sal Jr. plans to expand the business by bringing in two business school friends, Ellen and Wilbur, as investors. Sal Jr. will contribute the business and its assets (including a long-term commercial lease to its storefront location and goodwill), to the new operation. Ellen and Wilbur will invest cash in two ways: Each will pay cash in return for shares, and each will also lend money to the business in exchange for promissory notes, which will be repaid by the firm. Interest only will be paid by the business on the notes over a five-year period, with repayment of the principal amount at the end of the loan term. Ellen and Wilbur hope that in five to seven years they can sell their shares back to Sal Jr. at an increased price per share, or to another company wishing to buy into Sal's business. In the meantime, they are content to look to the interest payments on their notes as an adequate return on their investment in the business.

Sal Jr. will work as full-time manager of the business, which will continue to offer traditional copying services. In addition, the new capital will be used to expand into desktop publishing aimed at both the small business and the student markets.

Sal Jr., seeing that a change in business structure is needed to give Ellen and Wilbur a stake in the business, decides to incorporate. The investors like the corporate form because it limits their personal liability for its debts and other liabilities. Incorporating also should give the business a lift in its lending status at the local bank, which likes the fact that Sal Jr. is formalizing and expanding his business operations. Sal Jr. also realizes that forming a corporation will have tax advantages since it is one good way to split business income between the business entity, the investors, and himself. Specifically, the corporate form allows Sal to leave profits in the business, part of which will be used to pay back and retire Ellen's and Wilbur's promissory notes. Of course, the corporation will get to deduct Sal's salary and fringe benefits (as well as those of his employees) as well as the interest paid on the investors' notes. In short, the corporate form, with its built-in limited liability legal status, income- and tax-splitting capability, and stock ownership structure, suits Sal's new business needs to a T.

Comparing Business Entities at a Glance

In the tables that follow, we highlight and compare general and specific legal and tax traits of each type of business entity. We include a few technical issues in our chart to tweak your interest. Should any of the additional points of comparison seem relevant to your particular business operation, we encourage you to talk them over with a legal or tax professional.

RESOURCE

For an in-depth legal and tax comparison of limited liability entities, see *LLC or Corporation?* by Anthony Mancuso (Nolo).

What If You Operate a Website for Your Business?

If your company operates a website, it no doubt does so out of some physical location (your home or office). Of course, you may use servers located somewhere else, but you and your employees have some physical location where you do business related to the website (maintaining the site, taking and fulfilling orders, answering customer email). This location most likely represents your primary physical place of business, and most small business owners would reasonably decide to incorporate in the state where this workplace is located.

What about states where you sell products through your website to residents but have no physical presence? In that case, do you have to qualify to do business in that state? You don't have to qualify to do business in another state unless you engage in intrastate commerce in that state. Intrastate commerce refers to the fact that you either have a physical presence in that state (for example, a sales office or warehouse), or you have repeated and successive business transactions within that state (for example, your website enters into agreements with other companies in that state). You don't have to register if you are simply selling your products or services over the Internet to consumers in that state (interstate commerce). This is a general rule and the answer can vary depending on the type and amount of activity related to the website that you engage in. If you want to learn more about the issues surrounding operating an Internet business, see *LLC or Corporation,* Chapter 5 ("Doing Business Out of State").

Business Entity Comparison Tables—Legal, Financial, and Tax Characteristics						
	Sole Proprietorship	**General Partnership**	**Limited Partnership**	**C Corporation**	**S Corporation**	**LLC**
Who owns business?	sole proprietor	general partners	general and limited partners	shareholders	same as C corporation	members
Personal liability for business debts	sole proprietor personally liable	general partners personally liable	only general partner(s) personally liable	no personal liability of shareholders	same as C corporation	no personal liability of members
Restrictions on kind of business	may engage in any lawful business	may engage in any lawful business	same as general partnership	can't be formed for banking or trust business and other special businesses	same as C corporation —but has shareholder restrictions	same as C corporation; in California, many licensed professionals cannot form an LLC (lawyers, accountants, and architects— until 1/1/2019 for architects— can form RLLP instead)
Restrictions on number of owners	only one sole proprietor	minimum two general partners	minimum one general partner and one limited partner	one-person corporations allowed	same as C corporation, but no more than 100 shareholders allowed (who must be U.S. citizens or residents)	one-member LLCs allowed
Who makes management decisions?	sole proprietor	general partners	general partner(s) only (not limited partners)	board of directors; number of board members, if less than 3, must at least be equal to number of shareholders	same as C corporation	ordinarily members; or managers if manager-managed LLC
Who may legally obligate business?	sole proprietor	any general partner	general partner(s) only (not limited partners)	officers	same as C corporation	ordinarily any member; or any manager if manager-managed LLC

Business Entity Comparison Tables—Legal, Financial, and Tax Characteristics (continued)

	Sole Proprietorship	General Partnership	Limited Partnership	C Corporation	S Corporation	LLC
Effect on business if an owner dies or departs	dissolves automatically	dissolves automatically unless otherwise stated in partnership agreement	same as general partnership	no effect	same as C corporation	most LLC agreements say that LLC continues after a member leaves
Limits on transfer of ownership interests	free transferability	consent of all general partners usually required under partnership agreement	same as general partnership	transfer of stock may be limited under securities laws or restrictions in articles of incorporation or bylaws	same as C corporation —but transfers should be limited to persons and entities that qualify as S corporation shareholders	most LLC agreements require membership consent to admit new member
Amount of organizational paperwork and ongoing legal formalities	minimal	partnership agreement recommended	start-up filing required; partnership agreement recommended	start-up filing required; bylaws recommended; annual meeting of shareholders required	same as C corporation	start-up filing required; operating agreement recommended; meetings not normally required
Source of start-up funds	sole proprietor	general partners	general and limited partners	initial share-holders (in California, cannot invest with promise to perform services or to pay later (unless note is adequately secured))	same as C corporation —but cannot issue different classes of stock with different financial provisions	in California, members can invest by promising to perform services or contribute cash later

Business Entity Comparison Tables—Legal, Financial, and Tax Characteristics (continued)						
	Sole Proprietorship	**General Partnership**	**Limited Partnership**	**C Corporation**	**S Corporation**	**LLC**
How business usually obtains capital, if needed	sole proprietor's contributions; working capital loans backed by personal assets of sole proprietor	capital contributions from general partners; business loans from banks backed by partnership and personal assets	investment capital from limited partners' bank loans backed by general partners' personal assets	flexible; outside investors (may be issued various classes of shares); bank loans backed by shareholders' personal assets (if corporation has insufficient credit history); venture capital	generally same as C corporation—but can't have foreign partnership or corporate shareholders; must limit number of shareholders to 100; can't offer different classes of stock to investors except for share with different or no voting rights, hence venture capital opportunities are limited	capital contributions from members; bank loans backed by members' personal assets (if LLC has insufficient credit history)
Ease of conversion to another business form	may change form at will; legal paperwork involved	may change to limited partnership, corporation, or LLC; legal paperwork involved	may change to corporation or LLC; legal paperwork involved	may change to S corporation by filing simple tax election; change to LLC can involve tax cost and legal complexity	generally same as C corporation—may terminate S tax status to become C corporation but cannot reelect S status for five years after	may change to general or limited partnership or corporation; legal paperwork involved
Is establishment or sale of ownership interests subject to federal and state securities laws?	generally not	generally not	issuance or transfer of limited partnership interests is subject to state and federal laws	issuance or transfer of stock subject to state and federal securities laws	same as C corporation	generally not, if all members are active in the business

Business Entity Comparison Tables—Legal, Financial, and Tax Characteristics (continued)

	Sole Proprietorship	General Partnership	Limited Partnership	C Corporation	S Corporation	LLC
Who generally finds this the best way to do business?	owner who wants legal and managerial autonomy	joint owners who are not concerned with personal liability for business debts	joint owners who choose partnership tax treatment and some nonmanaging investors; general partners must be willing to assume personal liability for business debts	owners who want limited liability, the built-in formality and capital incentives of the corporate form, and the ability to split business income to lower overall taxes	owners who want limited liability, the built-in formality of the corporate form with the pass-through of corporate profits to individual owners	owners who want limited liability, a less formal legal structure, and automatic pass-through of profit
How business profits are taxed	individual tax rates of sole proprietor	individual tax rates of general partners, unless partners file IRS Form 8832 to elect corporate tax treatment	individual tax rates of general and limited partners, unless partners file IRS Form 8832 to elect corporate tax treatment	split up and taxed at corporate rates and individual tax rates of shareholders; $800 minimum state tax for second and subsequent tax years	individual tax rates of shareholders; $800 minimum tax for second and subsequent tax years	individual tax rates of members, unless LLC files IRS Form 8832 and elects corporate taxation; $800 minimum tax each year plus additional fees if gross income is $250,000 or more
Tax-deductible fringe benefits available to owners who work in business	sole proprietor may set up IRA or Keogh retirement plan	general partners and other employees may set up IRA or Keogh plans; can make corporate tax election to obtain corporate benefits	same as general partnership	employee-shareholders eligible for medical reimbursement, term life insurance, and equity-sharing plans	employee-shareholders owning 2% or more of stock are restricted to partnership rules	can get benefits associated with sole proprietorship, partnership, or corporation, depending on tax treatment of LLC

Business Entity Comparison Tables—Legal, Financial, and Tax Characteristics (continued)						
	Sole Proprietorship	**General Partnership**	**Limited Partnership**	**C Corporation**	**S Corporation**	**LLC**
Automatic tax status	yes	yes	yes, upon filing certificate of limited partnership with state filing office	yes, upon filing certificate of incorporation with state filing office	no; must meet requirements and file tax election form with IRS; revoked or terminated tax status cannot be reelected for five years	yes, one-owner LLC treated as sole proprietorship; co-owned LLC treated as partnership; one-owner and co-owned LLCs can elect corporate tax treatment
Deductibility of business losses	owner may use losses to deduct other income on individual tax returns (subject to active-passive investment loss rules that apply to all businesses)	partners may use losses to deduct other income on individual tax returns if at risk for loss or debt	same as general partnership, but limited partners may only deduct nonresource debts (for which general partners are not specifically liable)	corporation may deduct business losses (shareholders may not deduct losses)	shareholders may deduct share of corporate losses on individual tax returns, but must comply with special limitations	follows sole proprietorship, partnership, or corporate tax rules depending on tax status of LLC
Tax level when business is sold	personal tax level of owner	personal tax level of individual general partners	personal tax level of individual general and limited partners	two levels: shareholders and corporation are subject to tax on liquidation	normally taxed at personal tax levels of individual shareholders, but corporate level tax sometimes due if S corporation was formerly a C corporation	follows sole proprietorship, partnership, or corporate tax rules depending on tax status of LLC

CHAPTER

How California Corporations Work

This chapter gives you detailed information on the legal, financial, and practical considerations relevant to California corporations. Much of the information discussed here will help you decide whether to incorporate. Some information relates to the day-to-day operations of the corporation.

ONLINE RESOURCE

California Corporations Code is online. If you want to browse the California Corporations Code, go to www.leginfo.ca.gov, click "California Law," then select "Corporations Code" and click on "Search." The General Corporation law, which applies to California business corporations, is contained in Title 1, Division 1.

Types of California Corporations

California classifies corporations in several, sometimes overlapping, ways. The first classification is domestic versus foreign. A domestic corporation is one that is formed under the laws of California by filing articles of incorporation with the California Secretary of State. If you form a corporation in another state, even if the corporation does business in California, it is a foreign corporation. We've already taken a look at the relative advantages and disadvantages of setting up a foreign corporation in Chapter 1.

Corporations can also be classified as profit or nonprofit, although this distinction is breaking down somewhat with the introduction of California benefit and flexible purposes corporations. These corporations can be formed to make money as well as do good (see "New Hybrid California Social-Purpose Corporations," below). The California Corporations Code does not contain any precise definition of profit and nonprofit corporations, but does refer to regular profit corporations as business corporations to distinguish them from nonprofit corporations. We will refer to regular business corporations as profit corporations. A nonprofit corporation is one that is set up under the special provisions of the California Nonprofit Corporation Law.

Another corporate category is the professional corporation. This type of corporation is regulated by special statutes and, as its name implies, is a separate type of corporation formed for the purpose of engaging in the practice of certain professions.

Finally, the Corporations Code contains provisions for setting up a unique—and rarely used—type of profit corporation, the close corporation. A close corporation is one with a limited number of shareholders, who can enter into a shareholders' agreement that waives or alters many of the provisions of the Corporations Code.

Now let's briefly look at each of these types of corporations, starting with the privately held California profit corporation—the type of corporation we expect our readers to be interested in.

The Privately Held California Profit Corporation

This book shows you how to form a privately held profit corporation. The forms and information we provide will enable you to form a regular profit corporation that is eligible to issue its initial shares under the limited offering exemption contained in the Corporate Securities Law of California. Essentially, this means that your corporation can offer and issue its shares of stock privately, without public solicitation or advertisement. (The limited offering exemption is explained in detail in Chapter 3.) The remainder of this book explains the rules and procedures you will have to follow to organize and operate your corporation—and shows you, step by step, how to incorporate.

We occasionally use the term "closely held corporation." The Internal Revenue Code defines this term as a corporation in which five or fewer people own more than 50% of the value of the corporation's stock during the last half of the corporation's tax year. However, when we use this term outside of its technical tax context, all we mean is that the corporation is formed and operated by a small number of people who will be active in the affairs of the corporation, and that it will not rely on the resources and capital of outside investors or public subscribers to its shares. This is the type of corporation most readers will wish to set up.

Nonprofit Corporations

A nonprofit corporation is a corporation formed by one or more persons, for the benefit of the public, the mutual benefit of its members, or religious purposes. California public benefit nonprofit corporations are usually formed for tax-exempt purposes under Section 501(c)(3) of the Internal Revenue Code for religious, charitable, literary, scientific, or educational purposes. For example, child care centers, shelters for the homeless, community health care clinics, museums, hospitals, churches, schools, and performing arts groups normally incorporate as nonprofits.

With the exception of mutual benefit non-profit corporations, nonprofit corporations cannot distribute profits to their members. When they dissolve, most nonprofit corporations dedicate all corporate assets to another nonprofit corporation to comply with state and federal tax laws and to avoid paying corporate income tax (the main reason for organizing a nonprofit corporation). For example, if you establish a nonprofit corporation to educate the public about the need to preserve wetlands for birds, you might state that upon dissolution all remaining money will go to the Audubon Society.

New Hybrid California Social-Purpose Corporations

Effective January 1, 2012, the California legislature authorized the creation of two new types of hybrid business corporations: benefit corporations and flexible purpose corporations. Both these entities can be formed for the dual purpose of making money and doing good, without having to worry about shareholders lawsuits if they aren't making enough money. Some lawyers who have looked closely at the two entities think the flexible purpose corporation is the more practical and useful of the two.

Very few hybrid corporations have been formed as yet, but this may change as more investors decide that doing good can also improve the bottom line (taking the long-term view).

Neither of these entities is a pure nonprofit corporation and it seems unlikely that the IRS would consider either of them eligible for nonprofit 501(c)(3) income tax exemption.

For more information on these special social-purpose California stock corporations, see www.sos.ca.gov/business/be/forms/flexible-purpose-corp-and-benefit-corp.pdf

Nonprofit corporations, like regular profit corporations, have directors who manage the business of the corporation. The nonprofit can collect enrollment fees, dues, or similar amounts from members. Like regular corporations, a nonprofit corporation may sue or be sued, pay salaries and provide fringe benefits, incur debts and obligations, acquire and hold property, and engage in any lawful activity not inconsistent with its purposes and its nonprofit status. It also provides its directors and members with limited liability for the debts and liabilities of the corporation and continues perpetually unless steps are taken to terminate it. If you are interested in forming a California nonprofit, see *How to Form a Nonprofit Corporation in California*, by Anthony Mancuso (Nolo). To form a nonprofit corporation in another state, see *How to Form a Nonprofit Corporation*, by Anthony Mancuso (Nolo), a 50-state guide.

Professional Corporations

Certain specified groups of professionals must form professional corporations when incorporating their practices in California. There are special rules that govern how professional corporations must operate. In some cases, the professionals must obtain a certificate of registration from the governmental agency that regulates the profession (such as the State Bar for lawyers). Everyone who provides professional services through a professional corporation must be licensed to practice the particular profession in which the corporation is engaged. Only persons who hold such a California license in the primary (or a related) profession can own shares in the professional corporation. The corporation is subject to the rules, regulations, and disciplinary powers of the agency that regulates the particular profession. Special forms and procedures must be used to incorporate a professional corporation—we don't cover that process here.

TIP

Most professionals don't have to form a professional corporation. Only a few professions have to incorporate their practices as professional corporations. For example, engineers, computer scientists, real estate brokers, financial advisers, and most professions outside the areas of law, health care, and accountancy can incorporate as regular profit corporations (the type of corporation formed by using this book).

The professionals listed below can incorporate as professional corporations. Professions marked with an asterisk may incorporate either as a regular business corporation or as a professional corporation.

- accountant
- acupuncturist
- architect*
- attorney
- chiropractor
- clinical social worker
- dentist
- doctor (medical doctors including surgeons)
- marriage and family therapists
- naturopathic doctor
- nurse
- optometrist
- osteopath (physician or surgeon)
- pharmacist
- physical therapist*
- physician's assistant
- podiatrist
- psychologist
- shorthand and court reporter
- speech-language pathologist and audiologist
- veterinarian.*

CAUTION

Always check with your professional licensing board before deciding what type of corporation to form for your profession. The rules on licensing are not always clear as to which professions must, and which may, incorporate as professional corporations. Use the above list for general guidance but check with your licensing board about the rules for your profession before you decide which type of corporation to form.

Architects and veterinarians have the option to incorporate as a professional corporation or as a regular profit corporation. A physical therapy board ruling seems to indicate that physical therapists may form either a regular business or professional corporation. (See "Physical Therapy Corporation Ownership By a Layperson" on the Physical Therapy Board website at www.ptbc.ca.gov.) Attorneys and accountants and—until January 1, 2019—architects can also choose to organize their practice as registered limited liability partnerships. However, if you decide to form a corporation for your architecture, veterinary, or physical therapy business, check with your state licensing board to make sure you have the option of forming a regular for profit corporation instead of a professional corporation.

CAUTION

A flat corporate income tax rate applies for certain professionals. Professionals who work in the fields of health, law, engineering, architecture, accounting, actuarial science, or consulting will be subject to the maximum 35% federal corporate tax rate if substantially all the stock of the corporation is owned by the employees who perform professional services for the corporation (see "Federal Corporate Income Tax" in Chapter 4). It doesn't matter whether the corporation is a professional corporation or regular profit corporation. The 35% rate applies to all taxable income left in the corporation at the end of the tax year (and not paid out as salary, fringe benefits, or otherwise).

The Close Corporation

A California profit corporation with 35 or fewer shareholders may, by including special close corporation provisions in its articles of incorporation and on its stock certificates, elect to be organized as a California close corporation. Technically, California close corporations are referred to as statutory close corporations, because they are set up and

Registered Limited Liability Partnerships

Lawyers, accountants, and—until January 1, 2019—architects can form a special type of partnership, the registered limited liability partnership. This relatively new business entity gives the professional partners in an RLLP immunity from personal liability for the malpractice of other partners in the firm. (Normally, all partners are personally liable for their own and other partners' negligence in a professional partnership.) The only other way to achieve this type of personal protection in a business that is taxed as a partnership is to form a limited liability company. However, California licensed professionals are prohibited from forming an LLC (see "The Limited Liability Company" in Chapter 1).

Those California statutes are different from similar laws in other states (all states have adopted RLLP statutes) in that:

- California RLLP professionals are also personally protected against business debts, contracts, and other claims against the RLLP firm.
- California RLLP professionals are not personally liable for the negligence of people they supervise.
- Only three of California's 60+ licensed professions are allowed to form RLLPs.

If you are an accountant, lawyer, or, architect, you may want to consider forming an RLLP. Check with your state board and your legal and tax advisers. If you practice in another profession, then you may decide to incorporate to obtain limited liability protection.

operated under special California statutes, which allow them to establish their own operating procedures according to the terms of a close corporation shareholders' agreement. We usually refer to this type of corporation simply as a close corporation.

The primary reason for electing close corporation status is to operate the corporation under the terms of a close corporation shareholders' agreement, which can provide for informal management of the corporation and allow the corporate entity to operate under partnership-type rules. Through a shareholders' agreement, the close corporation can dispense with the need for annual director or shareholder meetings, corporate officers, or even the board of directors itself, and instead allow shareholders to manage and carry out the business of the corporation directly. As with a partnership, profits can be distributed without regard to capital contributions (stock ownership); thus a 10% shareholder could, for example, receive 25% of the profits (dividends). In effect, a close corporation can waive many of the statutory rules that apply to regular California profit corporations and establish its own operating procedures according to the terms of a close corporation shareholders' agreement.

> EXAMPLE: Kelley Greene, a successful junior tennis champion, together with her financial backer, forms her own California close corporation, What a Racquet, Ltd., a California limited partnership consisting of a general partner and ten limited-partner investors. In the close corporation shareholders' agreement, the limited partnership is given complete managerial control of the corporation and the limited partner investors are provided with a participation in 80% of the profits and liquidation proceeds of the corporation, while Kelley is assured an annual salary and a 20% share in corporate profits and liquidation proceeds.

Complex investment arrangements of this sort are the primary use of the close corporation. Most incorporators will not wish to organize their corporation as a close corporation. Indeed, fewer than 2% of all California profit corporations are formed in this manner.

There are a number of reasons for the lack of popularity of the close corporation. To begin with, most people do not need, or wish, to operate their corporation under informal or nonstandard close corporation shareholder agreement rules and procedures. In fact, many incorporators form a corporation in order to rely on the traditional corporation and tax statutes that apply to regular profit corporations. Second, shares of stock in a close corporation contain built-in (automatic) restrictions on transferability, and most incorporators do not want their shares to be subject to these transfer restrictions. Third, there are a number of potential problems related to the use of a close corporation shareholders' agreement, which make it inadvisable unless you first consult with an attorney and an accountant. If you are interested in forming a close corporation, you should see a lawyer.

Corporate Powers

Profit corporations have carte blanche to engage in any lawful business activity in California. Lawful doesn't just mean not criminal; it means not otherwise prohibited by law. Generally, this means that a corporation can do anything that a natural person can do. By way of illustration, the California Corporations Code lists the following corporate powers:

- to adopt, use, and alter a corporate seal
- to adopt, amend, and repeal bylaws
- to qualify to do business in any other state, territory, dependency, or foreign country
- subject to certain restrictions, to issue, purchase, redeem, receive, acquire, own, hold, sell, lend, exchange, transfer, dispose of, pledge, use, and otherwise deal in and with its own shares, bonds, debentures, and other securities
- to make donations, regardless of specific corporate benefit, for the public welfare or for community fund, hospital, charitable, educational, scientific, or civic or similar purposes
- to pay pensions and establish and carry out pension, profit-sharing, stock bonus, share pension, share option, savings, thrift, and other retirement, incentive, and benefit plans, trusts, and provisions for any or all of the directors, officers, and employees of the corporation or any of its subsidiary or affiliated corporations and to indemnify and purchase and maintain insurance on behalf of any fiduciary of such plans, trusts, or provisions
- except with respect to certain restrictions as to loans to directors and officers which we discuss later, to assume obligations, enter into contracts (including contracts of guaranty or suretyship), incur liabilities, borrow and lend money, or otherwise use its credit and secure any of its obligations, contracts, or liabilities by mortgage, pledge, or other encumbrance of all or any part of its property, franchises, and income
- to participate with others in any partnership, joint venture, or other association, transaction, or arrangement of any kind, whether or not such participation involves the sharing or delegation of control with, or to, others.

Corporate People

While a corporation is considered a legal person capable of making contracts, paying taxes, and so on, it needs real people to carry out its business. The law classifies corporate people in the following ways:

- incorporators
- directors
- officers, and
- shareholders.

These corporate people have varying powers and responsibilities which we discuss below.

In a Small Corporation, One Person Often Fills Several Roles

Distinctions between the different roles of corporate personnel often become blurred in a small corporation because one person may simultaneously serve in more than one, or all, of these capacities. For example, if you form your own one-person California corporation, you will be your corporation's only incorporator, director, officer, and shareholder.

Incorporators

Your incorporator is the person who signs the articles of incorporation and files them with the secretary of state to form the corporation. In a practical sense, incorporators are the key people who make the business happen. Typically, they are the entrepreneurs who arrange to get the money, property, people, and whatever else the corporation will need to make a go of it.

An incorporator (sometimes called a corporate promoter) is considered by law to be a fiduciary of the corporation. This means that he or she has a duty to make full disclosure to the corporation of any personal interest in, and potential benefit from, any of the business he or she transacts for the corporation. For example, if the incorporator arranges for the corporation to buy property in which he has an ownership interest, he must disclose his ownership interest and any personal benefit he plans to realize from the sale.

Incorporators May Be Liable for Contracts Signed Prior to Incorporation

The corporation is not bound by contracts the incorporator enters into with third persons before the corporation is formed, unless these contracts are later ratified by the board of directors or the corporation accepts the benefits of the contract (for example, it uses office space available through a lease the incorporator signed). On the other hand, the incorporator may be personally liable on these preincorporation contracts unless he or she signs the contract in the name of the corporation only and clearly informs the third party that the corporation does not yet exist, may never come into existence, and, even if it does, may not ratify the contract.

If you want to arrange for office space, hire employees, or borrow money before the corporation is formed, state clearly that you are acting on the corporation's behalf, and that your contracts are subject to ratification by the corporation when, and if, it comes into existence. The other party may refuse to do business with you under these conditions and tell you to come back after the corporation is formed. This is usually the best approach to preincorporation business anyway—namely, to postpone it until you file your articles.

Directors

Directors have the authority and responsibility for managing the corporation. The directors meet and make decisions collectively as the board of directors. For the board to take action, a majority of a quorum vote is usually necessary. However, the board may pass a resolution delegating most of the management of the corporation to an executive committee consisting of two or more directors. This arrangement is often used when one or more directors are unable or unwilling to assume an active voice in corporate affairs. The board of directors may also delegate management of the day-to-day operations of the corporation to a management company or others, as long as these people remain under the ultimate control of the board.

Directors normally serve without compensation. After all, they are intimately involved in the business and will gain financially if it does well by paying themselves a better salary and/or eventually selling the business. The corporation may pay its directors reasonable compensation, however, if it is for services they actually perform for the corporation. A director may also receive an advance or reimbursement for reasonable out-of-pocket expenses (for example, travel costs) incurred in the performance of corporate duties. Any compensation, advancement, or reimbursement paid to a director should be authorized before the payments are made.

Directors' Duties and Conflicts of Interest

Directors, like promoters, are fiduciaries of the corporation. This means they must act in the corporation's best interests and exercise care in making management decisions. In an effort to flesh out these responsibilities, the law says a director must act "in good faith, in a manner [which the] … director believes to be in the best interests of the corporation and its shareholders and with such care, including reasonable inquiry, as an ordinarily prudent person in a like position would use under similar conditions." This vague standard effectively leaves it up to the courts to define the duty of good faith a director owes the corporation. Courts, in turn, usually decide cases on an individual basis.

Broadly speaking, however, honest errors in business judgment are usually allowed, while fraudulent or grossly negligent behavior isn't. A director is allowed to rely on the apparently accurate reports of attorneys, accountants, and corporate officers in arriving at decisions, unless there was some indication that the director needed to look into the matter further. (Below, we discuss special provisions of California law that allow you to insulate your directors in many cases from personal liability for breach of their duty to the corporation or shareholders.)

The director also has a duty of loyalty to the corporation. This means, among other things, that a director usually must give the corporation a right of first refusal as to business opportunities he becomes aware of in his capacity as corporate director. If the corporation fails to take advantage of the opportunity after full disclosure or clearly would not be interested in it, the director can go ahead for himself.

The board of directors may vote on a matter in which one or more of the directors has a personal interest (the Corporations Code uses the term "material financial interest"), but only if:

- the director's interest in the transaction is fully disclosed or known to the board, and
- there are sufficient votes to pass the resolution without counting the vote of the interested director.

Alternatively, the board can approve such a contract if the contract or transaction is just and reasonable as to the corporation. (There are additional procedures for validating actions that benefit directors—see Cal. Corp. Code § 310.)

Subject to some exceptions, if the corporation lends money or property to, or guarantees the obligations of, directors, the shareholders must approve these transactions, either by a unanimous vote or by a majority vote of the shares not counting those held by benefited directors. Of course, the shareholders are entitled to full disclosure of the nature and extent of the benefit to the directors before votes are cast.

If a director violates one of the above rules, by grossly mismanaging or taking advantage of the corporation, receiving unauthorized or unwarranted compensation, or participating in unauthorized or unfair transactions, he or she can be subject to personal financial liability for any loss to the corporation, its shareholders, and its creditors. In addition to actual damages, the director can also be subject to monetary penalties (punitive damages), be temporarily or permanently ousted from directorship, and, in certain cases, face criminal penalties.

Of course, if you are forming a small corporation with, let's say, just you and a friend acting as the corporation's only directors, shareholders, and officers, much of this discussion will not apply to you. You will not have to worry about unfairly taking advantage of your own corporation or its shareholders because you cannot defraud or take advantage of yourselves—nor would you want to. When you and your closely held corporation have an identity of interest, it's not as important that you deal with the corporation at arm's length. However, if even a few others invest in your corporation, all the rules and legal principles regarding fair dealing discussed above apply.

Director Immunity and Indemnification Rules

California corporations can add provisions to their articles of incorporation that, in many cases, eliminate their directors' personal liability for monetary damages. They can also add provisions that allow the corporation to indemnify their directors (pay them back) for expenses, settlements, fines, judgments, and other costs associated with lawsuits brought against the directors beyond the indemnification limits provided by law. We discuss each of these optional provisions below.

Director immunity. California corporations can include language in their articles limiting or eliminating the personal liability of their directors for monetary damages, in suits brought by or on behalf of the corporation for breach of a director's duties to the corporation and its shareholders. (See Cal. Corp. Code §§ 204(a)(10) and 204.5.) You must include this language in your articles of incorporation for your corporation to qualify for this higher level of director protection. The articles of incorporation included in this book contain this director immunity language.

These provisions do not insulate directors from lawsuits brought by third parties (for example, a lawsuit for damages to an outsider caused by the act or omission of a director). They can be used, however, to protect directors from personal liability in shareholder derivative suits in many situations where the director is acting in good faith and according to law. A shareholder derivative suit arises when a shareholder sues the directors in the name of the corporation for damages caused to the corporation or its shareholders.

For example, if your board of directors makes what turns out to be a poor management decision that results in a monetary loss to the corporation (and a corresponding reduction in the value of the shareholders' stock), a shareholder—perhaps one who has been at odds with the directors for years—may decide to sue the directors personally in a shareholder's derivative action to allow the corporation to recoup this loss from the directors. In this situation, including a director immunity provision in your articles would protect your directors from liability. Of course, if a shareholder is injured personally (for example, by slipping and falling in the corporation's office), the shareholder could not bring a shareholder derivative suit on behalf of the corporation. Instead, the shareholder would have to sue the directors (and the corporation) in a regular third-party lawsuit—and the director immunity rules would not protect the directors from liability.

Even in shareholder derivative suits, there are some situations in which a director will be personally liable, regardless of the language in your articles. These exceptions, which generally involve illegal or unethical director conduct, are discussed below.

Indemnification. Although the director immunity rules may relieve a director of personal liability in certain types of lawsuits, there are many other costs that a director might incur in the course of defending or disposing of a lawsuit, such as settlement amounts, attorney fees, court costs, and other litigation-related expenses, which are not covered by the director immunity rules. Generally, California's indemnification rules allow the corporation to indemnify (pay back) a director (and officers, employees, and other corporate agents) for some or all of these additional types of lawsuit-related payments, if certain requirements are met. With the high incidence of out-of-court settlements (regardless of the actual merits of the case) and the mammoth costs of preparing for and defending even the most frivolous lawsuit, indemnifying your directors is essential.

Corporations can (and, in some cases, must) indemnify a director, officer, employee, or other corporate agent for expenses incurred in defending a shareholder's derivative suit, and for expenses, judgments, fines, and settlements incurred in third-party actions. Specific requirements must be met in all cases to fall within the indemnification provisions. These indemnification provisions used to be exclusive—that is, corporations could not indemnify directors and officers for circumstances and amounts not specifically allowed under the indemnification provisions set forth in Section 317 of the California Corporations Code.

However, this exclusivity rule has changed. Now, a California corporation can include language in its articles authorizing the indemnification of corporate agents beyond what is expressly permitted by Section 317. Under these new rules, the corporation can provide additional indemnification for directors and officers for breaching a duty to the corporation or its shareholders (shareholder derivative suits) and for acts or omissions affecting others (third-party liability suits). (See Cal. Corp. Code § 204(a)(11).) However, a corporation cannot indemnify corporate agents if they engage in certain types of wrongdoing—see "Exceptions to Special Director Immunity and Indemnification Rules," below.

In the articles of incorporation provided in this book, we include language which authorizes indemnification to the fullest extent permissible under California law. This language allows the corporation to indemnify directors and officers both for shareholder derivative suits and third-party liability suits. Article VII of the bylaws contains a general statement requiring indemnification of directors and officers in all cases not prohibited by the Corporations Code. This language should suffice for most small California corporations, but check this conclusion with your small business lawyer if indemnification is important to you. If you wish to provide your own language for director and officer indemnification, see Sections 317 and 204(a)(11) of the Corporations Code and refer to the discussion and suggestions in Chapter 5, Step 4.

Exceptions to Special Director Immunity and Indemnification Rules

You cannot protect your directors from personal liability (or provide additional indemnification for corporate agents) for:

- acts or omissions that involve intentional misconduct or a knowing and culpable violation of law
- acts or omissions that the director believes to be contrary to the best interests of the corporation or its shareholders, or that the director takes in bad faith
- any transaction from which the director derived an improper personal benefit
- acts or omissions that show a reckless disregard for the director's duty to the corporation or its shareholders in circumstances in which the director was aware, or should have been aware, in the ordinary course of performing a director's duties, of a risk of serious injury to the corporation or its shareholders
- acts or omissions that constitute an unexcused pattern of inattention that amounts to an abdication of the director's duty to the corporation or its shareholders
- liability arising under Section 310 (for certain unauthorized transactions between the corporation and a director of a corporation in which the director has a material financial interest) and Section 316 (for certain unauthorized distributions, loans, or guarantees made by directors) of the California Corporations Code
- liability for acts occurring prior to the effective date of the immunity or indemnification provisions in the articles (before your articles are filed), and
- liability for acts while acting as an officer of the corporation. You cannot limit or eliminate an officer's liability under these special rules, even if the officer is also a director or the directors have ratified the officer's actions.

Officers

Officers (president, vice president, secretary, and chief financial officer) are in charge of supervising or actually carrying out the day-to-day business of the corporation. For example, in smaller corporations, the president will often actively run the business and the chief financial officer (treasurer) will sign checks, make deposits, prepare invoices and receipts, and so on. In larger corporations, the officers will oversee various corporate departments or regular corporate personnel who will perform these day-to-day activities. The powers, duties, and responsibilities of the officers are set by the articles, bylaws, or board of directors.

Like directors, officers owe a fiduciary duty to the corporation and are subject to the same requirement of acting in good faith and in the best interests of the corporation. Although not specified by statute, the day-to-day authority of officers should not include authority to enter into certain major business transactions that are generally understood to remain within the sole province of the board of directors (for example, the mortgage or resale of corporate property). The board will have to delegate special authority to the officers if it wants them to handle major transactions.

In smaller corporations, the board of directors and the officers will often be the same people. However, the directors should still meet as a board to approve major corporate transactions, so that courts and the IRS recognize the business as a true corporate entity.

Officers are considered agents of the corporation. This means that the corporation can be held liable for their negligent or intentional acts, if they are committed within the course and scope of their employment. The corporation, moreover, is bound by the contracts and obligations entered into or incurred by the corporate officers, as long as they had legal authority to transact the business. This authority can be actual authority (a bylaw provision or resolution by the board of directors), implied authority (a necessary but unspecified part of duties set out in the bylaws or a board resolution), or apparent authority (where a third party reasonably believes that the officer has authority).

Apparent authority is a tricky concept. Basically, any third party can rely on the signature of the president or chairman of the board, vice president, secretary, assistant secretary, chief financial officer, or assistant treasurer, whether or not this officer has any actual or implied authority to sign for the corporation, as long as the third party did not actually know that the corporate officer didn't have the authority to sign.

Furthermore, one signature on a corporate instrument is sufficient to bind the corporation if the person holds both of the required positions (for example, if he or she is both the president and secretary of a one-person California corporation).

Any act performed by an officer without legal authority can still bind the corporation if the corporation accepts the benefits of the transaction or if the board of directors ratifies it after the fact.

Corporate officers are normally compensated for their services to the corporation, either as officers or simply as employees of the corporation. The compensation should be reasonable and should be paid only for services actually performed for the corporation.

> **EXAMPLE:** Jason Horner and Elmore Johnson form their own publishing company. Jason is the president and Elmore is the treasurer of the corporation. Jason is paid a salary for acting as the publisher (not for serving as president). Elmore is paid a regular annual salary as treasurer (for the bookkeeping, bill paying, and other ongoing work related to the

financial operations of the corporation). The title of the person being paid is not critical. What matters is the nature and extent of the work for which the person is being compensated.

The rules that apply to approving loans and guarantees made to directors (see "Directors' Duties and Conflicts of Interest," above) also apply to officers. Officers, like directors, can be insured or indemnified against liabilities under the insurance and indemnification rules discussed above in "Director Immunity and Indemnification Rules." The special indemnification rules for directors also apply to officers.

Shareholders

Shareholders invest in a corporation and participate in some of its important decisions. Shareholders also have the right to participate in the profits of the corporation through dividends and the right to a share of the liquidation proceeds of a dissolved corporation, after the creditors are paid. In practice, shareholders of small corporations won't pay themselves dividends, preferring instead to pay themselves directly as employees, through deductible salaries and bonuses.

Shareholders vote for the board of directors and, therefore, have an indirect but strong voice in the management of the corporation. In addition, certain acts require shareholder approval including, with some exceptions:

- the amendment of the articles of incorporation after the issuance of stock
- the sale, option, or lease of all, or substantially all, of the corporate assets other than in the usual and regular course of business, except for mortgages and the like given to secure corporate obligations, and
- decisions with respect to certain mergers, or other reorganizations, of the corporation.

Shareholder approval may be sought to approve loans, guarantees, or indemnifications that the corporation makes in favor of a director or officer. Shareholders also have the power to act independently of the board of directors to make certain decisions, including:

- amending the bylaws of the corporation
- removing any or all of the directors from the board, and
- dissolving the corporation.

In the absence of provisions to the contrary contained in the articles or bylaws, shareholders are given one vote per share. For instance, if you own 100 shares, you cast 100 votes for or against a shareholder action. A majority of a quorum vote is usually necessary to decide an issue subject to shareholder approval.

Unlike directors or officers, shareholders are not normally considered fiduciaries of the corporation with the responsibility of acting in its best interests. They are required, however, to pay the corporation the full value of the shares they purchase. Moreover, in some cases involving larger corporations, courts have treated majority shareholders as fiduciaries with a duty of full disclosure and fairness to the corporation and the minority shareholders when transferring their majority interests to outsiders. Remember, the general rule is that shareholders enjoy the protection of limited liability and are not usually personally liable to or for the corporation.

Like any other person, a shareholder can sue the corporation for personal wrongs or damages suffered on account of corporate action. However, if the shareholder is damaged in his or her capacity as a shareholder (for example, the officers or directors waste corporate assets, which devalues the shareholder's stock), the law says that the real injury is to the corporation, not the shareholder. In this case, the shareholder must ask the board of directors to bring suit or take other appropriate action. Of course, where the damage was caused by mismanagement, negligence, or fraud by the directors, the shareholder is asking them to take action against themselves—as you might guess, this doesn't always bring immediate results.

If the shareholder can't get the directors to bring suit, the shareholder can sue in his or her own name. This legal action is called a shareholder's derivative suit since, as the theory goes, the shareholder derives the right to sue from, and on behalf of, the corporation. The corporation, somewhat inconsistently, is required to be named as a defendant along with the officers and directors who are responsible for the alleged damage. The court, however, treats the corporation as the coplaintiff of the shareholder for whose benefit the suit is brought. If, after initiation of the suit by the shareholder, the directors decide to bring the action themselves against those who are responsible for the injury, the court will dismiss the shareholder's derivative suit and litigate the case in this second action.

How Many People May Organize the Corporation?

A corporation may be formed by one or more people who execute and file articles of incorporation with the California Secretary of State. The person (or persons) filing the corporation's articles are legally referred to as the corporation's incorporator(s).

California does not impose age, residency, or other requirements on any corporate person (incorporator, director, officer, or shareholder). However, in order to avoid contractual problems, your incorporator(s) (the person(s) who sign your articles), directors, and officers should be at least 18 years of age.

Under California law, the bylaws of your corporation must provide for at least three directors if your corporation has three or more shareholders. However, a corporation with two shareholders is allowed to have only two directors. Further, a corporation with only one shareholder is allowed to have only one or two directors.

A California corporation must have the following officers: a president (or chairman of the board), a secretary, and a chief financial officer (or treasurer).

In sum, your corporation must have the following minimum number of titled positions:

- with one shareholder: one incorporator, one director, one president, one secretary, and one treasurer
- with two shareholders: one incorporator, two directors, one president, one secretary, and one treasurer, or
- with three or more shareholders: one incorporator, three directors, one president, one secretary, and one treasurer.

These are the minimum number of titled positions, not the minimum number of actual people required to serve in those positions. One person can act as an incorporator, director, president, secretary, and treasurer of the corporation. In other words, the same person may be an incorporator, a director, and hold all of the officer positions. One person, however, cannot occupy more than one director position. This means that a corporation can be organized and operated by the following minimum number of people:

- one shareholder: one person
- two shareholders: two people (two directors), or
- three or more shareholders: three people (at least three directors).

These are the minimum number of positions and people necessary to incorporate a business. However, a corporation may have as many incorporators, directors, officers, and shareholders as are desirable or expedient to carry out its business. As a practical matter, major corporate shareholders will probably want not only to fill a director position, but also to participate as officers in the day-to-day operations of the corporation. As long as you meet the minimum requirements, the details of these arrangements are up to you.

Capitalization

A corporation needs people and money to get started. The money or dollar value of assets used to set up a corporation is called capital, and the process of raising the money or other assets is called capitalizing the corporation. There are no minimum capitalization requirements for corporations in California—theoretically, you could start a corporation with next to no money, property, or other assets. The corporation must receive some consideration (for example, money or property) for shares, even if it's only a one-person corporation, but no statute dictates how much consideration is necessary.

While it may be tempting to start your business on a shoestring and learn as you earn, starting a corporation without any money or assets is usually impractical. Profit corporations are in business to make money, and you will usually need at least some assets to start operations. An undercapitalized corporation may also be risky from a legal and tax standpoint. Even though California doesn't require that a corporation have any minimum amount of assets, the courts and the IRS look at "thin" (undercapitalized) corporations with a leery eye, and occasionally subject the shareholders of such corporations to personal liability for corporate debts and taxes (see "Piercing the Corporate Veil," below). To give yourself the best chance of making a success of your corporation and to protect yourself from such individual liability, you should fund your corporation adequately to start operations and cover your short-range expenses and debts.

There are several ways to get the assets necessary to capitalize a corporation. Perhaps the most common is to transfer the assets of an existing unincorporated business to the new corporation in return for shares of stock. In most other situations, a corporation is capitalized with money or property contributed to the corporation in return for its initial shares of stock, or with money loaned to the corporation in return for a promissory note.

The term capitalization refers loosely to the assets a corporation has when it starts out. In bookkeeping terms, however, capitalization has a specific meaning: It refers to the way the organizational assets are carried on the corporate books—either as equity or debt. Equity capital is, generally, the amount of money or dollar value of property transferred to the corporation in return for shares of stock. Debt is, quite logically, money borrowed by the corporation in return for promissory notes or other debt instruments.

Often, the nature of the assets capitalized will determine whether these assets will be carried on the books as equity or debt. In many cases, however, particularly in closely held corporations, the incorporators can choose whether their contribution to the corporation will be handled as an equity or debt transaction. For example, they can lend money to the corporation, contribute it in return for shares of stock, or, as is customary, elect a combination of both techniques. Because there are significant practical, legal, and tax differences between equity and debt capital, you should seek the advice of an experienced accountant or other financial adviser before opting for a particular capitalization method. However, we'll take a brief look at these differences here to give you a general idea of some of the considerations relevant to your decision.

CAUTION

Watch out when capitalizing your new corporation with assets and a note. If you are incorporating an existing business and plan to transfer your business's assets to your new corporation partly for shares and partly for a promissory note—be careful. This type of transaction is likely to be treated as a taxable exchange under Section 351 of the Internal Revenue Code. See "Potential Problems With Section 351 Tax-Free Exchanges" in Chapter 4 for more on this topic and check with an accountant or expert before you do one.

In practical terms, a contribution of equity capital to a corporation in return for shares of stock is a risky investment. The shareholder will receive a return on this investment if, and only if, the corporation makes a profit and is able to distribute dividends to shareholders or, upon its dissolution, has assets left after payment of the corporate creditors to distribute to the shareholders. When equity contributions are made to a new corporation that has not operated previously in any form, this is indeed a high-risk investment. Although still risky, a debt transaction is more certain, safer, and generally more short-term, with the lender relying on the terms of a promissory note as to the date or dates of repayment and the rate of return (interest).

A bank that makes a loan to a new business will often demand that the personal assets of the incorporators be pledged as security for the loan. A standard note, however, unlike a stock certificate, doesn't carry with it the attractive possibility of providing the lender with a percentage of the profits or the liquidation assets of a successful enterprise.

The situation is altered somewhat for a closely held corporation. The shareholders of the corporation are not normally passively investing in an enterprise but are simply incorporating their own business, which will pay them a salary in return for their efforts and provide them with favorable corporate tax advantages. Nonetheless, if the incorporators lend money to the corporation, they, too, will be able to look to the specific terms of a promissory note in seeking a guaranteed rate of return on their investment, rather than relying solely on the profits of the corporation to pay them money by way of salary.

For tax purposes, an equity contribution may result in taxable income to the shareholders. Dividends paid to shareholders are taxed to them as income, currently at a special 15% or lower federal dividend tax rate. (Dividends are rarely paid out in a small closely held corporation precisely because of this extra dividends tax rate.) In addition, payment of dividends to shareholders is a distribution of profits, and the corporation is not allowed a business expense deduction for these payments. Debt capital, on the other hand, provides certain tax advantages to the corporation and to the noteholder. Interest payments are taxed to the recipient as income at regular income tax rates, but the repayment of principal is simply a return of capital, which gives rise to no individual tax liability. The corporation, moreover, is allowed to deduct interest payments as a business expense on its tax return.

CAUTION

Keep loan transactions reasonable. If shareholders lend money to the corporation, it's best not to overdo it—some tax advisers think it's dicey to have a debt-to-equity ratio that exceeds 3 to 1, while others are more aggressive and balk only if the ratio gets close to 10 to 1. Ask your tax adviser for specific advice.

There are several reasons for caution with shareholder loans. First, the IRS may become suspicious of a corporation that has a high ratio of debt to equity or very loose shareholder loan arrangements. For instance, if a disproportionate amount of money is "loaned" to a closely held corporation rather than paid in for stock, and the repayment terms are unduly permissive or generous, the IRS or a court may find that the contribution was, in essence, an equity transaction contrived as debt to obtain favorable tax treatment (deduction by the corporation of interest payments on the debt). In this situation, the interest payments on the loan can be treated as dividends, which means the corporation cannot deduct these payments as a business expense and the lender-shareholder has to report repayment of the principal of the loan as dividend income rather than a return of capital.

Another practical reason for watching your debt-to-equity ratio is that banks are unlikely to lend money to your corporation if this ratio is particularly lopsided (too much debt/not enough equity).

Your debt arrangement is most likely to survive scrutiny if the debt instrument is drawn up as a regular promissory note with a fixed maturity date and a specified rate of interest, and the corporation has the right to enforce the terms of the note. The corporation should not arbitrarily grant the person making the loan any special preferences over other lenders or allow this person to postpone payments on the note. If the corporation has a high ratio of debt to equity, can obtain loan funds from outside lenders, or uses the loan proceeds to acquire capital assets, the loan is more likely to be disallowed and treated as an equity contribution.

Loans Are Securities

Notes issued by a corporation to lenders (shareholders, investors, and so on) are considered securities and must be qualified by the Commissioner of Corporations—usually by a somewhat complicated and costly procedure requiring the assistance of an attorney—unless the notes are exempt from qualification under a special rule. As you'll see in Chapter 3, we assume all the initial securities issued by your corporation to your shareholders (including shareholder loans) will be exempt from qualification under the California limited offering exemption. Many small corporations do not substantially capitalize their corporation with loans. Even if they do, their loan transactions should be exempt from qualification under the California limited offering discussed in the next chapter. Nonetheless, because of the technicalities involved with this area of law, you should consult with a lawyer if you capitalize your corporation with loan proceeds.

Selling Stock

Corporate stock may be sold for:

- money
- labor done
- services actually rendered to or for the benefit of the corporation in its formation or reorganization
- cancelled debts, and
- tangible or intangible property actually received by the corporation.

If shares are sold for something other than money, the board of directors must state, by resolution, the fair value to the corporation in monetary terms (that is, they must state a dollar amount which represents the fair market value) of the services, property, or other form of payment given for the shares.

In California, shares cannot be sold in return for promissory notes of the purchaser (shareholder) unless secured by collateral other than the shares themselves, nor can they be sold in return for the performance of future services (unless as part of an employee or director stock purchase or option plan).

> EXAMPLE: Thomas and Richard, after a bit of brainstorming, decide to form a Beverly Hills hang gliding tour service called "Two Sheets in the Wind, Inc." Unfortunately, they know only one person who would be willing to actually strap himself in as their tour guide—a fellow flying enthusiast, Harold. Harold sees the unique possibilities associated with this enterprise and insists on owning shares in the corporation rather than being a mere employee. Everyone agrees that not just any Tom, Dick, or Harry would be willing to assume this position, so they agree to give Harold one-third of the corporation's shares in exchange for his agreement to enter into an employment contract with the corporation. Although this arrangement may seem fair to all the parties involved, it isn't allowed because shares cannot be issued in return for future services. Harold suggests that the corporation instead issue shares to him in return for an unsecured long-term note (he'll pay for them after he's survived a few tours). This also won't work because shares cannot normally be issued in return for a promissory note. Harold decides to pay cash (or borrow enough cash) to purchase his shares outright.

Paying Dividends

There are restrictions on a corporation's right to declare dividends. Before dividends can be paid to shareholders, certain legal and financial tests must be met. For the most part, the law applies generally accepted accounting procedures to determine the validity of dividend payments (or distributions to shareholders).

A dividend cannot be paid unless:

- the amount of retained earnings of the corporation, immediately prior to the payment of the dividend, equals or exceeds the amount of the proposed dividend (plus amounts owed to preferred shareholders), or
- immediately after the distribution, the value of the corporation's assets would equal or exceed the sum of its total liabilities (plus amounts that would be owed to preferred shares upon dissolution of the corporation).

In addition, no dividend can be paid if the corporation is, or as a result of the payment of a dividend would be, likely to be unable to meet its liabilities as they become due.

The rules for determining the validity of distributions to shareholders apply technical computations and accounting standards, and you should consult an accountant or a lawyer before declaring and paying a dividend. If a dividend is paid and does not meet the appropriate tests, the directors of the corporation may be held personally liable to the creditors and shareholders of the corporation for the amount of the illegal dividend.

Dissolving a Corporation

We're sure the dissolution of your corporation is the last thing on your mind at this point. Nevertheless, it might be comforting to know that you can wind up the affairs and business of your corporation with a minimum of legal formality. Here is a quick look at the basic rules that apply when voluntarily dissolving a California corporation.

Any California corporation may, on its own motion and out of court, elect to voluntarily wind up and dissolve for any reason. This act requires the vote of at least 50% of the voting power of the shareholders.

In addition, the board of directors may elect to dissolve the corporation without shareholder approval if any of the following conditions apply:

- The corporation has not issued any shares.
- An order for relief has been entered under Chapter 7 of the federal bankruptcy law for the corporation.
- The corporation has disposed of all its assets and hasn't conducted any business for the past five years.

Upon the request of the corporation, three or more creditors, or other interested parties, a corporation's voluntary dissolution may be subject to court supervision.

In any dissolution, whether voluntary or involuntary, the corporation must stop transacting business except to the extent necessary to wind up its affairs and, if desired, to preserve the goodwill or going-concern value of the corporation pending a sale of its assets. All shareholders and creditors on the books of the corporation must be notified of the dissolution. All debts and liabilities, to the extent of corporate assets, must be paid or otherwise provided for, with any remaining assets distributed to shareholders in proportion to their stockholdings and any special stock preferences. A certificate of dissolution must be filed with the secretary of state.

Corporate dissolutions subject to superior court supervision must publish a notice to creditors at least once a week for three successive weeks in the county in which the court is located. Creditors who don't file claims within a specified period are barred from participating in any distribution of the general assets of the corporation.

RESOURCE

What about involuntary dissolutions? The rules in this section deal with a voluntary dissolution of the corporation (where a majority of your shareholders mutually agree to dissolve the corporation). There are also involuntary dissolution procedures. In an involuntary dissolution, the court is petitioned by dissatisfied or deadlocked shareholders, directors, or the attorney general to force the dissolution of a corporation. (If you're interested in these special rules, see the Corporations Code, starting with Section 1800.)

Voluntary Dissolution—How to Do It

The dissolution of a small corporation is usually a relatively simple procedure. You must prepare and file one or more forms with the California Secretary of State. First, you file a certificate of election to wind up and dissolve. You don't have to file a certificate of election if the election to dissolve was approved by all outstanding shares, and you note this fact on your certificate of dissolution. Then, after the creditors have been paid and any remaining assets have been distributed to the shareholders, you file a certificate of dissolution. The certificate of dissolution or a separate statement attached to it must indicate that a final corporate franchise tax return has been or will be filed with the California Franchise Tax Board. These formalities are simple, and there is no fee for filing these forms. For further information on the voluntary dissolution of a California corporation, together with sample forms and instructions, go to the California Department of Corporations website, at www.corp.ca.gov.

Piercing the Corporate Veil

After you've set up a corporation, you must act like one if you want to qualify for the legal protections and tax advantages the corporate form offers. Filing your articles of incorporation with the secretary of state brings the corporation into existence and transforms it into a legal entity. However, this is not enough to ensure that a court or the IRS will treat you as a corporation.

Courts occasionally scrutinize the organization and operations of corporations, particularly closely held corporations where the shareholders also manage, supervise, and work for the corporation as directors, officers, and employees. If a corporation is inadequately capitalized, doesn't issue stock, diverts funds for the personal use of the shareholders, doesn't keep adequate corporate records (for example, minutes of annual or special meetings), or, generally, doesn't pay much attention to the theory and practice of corporate life, a court may decide that your corporation is a bogus legal entity you are using to avoid liability. If this happens, the court can disregard the corporate entity and hold the shareholders liable for the debts of the corporation. Using the same criteria, the IRS has been known to treat corporate profits as the individual income of the shareholders. This is called piercing the corporate veil.

Piercing the corporate veil is the exception, not the rule. However, to avoid problems, your corporation should be adequately capitalized; issue its stock; keep accurate records of who owns its shares; keep corporate funds separate from the personal funds of the shareholders, officers, and directors; and keep accurate records of all votes and decisions that occur at formal meetings of the board of directors and the shareholders. These formal meetings should be held at least annually and whenever you wish to document a change in the legal or tax affairs of your corporation (such as an amendment of your bylaws or board approval of an important tax election) or an important business transaction (like the purchase of corporate real estate or authorization of a bank loan).

For one-person or other small corporations, your formal meetings will often be held on paper, not in person, to document corporate actions or formalities that have already been agreed to ahead of time by all the parties.

RESOURCE

For help with ongoing corporate formalities, see *The Corporate Records Handbook*, by Anthony Mancuso (Nolo). This book shows you how to hold and document ongoing corporate meetings of your board and shareholders. It also contains corporate resolutions to insert in your minutes to handle common legal, tax, and business transactions that occur after incorporating.

CHAPTER

Issuing and Selling Stock

This chapter will explain how to offer and sell your stock shares without running afoul of California and federal securities laws. In California, most small private corporations qualify for the limited offering exemption, which allows you to make an initial private stock offering without getting a permit from the state commissioner of corporations. If you don't fall within this exemption, you'll have to submit lots of complicated paperwork to get your permit—this book doesn't cover that process, because most readers will qualify for the exemption.

Because all stock transactions are also subject to the federal securities laws, we provide information on exemptions under the federal Securities Act and its regulations.

On first impression, some of the information in this chapter may seem complicated. If so, don't despair—it will make sense when you actually go through the steps in Chapter 5 to prepare the documentation necessary to issue your initial shares under the limited offering exemption. So for now, relax, read this information carefully, and, if it still seems muddy, read it again when you go through Steps 8 and 9 of Chapter 5.

CAUTION

You must qualify for the limited offering exemption to use this book. If you conclude, after reading this chapter, that you are not eligible to form a California corporation using the limited offering exemption, or if you have any questions, see a lawyer.

Securities Laws and Exemptions

One of the most important steps in forming your corporation is the issuance of your initial shares of stock. You are responsible for making sure that your shares are offered and sold in strict compliance with the securities laws of California and the federal Securities Act. Federal securities law is intended to ensure that corporations fully disclose all relevant facts to all prospective purchasers of shares. California law goes a step beyond this: Its purpose is to make sure that the stock issuance transaction is fair, just, and equitable to all offerees and purchasers of stock (that is, your shareholders). The California system is therefore referred to as a merit system (as opposed to the federal disclosure system), and is considered by many securities specialists to be the most rigorous in the nation.

CAUTION

Selling shares outside of California will subject you to other states' laws. The securities laws of another state may also apply to your stock issuance transaction if you offer to sell your shares outside of California or your offer to sell shares is directed to people in another state. Many states provide exemptions similar to California's limited offering exemption for shares privately offered and sold to a limited number of people within the state. However, we don't cover those laws here. If you plan to offer or sell shares in another state, see a lawyer. Remember, technical violations of the securities laws (even though no one is defrauded or unfairly treated) can come back to haunt you later on—this is particularly true if you decide to have distant (out-of-state) investors in your corporation.

In California, your stock issuance must be qualified (approved) by the commissioner of corporations, usually by means of obtaining a permit for the issuance of shares, unless you fall within an exemption. Under federal law, you must register your stock issuance with the Securities and Exchange Commission (SEC) unless a federal exemption is available. Qualifying or registering a stock issuance requires the preparation and submission of complex legal and financial statements, takes time, and can be expensive due to accountant, attorney, and filing fees.

Fortunately, stock issuance exemptions exist in California and at the federal level that allow most small, closely held corporations to privately offer and sell their initial shares of stock without having to obtain a permit from the department of corporations or register with the SEC. Most small, closely held corporations should be able to qualify for the California limited offering exemption. As you'll see, one-person corporations, small family corporations, and preexisting businesses that are incorporating their current operations should find it particularly easy to meet the requirements of this exemption.

TIP

There are other simplified California public offering exemptions. The exemption we discuss in this chapter is for a privately held corporation. California also has exemptions for corporations whose owners wish to make small offerings of shares to the public.

The first is a simplified securities permit procedure that allows a corporation to raise up to $1 million in a small public offering. The corporation must file a relatively simple question-and-answer form, Form U-7, commonly referred to as a *Small Corporate Offering Registration* or SCOR form. A fee of $2,500 is charged, plus up to $1,000 more based upon the Department of Corporations' average cost of processing the form for all SCOR applicants. A number of other states recognize Form U-7; it may soon be the best way to obtain moderate amounts of equity capital from investors under state securities registration laws. Certain restrictions apply—for example, your stock price must be at least $5. If you are interested in raising capital through a small stock promotion, you may wish to check out this simplified permit procedure with a lawyer or order a SCOR form (Form U-7) from the nearest office of the California Department of Corporations.

A second exemption allows issuers—corporations —to make a general announcement of the sale of shares to the public. The announcement must contain certain information and meet conditions related to its dissemination to the public. You must file two notice forms; the first one requires a filing fee of $600. Unlike the limited offering exemption, we believe you always need a lawyer to rely on this exemption. For more information, call the nearest Department of Corporations office and ask for the 25102(n) packet.

The Limited Offering Exemption

The limited offering stock issuance exemption is available if you will be issuing shares privately to your shareholders without advertisements or public solicitation for your shares. There are other rules and requirements related to your stock issuance that you must meet that we discuss below. Most small, closely held corporations should not have any trouble meeting these rules, since they reflect the way most small corporations actually sell their shares.

RESOURCE

Where to get more information on the limited offering exemption. You can find the limited offering exemption at Section 25102(f) of the Corporations Code. The regulations that interpret the statute are contained in Title 10 of the California Code of Regulations, §§ 260.102.12 through 260.102.14.

Additionally, your shareholders must meet certain requirements, which we discuss below. Finally, we give you a series of down-to-earth examples to put this rather technical information in a more practical context.

CAUTION

This book doesn't cover future stock issuances. The limited offering exemption contains technical rules relating to future stock issuances, which we do not cover here. If you issue shares again after your initial stock issuance, make sure this future stock offering meets the requirements of the securities laws. Otherwise, you could jeopardize your initial stock issuance.

General Rules of the Limited Offering Exemption

Here, we discuss the general requirements of the limited offering exemption. Most small corporations planning a limited, private offering and sale of their initial shares should not have a problem meeting these basic requirements.

The Investment Representation Rule

All purchasers of shares issued under the limited offering exemption are required to state, in writing, that they are purchasing their shares for their own account and not to resell to others. Shareholders in small, closely held corporations should not have any problem making this representation.

RELATED TOPIC

This investment representation is included in the tear-out shareholder representation letter contained in Appendix B.

The No-Advertising Rule

Your offer or sale of shares must not be accompanied by the publication of any advertisement. Advertisement is defined as any written or printed communication, recorded telephone messages, or radio, television, or similar communication, published in connection with the offer or sale of stock. Publish means to publicly issue or circulate by newspaper, mail, radio, or television, or otherwise to disseminate to the public. A public advertisement also includes sales pitches at seminars or meetings to which attendees have been invited by general advertising or solicitation. Although these terms cover a lot of ground, they do not prohibit circulation of disclosure materials to offerees, as long as these materials are not disseminated to the public.

If you disclose material about your stock issuance only to people reasonably believed to be interested in purchasing the shares or to persons whom the corporation reasonably believes may meet the qualifications required of purchasers under this exemption, you should not run afoul of these rules (as long as neither the corporation nor an agent acting on its behalf offers or sells shares through general solicitation or general advertising). Use common sense in communicating the fact that you are setting up a corporation and will be issuing your initial shares. Obviously, you should keep these types of discussions with potential investors on a private level and not disclose the availability of your shares publicly.

For example, you won't want to advertise your new corporation in the business opportunities section of the classifieds or use mailing lists as a means of targeting potential shareholders. Perhaps less obviously, you shouldn't invite the public to a seminar or a meeting where you plan to make even a soft pitch for your shares.

Most incorporators of small, closely held corporations will naturally limit any overtures to invest in the corporation to close friends, relatives, or business associates who are considered suitable purchasers under this exemption (that is, purchasers who fit within one of the specific limited offering categories as explained in "Special 35-Shareholder Rule," below). This will usually be done in the context of a one-to-one conversation. If you do this, you should not have a problem complying with this no-advertising rule.

The California Small Offering Exemption

If your proposed stock issuance does not qualify under the California limited offering exemption discussed in this chapter, you may be able to rely on another California stock issuance exemption—the small offering exemption. In practice, this exemption may serve as a useful alternative if you will be issuing stock to all your shareholders for cash only. The other situations covered by the small offering exemption are also covered by the limited offering exemption, although in broader terms.

Under the small offering exemption, a lawyer is required to sign an opinion of counsel statement on a notice form stating that in the lawyer's opinion, the stock offering and issuance meets the requirements of the small offering exemption. You file this with the Department of Corporations.

Because the small offering exemption is truly limited in scope and requires a lawyer's opinion, this book does not include the small offering exemption notice form or discuss its various requirements. However, if you experience any difficulty in understanding or meeting the (sometimes subjective) requirements of the limited offering exemption, we urge you to discuss this alternative with a lawyer.

TIP

The forms contained in Appendix B of this book, such as the articles of incorporation, bylaws, and most of the resolutions in the minutes of your first meeting, will work fine if you utilize the small offering exemption instead of the limited offering exemption.

The Consideration for Shares Rule

You may only issue shares in exchange for something of value (consideration). The consideration you may receive for stock includes money paid, tangible or intangible property received by the corporation, labor done for or services rendered to the corporation, or the cancellation of debts owed by the corporation to the person receiving the shares. Shares cannot be issued under California law in return for future services or promissory notes (unless the notes are adequately secured by collateral other than the shares themselves). This means, for example, that you shouldn't issue shares to a key employee in return for her entering into an employment contract with the corporation—this is really issuing shares in return for the performance of future services. Similarly, you can't normally issue shares in return for the promissory note of a shareholder who promises to pay for the shares over time or at some later date. (For further details on how to issue shares in return for different types of consideration, see Chapter 5, Step 9.)

The Notice of Transaction Rule

Your corporation must file a notice of transaction form with the Department of Corporations within 15 calendar days after the first sale of a security in this state.

RELATED TOPIC

You will prepare this notice form as part of Step 8 of Chapter 5. As you'll see, you will prepare and file this notice just before the actual issuance (sale) of your shares to stay on the safe side of this deadline date.

The Disclosure of All Material Facts Rule

Although the limited offering exemption does not contain any specific requirements relating to the disclosure of specific facts to shareholders, it is illegal "to offer or sell a security in this state or buy or offer to buy a security in this state by means of any written or oral communication which includes an untrue statement of a material fact or omits to state a material fact necessary in order to make the statements made, in light of the circumstances under which they were made, not misleading." (Cal. Corp. Code § 25401.)

Since you will undoubtedly be making at least oral communications in issuing your shares, you must make sure you are completely honest in your dealings with potential shareholders and that you disclose all material facts concerning your incorporation and share issuance to them.

Special Shareholder Suitability Rules

The limited offering exemption requires you to make sure that each of your shareholders qualifies to be issued shares under the limited offering exemption. Specifically, each purchaser must fit within one of six categories (although the statute includes only three categories, we've divided them into six to make them easier to understand). The basic purpose of these suitability categories is to ensure that each of your shareholders is able to protect him- or herself when purchasing shares in your corporation.

Our discussion of suitable shareholders looks only at types of shareholders who are most relevant to small corporations issuing shares to individual shareholders. We have excluded rules relating to affiliates and other types of shareholders that are unlikely to apply to you.

TIP

Most shareholders fit into Categories 1 and 6. Most incorporators will not need to get bogged down in the more technical categories discussed below. In the usual case, all your shareholders will fit nicely into Category 1 (inside shareholders such as directors or officers) and Category 6 (spouses or relatives of another suitable shareholder). Because each shareholder only need fit within one suitability category, most readers will be able to review these two categories and then skip ahead to the next section of this chapter.

Category 1. Inside Shareholders

The most common types of suitable shareholders under the limited offering exemption are those with a close relationship to the corporation, whom we refer to as inside shareholders. Many small corporations will find that most, if not all, of their shareholders will fall into one of the inside shareholder definitions discussed here.

These shareholders (sometimes referred to as uncounted shareholders by lawyers) are automatically suitable under the limited offering exemption—this means that they do not have to meet one of the subjective suitability standards discussed in Categories 2 and 3 of this section. Here's a list of the different types of shareholders who fit within this inside shareholder category:

- **Directors or officers of the corporation.** Because many small corporations will only issue shares to directors or officers, all of their shareholders will be suitable shareholders and their stock issuance will, therefore, easily meet the requirements of the limited offering exemption.
- **Executive officers of the corporation.** The law defines executive officers of the corporation as "persons who occupy a position with the corporation with duties and authority substantially similar to those of an executive officer." The background material to this exemption indicates that this rule applies to people who function more or less as directors

or officers but have different titles. If you find that you will be issuing some of your initial shares to a managerial or supervisory employee who isn't a director or officer of the corporation, and you cannot qualify this shareholder under any other shareholder suitability category, this inside shareholder suitability rule may come in handy.

- **Promoters of the corporation.** In this context, the word promoter means any person who, acting alone or with others, takes the initiative in founding and organizing the business or enterprise of the corporation. Readers of this book who form their own corporation should be considered the promoters of their corporation. However, you won't normally need to have to rely on this promoter status, because your promoters will usually serve as the directors or officers of your corporation and therefore already be qualified as inside shareholders. However, this rule may come in handy if some person instrumental in organizing your corporation does not meet another shareholder suitability test of the limited offering exemption.

If you find that all of your shareholders qualify as inside shareholders because they will be directors or officers (or, less commonly, because they can be considered executive officers or promoters) of your corporation, you don't have to bother with the more complex shareholder suitability requirements discussed in Categories 2 through 6 of this section.

Category 2. Shareholders With an Existing Relationship to Directors or Officers

Shareholders with a preexisting personal or business relationship with the corporation or any of its officers, directors, or controlling persons are also considered suitable shareholders under the California limited offering exemption. A controlling person is a promoter of the corporation. The rules give a general (and not very helpful) description of this kind of relationship as follows:

"... any relationship consisting of personal or business contacts of a nature and duration such as would enable a reasonably prudent purchaser to be aware of the character, business acumen and general business and financial circumstances of the person with whom such relationship exists."

As you can see, this language requires a subjective determination of the suitability of a shareholder under this category. The rules state that the relationship of employer-employee, or of a shareholder of the corporation, will not necessarily meet this test—if you issue shares to someone who is already an employee of the business, you can't automatically assume that this person meets this relationship requirement. For simplicity, we assume that a shareholder will need to have an existing personal or business relationship with a director or officer of your corporation to qualify under this category.

EXAMPLE: You and three other business friends plan to incorporate your existing software development business, "Bits and Pieces, Inc." (The three of you will be directors of the corporation and will therefore qualify as inside shareholders under Category 1, above). For the past five years, you have worked closely with Jessica, a professional outside programmer, in developing and marketing various programs, and you plan to bring her in as an initial shareholder in your corporation. Because Jessica has been closely associated personally and financially with you and the other principals of your corporation over a continuous and extended period of time, you conclude that she has the required relationship with you and the other directors to meet the preexisting relationship test of this category.

CAUTION

Additional rules may apply. If any of your shareholders qualify under this Category 2, you'll need to look at "Special 35-Shareholder Rule," below, which contains information on another requirement you may have to meet.

Category 3. Sophisticated Shareholders

Shareholders who, by reason of their business or financial experience, can reasonably be assumed capable of protecting their interests in connection with the stock transaction are also considered suitable shareholders under the limited offering exemption. We refer to these suitable shareholders as sophisticated shareholders.

EXAMPLE: You and your spouse are forming your own California corporation. Over a mixed doubles tennis match, your friends, Althea and Walter, each ask if they can invest as shareholders in your new venture. Althea is a CPA and Walt is an investment adviser and active trader of his own large portfolio of stocks. You conclude that both meet the sophisticated investor test and will qualify as suitable shareholders under this category.

CAUTION

Additional rules may apply. If any of your shareholders qualify under this Category 3, you'll need to look at "Special 35-Shareholder Rule," below, which contains information on another requirement you may have to meet.

Category 4. Major Shareholders

Certain types of major shareholders (this is our term, used for convenience to help characterize this category) qualify as suitable shareholders under the limited offering exemption. These major shareholders must either make a specified investment in the corporation or be able to meet either a net worth or an income test (and meet additional requirements, explained below). Here is a list of the types of major shareholders suitable under this category:

- **A shareholder who purchases $150,000 or more of the corporation's shares.** The shareholder's investment must not exceed 10% of his or her net worth or joint net worth with his or her spouse; if it does, the corporation must reasonably believe that the shareholder, or the shareholder's professional adviser, has the capacity to protect his or her own interests in connection with the stock purchase.
- **A shareholder who qualifies as an accredited investor under the federal Regulation D securities law exemption (discussed in "Federal Securities Act," below).** An accredited investor includes persons who come within, or whom the corporation reasonably believes come within, any of the following categories at the time of the sale of shares to the person (we don't list categories unlikely to apply to small corporations or those already included in another suitability category under the California limited offering exemption):
  - a person whose individual net worth, or joint net worth with the person's spouse, exceeds $1,000,000 at the time of the purchase of shares, or
  - a person who had an individual income in excess of $200,000 in each of the two most recent years, or joint income with the person's spouse in excess of $300,000 in each of those years, and has a reasonable expectation of reaching the same income level in the current year.

We won't dwell on these requirements here. In the unusual event that you do need to use one of these major shareholder tests, it will usually be to qualify an outside shareholder (one who is passively investing in your corporation). Because these shareholders are outsiders and should have financial resources, your best bet is to ask them to check with their lawyer to make sure they meet the technical requirements of this suitability category. Or you can ask them to designate a professional adviser who will protect their interests in connection with their purchase of shares in your corporation (as explained in Category 5, just below).

Category 5. Reliance on Professional Advisers

Shareholders who, by reason of the business or financial experience of their professional adviser, can "reasonably be assumed capable of protecting their interests in connection with the stock transaction" are suitable shareholders under the limited offering exemption. This is similar to Category 3, but here, the shareholder is relying on the business and financial experience of a professional adviser, not on his or her own individual experience.

A professional adviser is defined as "a person who, as a regular part of such person's business, is customarily relied upon by others for investment recommendations or decisions, and who is customarily compensated for such services, either specifically or by way of compensation for related professional services, and attorneys and certified public accountants." Besides lawyers and CPAs, professional advisers also include persons licensed or registered as broker-dealers, agents, investment advisers, banks, and savings and loan associations.

Professional advisers must not be affiliated with, or compensated by, the corporation. If a shareholder relies upon a professional adviser to qualify under this category, he or she must designate the adviser in writing. We discuss professional advisers further in Chapter 5, Step 7, of the book, which also shows you how to designate a professional adviser for one or more of your shareholders when preparing the tear-out shareholder representation letter contained in Appendix B.

TIP

This professional adviser category can be very helpful in qualifying any shareholder who does not neatly fit within any of the other categories. For example, if you wish to issue shares to an outside investor and are not sure if he meets the requirements of another category (for example, if the only other possible category is 3, and you don't feel comfortable in classifying the shareholder as a sophisticated investor under the language of that category), simply have the shareholder designate a professional adviser (as further explained in Chapter 5, Step 7) in order to meet the more certain requirements of this category.

CAUTION

Additional rules may apply. If any of your shareholders qualify under this Category 5, you'll need to look at "Special 35-Shareholder Rule," below, which contains information on requirements you may have to meet.

Category 6. Relatives of Other Suitable Shareholders

Spouses, relatives, or in-laws of another shareholder who have the same principal residence as this other shareholder are automatically considered suitable as shareholders under the limited offering exemption.

This means that once you have determined that a particular shareholder is suitable under any of the above limited offering exemption suitability categories (Categories 1–5), then the spouse, relatives, and in-laws of this shareholder who share the same principal residence with this shareholder qualify as suitable shareholders.

The rules indicate that the term relative means a person who is related by blood, marriage, or adoption. If, as is common, you are only issuing shares to the directors and officers of your corporation and to their spouses (assuming that the spouses share the same principal residence), then all of these shareholders will automatically qualify as suitable shareholders under the limited offering exemption: The directors and officers qualify as inside shareholders under Category 1; the relatives qualify under this Category 6. As we've said, most small, closely held corporations will only need to rely on Categories 1 and 6 in qualifying their shareholders as suitable under the limited offering exemption.

Special 35-Shareholder Rule

The limited offering exemption contains a special rule that prohibits you from having more than 35 shareholders who fall within Categories 2 (Existing Relationship), 3 (Sophisticated Shareholders), or 5 (Reliance on Professional Advice). This rule is very unlikely to apply to you for the following reasons:

- It's unusual for privately held corporations to issue initial shares to more than 35 shareholders from all categories.
- Even if you do plan to issue initial shares to more than 35 shareholders, the odds are that you won't have more than 35 shareholders in just these three special categories (Categories 2, 3, or 5). Remember, most shareholders of closely held corporations will be directors or officers (Category 1) or their spouses, live-in relatives, and in-laws (Category 6).

If you plan to have more than 35 shareholders who fit within just these three special categories, we suggest you see a lawyer to find out whether this rule poses a problem for you.

CAUTION

Other rules apply to organizational shareholders. Here, we cover only the rules that relate to individual shareholders. If you plan to have corporate, partnership, institutional, or other types of organizational shareholders, you should check with a lawyer concerning counting rules for these special types of shareholders.

Applying the Limited Offering Exemption

Now that we've thrown a basketful of legal technicalities at you, let's look at the limited offering exemption in a more down-to-earth, real-life context.

EXAMPLE 1: Bob wants to form his own corporation and be the sole director and shareholder and fill all of the required officer positions himself. He will qualify as a suitable shareholder because, as a director and officer, he fits within the inside shareholder Category 1.

EXAMPLE 2: Now let's assume that Bob wants to make his wife, Blanche, a shareholder, together with his mother-in-law, Beatrice, who has been living with them for the last 15 years. No problem here. Blanche and Beatrice qualify as relatives of a suitable shareholder under Category 6: Blanche is Bob's wife; Beatrice is related to Bob's wife; and they both share the same principal residence as Bob.

EXAMPLE 3: Let's assume that Bob would like to incorporate his preexisting partnership, Bob & Ray's delicatessen. Ray is Bob's brother and has decided to stay with the deli only as a part-time employee, allowing his half-interest in the business (worth $75,000) to be transferred to the corporation in return for half of the initial shares. Bob will manage the corporation as its only director.

Ray does not qualify as an inside shareholder under Category 1 because he will not be a director, officer, founder, or promoter of the corporation. He does not qualify as a major shareholder under Category 4, because he cannot meet any of the three alternate tests of this category: He will not be purchasing $150,000 of the corporation; he does not have a net worth of $1 million; and he has not, and does not expect to, earn $200,000 annually (you'll have to take our word for it). Further, although Ray is related to Bob (Bob is a suitable purchaser), he does not qualify as a relative of a suitable shareholder (Category 6) because Bob and Ray don't share the same principal residence.

Does Ray qualify as a suitable shareholder under any of the other categories? The logical choice here is Category 2 (shareholders who have a sufficient preexisting personal or business relationship with the corporation, its directors, officers, or controlling persons). Ray should be able to fit in this category in view of the fact that Bob and Ray have been doing business together for the past ten years. This should give Ray the type of preexisting personal and business relationship with a corporate director (Bob) sufficient to allow him to "be aware of the character, business acumen and general business and financial circumstances" of that person. Of course, if Blanche and Beatrice still wanted to be let in as shareholders (let's say for cash), there would be no problem. They would qualify as suitable shareholders under the reasoning set out in Example 2, just above.

EXAMPLE 4: Now, let's go one step further in this fantasy and say that Bob, in one of his infrequent yet customary calls to his stockbroker Bernie to check on the status of his small investment in pork belly futures, casually mentions that he is forming a corporation. Because the hogs have been good to Bernie, too, he has a little extra money and thinks it would be a neat idea to purchase a few shares in a business that will get the hogs to market (and, hopefully, bring in a little bacon on the side). Bernie should be able to qualify as a sophisticated shareholder under Category 3, because he could be reasonably assumed to have the capacity to protect his own interests in connection with the purchase of his shares by reason of his own business and financial experience.

EXAMPLE 5: Now let's assume that Bob, Blanche, Beatrice, Bernie, and Ray succumb to pressure from Beatrice's younger brother Biff, who lives in the next town, and decide to let Biff in on this golden opportunity. Biff is a successful guitarist but lets his business manager take care of most of the details of the business side of his career. Biff doesn't stay in constant contact with the family, preferring to limit his visits to major holidays and occasional family get-togethers. Moreover, he rarely discusses family finances or business with his relatives and has never had anything to do with the deli. Biff will not qualify under the tests of Categories 1, 2, 3, 4, or 6. He is not an insider under Category 1; does not have a sufficient preexisting personal or business relationship under Category 2; is not a sophisticated shareholder under Category 3 (he does not have sufficient business or financial experience to be reasonably assumed to have the capacity to protect his own interests in the stock issuance transaction); cannot meet any of the tests for major shareholders contained in Category 4; and does not satisfy the relationship test of Category 6 (although he is related to the spouse of a suitable shareholder—he is the brother of Blanche, Bob's wife—he does not share Bob's principal residence).

Therefore, the only way Biff could qualify as a suitable shareholder is under Category 5, if he designates a professional adviser such as a CPA or attorney who can protect his interests for him. (We discuss the rules relating to professional advisers further in Chapter 5, Step 7.)

EXAMPLE 6: As a final scenario, let's assume that Bob, Blanche, Beatrice, Bernie, Biff, and Ray all decide, in separate moments of sober reflection, that the idea of an incorporated delicatessen is silly, and the incorporation is called off. As an alternative, Bob decides to go ahead with an idea that he's had for some time: manufacturing and marketing an extremely efficient and novel sausage stuffing machine of his own invention. Some of his friends and neighbors who are regular customers of the deli have seen his machine in operation and, favorably impressed, have expressed an interest in investing in Bob's creation. Bob, who knows these people only casually, decides to see if any of them are interested in becoming shareholders in a corporation set up to exploit his invention.

Assuming that none qualify as major shareholders under Category 4 (a logical assumption in most cases), each of these people must qualify under Categories 2, 3, or 5 (none are insiders such as directors or officers or related to another suitable purchaser). Of course, if a particular shareholder qualifies under Category 2, 3, or 5, then his or her spouse or other live-in relative would automatically qualify as a relative of a suitable shareholder (Category 6). Because these people don't know Bob or his business except as customers of the deli, none of them will qualify as having a preexisting personal or business relationship with him and therefore won't qualify under Category 2. What about Category 3? To qualify under this category, each prospective shareholder must have the requisite financial or business experience discussed above. As a practical matter, it is unlikely that all of these people will be able to meet this test. Some, if not most, will have to designate and seek the advice of a professional adviser under Category 5 if the shares are to be issued under the limited offering exemption.

The alternative to the limited offering exemption in this type of situation is, as we've said, to have the corporation's initial stock offering and issuance qualified by obtaining a permit from the Department of Corporations (or issue shares for cash under the California small offering exemption—see "The California Small Offering Exemption," above). Because Bob is dealing with so many outsiders, it may be best to hire a lawyer to obtain a permit for his stock issuance rather than to try to qualify each one of these people as suitable purchasers.

The point of these last two examples is that you should be careful about considering relatives, friends, neighbors, business associates—and particularly casual acquaintances, customers, or clients of your business—as meeting the suitability standards of this exemption. They may not have a close enough personal or business relationship with one of the corporation's directors or officers or may not have sufficient personal business or financial experience to enable them to make an informed investment decision and protect their own interests. When making distinctions of this type, use your common sense, be a bit conservative, and, if you have any doubts about the suitability of a prospective purchaser, make sure that their interests are protected by a qualified professional adviser (Category 5).

Federal Securities Act

The federal Securities Act also applies to the offering of shares by a corporation. You must register your initial offering of stock with the federal Securities and Exchange Commission (SEC) unless you qualify for an exemption. There are several exemptions available—most small, closely held California corporations eligible for the California limited offering exemption should qualify under at least one of them.

Traditionally, most small, closely held corporations wishing to privately issue their initial shares to a limited number of people have been able to rely on the federal private offering exemption. Readers using this book (who will be eligible for the California limited offering) will probably also qualify for this federal exemption—as you'll see, the basic requirements of the two exemptions are similar. The federal private offering exemption is a one-line exemption contained in Section 4(2) of the Securities Act for "transactions by an issuer [corporation] not involving any public offering." The courts have discussed the basic elements that should be present when relying on this exemption (a leading case on this exemption is *SEC v. Ralston Purina Co.,* 346 U.S. 119 (1953)):

- The offerees (people to whom shares are offered) and purchasers are able to fend for themselves due to their previous financial or business experience, relationship to the issuer (the corporation, its directors, or officers), and/or significant personal net worth.
- The transaction is truly a nonpublic offering involving no general advertising or solicitation.
- The shares are purchased by the shareholders for their own account and not for resale.
- The offerees and purchasers are limited in number.
- The offerees and purchasers have access to or are given information relevant to the stock transaction in order to evaluate the pros and cons of the investment—for example, financial statements or a business plan.

In order to better explain the factors which should, and should not, be present when relying on this exemption, the SEC has issued Release No. 33-4552. This release includes several statements and examples regarding the private offering exemption—please see "SEC Release 33-4552," below, for a summary.

The guidelines contained in this release and the language of the court decisions are very general but, as you can see, they are similar to the general requirements of the California limited offering exemption. In order to make things a little clearer, the SEC has issued Rule 506 (this rule is part of a series of provisions referred to as Regulation D), which provides a safe harbor set of rules and procedures under Section 4(2) of the federal Securities Act, intended to show you a safe way to issue shares to others in a qualified private offering.

Here are some of the requirements of Rule 506 (although you don't have to follow these rules, we suggest you do to increase the likelihood that you will qualify under this exemption):

- There can be no more than 35 purchasers of shares. However, certain purchasers of shares are not counted, including certain accredited investors and the spouses, relatives, and relatives of spouses of another purchaser, if they share the same principal residence as the other purchaser. Accredited investors include directors and executive officers of the corporation and individuals with a net worth of more than $1 million or with two years' prior individual income in excess of $200,000 (or joint income with a spouse in excess of $300,000). These categories of uncounted purchasers under the federal rule are similar to, but narrower than, Categories 1, 4, and 6 under the California limited offering exemption.

- The shares cannot be offered or sold by any form of general solicitation or advertising. The rules restricting the manner of offering and selling the shares are similar to those which apply under the limited offering exemption. (See "The No-Advertising Rule," above.)
- The corporation must reasonably believe that each purchaser who is not an accredited investor (either alone or together with his or her purchaser representative) has such knowledge and experience in financial matters that he or she is capable of evaluating the merits and risks of the prospective investment. This requirement resembles the sophisticated investor test under the limited offering exemption Category 3. This rule allows a purchaser to rely on the experience of his or her purchaser representative, a concept similar to that of reliance on the financial or business experience of a professional adviser under the limited offering exemption Category 5. As with the limited offering exemption, this purchaser representative must be designated by the purchaser in writing.
- The corporation must furnish specific types of information (financial statements, written disclosure of resale restrictions, and so on) to nonaccredited investors within a reasonable time prior to sale of the shares. To be safe, the regulation suggests that this information be disclosed to accredited investors as well.
- The corporation must give each purchaser the opportunity to ask questions and receive answers about the terms and conditions of the offering and to obtain any additional information which the corporation possesses, or can acquire without unreasonable effort or expense, that is necessary to verify the accuracy of information already furnished to the purchaser. The rule also indicates that the antifraud provisions always apply to any offer or sale of securities, and that the corporation must, generally, provide all material information to ensure that purchasers are not misled.
- The corporation must make a reasonable inquiry to determine whether the purchaser is acquiring the securities for him- or herself (and not for resale to other persons). Actions the corporation should take include: (1) making a written disclosure to each purchaser, prior to the sale, that the securities have not been registered under the Act and cannot be resold unless they are registered or are exempt from registration; and (2) placing a legend on the share certificates indicating that the securities have not been registered and referring to these restrictions on the transferability and sale of the shares.
- A *Notice of Sales of Securities* form (Form D) must be filed electronically with the SEC.

It is not coincidental that Rule 506 so closely resembles the California limited offering exemption. Both were passed at approximately the same time, and were drafted and amended so as to achieve uniformity between federal and state security law exemptions. Perhaps the most significant procedural differences between the California limited offering exemption and Rule 506 is that the latter requires you to furnish specific information to certain purchasers of

SEC Release 33-4552

The SEC issued this release to explain the scope of the federal private offering exemption. Here are some of the key factors it covers:

- Whether a transaction is truly private is essentially a question of fact. The SEC will consider all surrounding circumstances, including such factors as the relationship between the offerees and the issuer (corporation) and the nature, scope, size, type, and manner of the offering.
- The number of persons to whom shares are offered doesn't determine whether this exemption is available. What's important is whether these people have sufficient association with and knowledge of the issuer so as to make the exemption available.
- If you talk to, negotiate with, or solicit an unrestricted and unrelated group of prospective purchasers to figure out who would be willing to buy stock, the transaction is a public offering—even if only a few knowledgeable purchasers ultimately buy the shares.
- Offering shares only to key employees may not be sufficient to qualify for this exemption. However, an offering made to executive personnel who, because of their position, have access to the same kind of information that the Act would make available in the form of a registration statement (financial statements and so on) may qualify for the exemption.
- The sale of stock to promoters who take the initiative in founding or organizing the business falls within this exemption.
- If the amount of the stock offering is large, it may be considered a public offering not eligible for the exemption.
- If the purchasers acquire shares with the intent to resell them, the exemption may not apply—and the corporation may be liable for civil penalties.
- The corporation should consider the nature of the purchaser's past investment and trading practices or the character and scope of his or her business to make sure the shares won't be purchased for resale. In particular, purchases by individuals engaged in the business of buying and selling securities require careful scrutiny.
- The issuer can help control the resale of the securities and thereby make reliance on this exemption a little safer. For example, the corporation may secure a representation from the initial purchasers that they are acquiring the securities only for investment and place a legend to this effect on the stock certificates.
- What may appear to be a separate offering to a properly limited group will not be considered exempt if it is one of a related series of offerings (if, for example, you offer and sell shares after your initial stock offering, this future issuance, if similar in structure, purpose, and scope, may be considered part of your initial stock issuance and may jeopardize your initial exemption).
- Regardless of whether an exemption is available for your stock offering, you cannot engage in any fraudulent activity (and should disclose all material facts to all potential shareholders) to avoid civil penalties.

shares, including the disclosure of transfer restrictions on these shares to purchasers and the placement of a legend to that effect on the share certificates.

As mentioned above, we assume that you should be able to meet most of the general guidelines to the federal private offering exemption under Section 4(2) of the federal Securities Act when issuing your initial shares under the California limited offering exemption, and you should also be able to simultaneously meet most of the safe harbor provisions of Rule 506 just discussed.

TIP

Our documents contain some of the Rule 506 language. To help conform your limited offering stock issuance to some of the additional required and suggested procedures of Rule 506, we have: (1) included a statement of the restrictions on transfer of shares in the shareholder representation letters prepared in Step 7 of Chapter 5; and (2) placed a nonregistration legend on the share certificates contained in Appendix B of this book.

We have provided a practical and traditional method of issuing your shares under the general guidelines of the federal private offering exemption promulgated under Section 4(2) of the federal Securities Act and under some of the provisions of Rule 506. However, we can't anticipate the particular facts and circumstances surrounding your incorporation, and, of course, we can't guarantee that the federal private offering exemption will apply to you. Technical provisions of law (particularly of the securities laws) can be analyzed ad infinitum, and entire volumes, indeed libraries, have been devoted to the task. What we can do is provide you with (hopefully) helpful information, and repeat the reminder that you are ultimately responsible for making sure that you comply with the securities laws. We recommend you also ask an experienced business lawyer to review your proposed stock issuance to ensure compliance with federal and state securities laws.

Finally, one other point bears repeating: Remember to disclose, disclose, disclose all material information to every investor in your new corporation. This makes good business sense—and can help you steer clear of the SEC's antifraud rules.

Other Regulation D Exemptions

Federal Regulation D contains two other stock offering exemptions, which you may wish to discuss with a small business lawyer:

- Rule 504 exempts limited offerings up to $1 million. Although this rule does not limit the number of purchasers, it does prohibit general advertising, and no more than $500,000 of the stock can be sold without registering the sale with the state.
- Rule 505 exempts limited offerings up to $5 million. Generally no more than 35 nonaccredited investors are allowed, no general advertising is permitted, and specific information must be disclosed if any nonaccredited investors are included in the offering.

RESOURCE

For more information on SEC small business securities law exemptions, go to www.sec.gov and search under information for "Small Business."

CHAPTER

Corporate Taxation

Most profit corporations, like individuals, must pay state and federal income taxes. (S corporations, discussed below, are exceptions.) In this chapter, we discuss the principal tax consequences of starting and operating a corporation and review special tax elections many small corporations will want to make. This information is meant to introduce you to the most important areas of corporate taxation and to provide you with enough background information to discuss them in greater depth with a tax expert.

RESOURCE

Keep up with changing tax rules. Tax laws and regulations are constantly changing, and corporate and individual tax rates may change over the next year (including dividend and capital gains tax rates). To keep up to date, see the most recent IRS and California tax publications. (See the tax publications listed in "Tax Forms—Federal" in Chapter 6.) For information on deductible business and home office expenses, see *Deduct It!* by Stephen Fishman (Nolo) and *Tax Savvy for Small Business,* by Frederick W. Daily (Nolo). Also, consult a tax adviser with small business experience on a regular basis to make sure you understand how all the latest tax wrinkles apply to your business.

California Taxes

Let's start by looking at the taxes and tax elections built into the California corporate tax scheme.

California Corporate Franchise Tax

California profit corporations must pay an annual corporate franchise tax—a fee you pay to the state for the privilege of doing business as a corporation. The tax is computed each year on the basis of the net income your corporation earned in the previous year from business activity in California (and, sometimes, outside California). The California franchise tax rate is 8.84% of the corporation's taxable income, with a minimum yearly payment of $800 regardless of the amount of annual income or profits. For your first tax year, you don't have to pay the minimum franchise tax, but you must estimate and pay any actual franchise taxes owed.

Corporations must estimate and pay franchise taxes during the year. (See "Corporate Estimated Tax Return" in Chapter 6.)

You must take your responsibility to estimate and pay corporate taxes seriously. If you fail to file state corporate tax returns or pay state corporate income taxes on time, your corporate privileges can be taken away. (You'll find a more detailed discussion of other taxes for which your corporation may be liable in Chapter 6.)

California Personal Income Tax

Corporate employees must report salaries and bonuses on their personal income tax returns, and pay tax on them at their personal state income tax rates. The fact that a corporate employee is also a corporate shareholder does not affect how income tax is calculated. As long as salaries and bonuses are reasonable (most are), the corporation can deduct these amounts as an ordinary and necessary business expense. This means that only the individual employee-shareholder pays income tax on corporate earnings paid out as salaries—the corporation does not.

In contrast, corporate profits paid to shareholders in the form of dividends are taxed twice. First, the corporation pays taxes at the corporate level, then the shareholders pay taxes on the individual distribution.

Unlike salaries, the corporation cannot deduct dividend payouts to shareholders as a business expense on its income tax return. As a practical matter, however, double taxation is rare. Small corporations usually don't have to pay out profits as dividends. Instead, corporations can retain excess earnings in the corporation, where they are taxed only at corporate tax rates, or pay this money to the employee-shareholders in the form of salaries, bonuses, and fringe benefits, in which case they are taxed to the employees (and the corporation gets to treat them as tax deductible business expenses). Either way, only one tax is paid (corporate or individual).

California S Corporation Tax Election

Some California corporations may wish to elect federal S corporation tax status. If the federal election is made, the corporation will automatically be treated as an S corporation under California state tax laws as well (unless the corporation opts out by filing FTB Form 3500). Making the federal S corporation election allows the corporation to bypass regular corporate level taxes on corporate taxable income. The state still assesses a small tax, as explained in "California S Corporation Tax Treatment," below, with the taxable income of the corporation passed through to the shareholders to be taxed only once on their individual tax returns. We explain how these special S corporation tax elections work later in this chapter.

California S Corporation Tax Treatment

California corporations that are qualified for, and have elected, federal S corporation tax status are automatically treated as S corporations in California, unless they opt out of S corporation tax treatment by filing FTB Form 3500. This state S corporation tax treatment means the corporation avoids the full California corporate franchise tax rate on state corporate net taxable income. Instead, the corporation's taxable California income passes through to the individual state tax returns of the corporation's shareholders. We explain the requirements, advantages, and disadvantages of the federal S corporation tax election in detail in "S Corporation Tax Status," below.

However, before electing federal S corporation tax status consider the following:

- A new business is generally better off organizing as an LLC rather than an S corporation. An LLC gives you the same pass-through tax status as an S corporation and the same limited personal legal liability protection for all business owners. And an LLC is easier to organize and operate than an S corporation, and does not burden the owners with the special requirements that apply to S corporations.
- As opposed to federal S corporations, which normally don't pay any federal corporate income taxes, California S corporations still have to pay the California Franchise Tax Board a 1.5% tax on net California corporate income. They must also pay the minimum $800 corporate franchise tax each year (except for their first tax year).

Federal Taxes

In this section, we look at how the federal corporate tax rates compare to individual tax rates. We also show you how to enjoy one of the best built-in benefits of forming a corporation: splitting income between the corporation and individual tax brackets to achieve overall tax savings for the owners of the business.

Federal Corporate Income Tax

Federal Corporate Tax Rates

Federal corporate income taxes and tax rates are as follows:

Corporate Taxable Income	Corporate Tax
$0–$50,000	15% of taxable income
$50,001–$75,000	$7,500 + 25% of taxable income over $50,000
$75,001–$100,000	$13,750 + 34% of taxable income over $75,000
$100,001–$335,000	$22,250 + 39% of taxable income over $100,000
$335,001–$10,000,000	$113,900 + 34% of taxable income over $335,000
$10,000,001–$15,000,000	$3,400,000 + 35% of taxable income over $10,000,000
$15,000,001–$18,333,333	$5,150,000 + 38% of taxable income over $15,000,000
over $18,333,333	35%

As you can see, the first $50,000 of taxable corporate income is taxed at only 15%, and the next $25,000 at 25%. Because these rates are lower (as compared to most individuals' marginal (top) personal income tax rates), and especially if your corporation needs money to expand, retaining corporate profits that get taxed at these lower corporate tax rates is often an excellent tax strategy.

You will also notice that corporate taxes go way up—to 39%—after you retain $100,000 of income at the corporate level. This structure requires larger corporations to pay back the benefits of the lower graduated tax rates of 15% and 25%. But even corporations subject to this 39% bracket still pay tax at an effective rate of 34%, when the lower brackets are averaged in. For highly profitable corporations, a 35% tax rate is applied to taxable incomes over $10,000,000, with an additional 38% bubble set up to make corporations with incomes over $18,333,333 pay taxes at a flat 35% tax rate (to eliminate the advantage of the lower graduated tax brackets below 35%).

A Higher Corporate Tax Rate Applies to Corporations That Provide Personal Services

Under Internal Revenue Code Section 11(b)(2), many incorporated professionals and others who provide personal services (called personal service corporations) pay a flat corporate tax of 35% on corporate taxable income.

This flat tax rate applies to corporations in which:

- substantially all the stock of the corporation is held by the employees performing professional services for the corporation, and
- substantially all the activities of the corporation involve the performance of one of the following professions or activities:
  - health
  - law
  - engineering
  - architecture
  - accounting
  - actuarial science
  - performing arts, or
  - consulting.

Because professionals in these fields (except architecture, actuarial science, engineering, performing arts, and consulting) are required to incorporate as California professional corporations rather than regular California for-profit corporations (see "Professional Corporations" in Chapter 2), this tax will not apply to most readers of this book.

Federal tax law provides deductions for corporate income derived from United States manufacturing and other "domestic production" activities. The deductions started at 3% in 2005 and increased to 6% for 2007 through 2009 and are at 9% for 2010 and thereafter. This means that a corporation in the top corporate tax bracket level may be able to lower its tax rate by 3% in 2010 by taking advantage of this tax break. For example, if you have an effective corporate tax rate of 33⅓%, then a 9% deduction in income results in a 3% tax rate deduction (⅓ × a 9% deduction = a 3% tax rate deduction). For more information, see IRS Form 8903, *Domestic Production Activities Deduction*, and Section 199 of the Internal Revenue Code.

Federal Individual Income Tax

The federal government levies an income tax on shareholders when corporate profits are distributed to them as either dividends or salaries. Currently, dividends are taxed at a 15% federal tax rate (5% for low-income taxpayers). But because dividends are taxed both to the corporation and shareholders, owners of small corporations normally prefer to avoid double taxation by paying out corporate profits in the form of tax deductible salaries, bonuses, or employee fringe benefits, or under the terms of a consulting contract.

A big advantage of incorporating a business in which you actively participate is that you can split business income between two tax entities, your corporation and yourself. You can pay yourself a salary, which will be taxed at your individual federal income tax rate (and is tax deductible by your corporation), and at the same time, retain earnings in your corporation (the first $75,000 of which will be taxed at the lower federal corporate tax rates of 15% or 25%). The IRS allows most corporations to accumulate up to $250,000 of earnings in the corporation for this type of income splitting, no questions asked (personal service corporations get a lower automatic credit of $150,000). Amounts above the automatic credit limit can be left in the corporation, if they are accumulated to meet the reasonable business needs of the corporation.

CAUTION

Unreasonable accumulations get hit with a tax penalty. Most corporations accumulate profits for valid business purposes, such as maintaining inventory levels, paying off debt, expanding the business, and the like. The IRS will not challenge these business-related accumulations. But if you do something silly—like accumulate $1 million cash in your corporation simply to avoid paying individual income taxes on these profits—the IRS may challenge you. If you can't show a valid business reason for keeping these profits in your corporation, the IRS will make you pay an extra tax on the accumulation at the current top dividend tax rate of 15%.

LLCs Can Choose to Be Taxed as Corporations

While limited liability companies (LLCs) are normally taxed as pass-through entities, with LLC income and losses reported and taxed on the personal income tax returns of the owners, they have the option to be treated and taxed like a corporation. To do this, the LLC owners must complete and file IRS Form 8832, *Entity Classification Election*, checking the box on the form that asks the IRS to treat the LLC as a corporation for tax purposes. Once this form is filed, the LLC files regular corporate income tax returns and can split income between the business and the owners. Your tax adviser can tell you if this corporate tax strategy makes sense for an unincorporated co-owned business. (See Chapter 7.)

Beware of the Personal Holding Company Penalty

IRC Sections 541 through 547 impose an extra tax—equal to the highest dividend tax rate of 15%—on the income of personal holding companies (PHCs). Generally, a corporation is a PHC if five or fewer shareholders own 50% or more of the corporation's stock and if 60% or more of the corporation's gross income for the tax year comes from "personal service contracts"—contracts for personal services that name the person who must perform the services—or from passive sources like dividends, interest, rents, or royalties.

Most small business corporations don't need to worry about being classified as PHCs and having to pay this tax, even if they have five or fewer shareholders. It's usually easy to avoid by having a tax adviser tell you how to use a corporate services contract that won't be classified as a personal services contract, and because most small corporations do not have significant passive income. Also, the PHC rules state that rental income and software royalties—two of the categories of passive income most likely to be earned by small corporations—won't be counted to determine if a corporation is a PHC. Even if the IRS finds that a corporation is a PHC and assesses the surtax, the corporation can usually avoid the tax by making dividend payments (direct payments out of current earnings) and profits to shareholders. In other words, you can pay your profits to your shareholders, not to the IRS in the form of a PHC tax.

The PHC rules are too complicated to fully explain. If your corporation has five or fewer shareholders and performs services or earns passive income, check with a tax adviser to make sure you avoid the PHC surtax.

If you find that being taxed as a corporation will subject you to higher taxes than you would pay if all income were passed through to you and the other shareholders and taxed at your personal income tax rates, you have an alternative. You may be able to elect federal S corporation tax status. As explained below in "S Corporation Tax Status," if you make this federal tax election, corporate income is passed through to your shareholders where it is reported and taxed on their individual federal tax returns only.

Comparing Individual and Corporate Tax Rates and Payments for Owners of Smaller Corporations

Incorporating and paying taxes as a corporate entity can result in business owners paying less tax on business income than they would pay as an individual. This is because income retained in a corporation may be taxed at the 15% and 25% corporate tax rates, instead of the higher marginal tax rates of the corporate owners, which can be as high as 35%

EXAMPLE: Sally and Randolph run their own incorporated lumber supply company (S & R Wood, Inc.). With the boom in home renovations, their sales increase. After the close of the third quarter, S & R's accountant reports that they are on course to make $100,000 in taxable profits, even after dipping into the increased earnings to pay deductible bonuses and other operating expenses. Sally and Randy already receive a generous salary from their corporation, so they decide to keep the profits in the business to fund expansion in the following tax year. If S & R was taxed as a pass-through entity (a regular LLC or a general partnership), rather than as a corporation, the $100,000 would pass through the business and be taxed at Sally's and Randy's marginal (top) individual income tax rate of 35%. Instead, by retaining the money in the business, S & R Wood will pay corporate taxes at a rate of 15% and 25% for the first $75,000 of retained taxes, thus saving overall taxes for an effective tax rate of about 22%—a tax savings of $16,350 over what they would have had to pay at their individual tax rates (35% × $100,000, or $35,000).

TIP

Even corporations with sales of $1 million often benefit from the lower corporate tax rate. Why? Because after the corporation pays deductible salaries, bonuses, and corporate fringe benefits to the owner-employees of the corporation (and to other corporate personnel), and deducts other corporate business expenses, actual profits will be substantially reduced—often below the $75,000 threshold, where only the 15% and 25% corporate tax rates apply

CAUTION

Don't forget to factor in other income earned by individual taxpayers. Individual taxpayers need to consider the money they are already earning—as salary and bonuses from their corporation and/or outside income—before comparing corporate versus individual tax rates. Many individuals will be paying taxes in one of the top individual tax brackets (33% or 35%) on individual income (this is their marginal tax bracket), and this is the rate that will apply to any additional income they earn. If income is not retained in the corporation, it will be taxed to them at this marginal rate—a rate that normally is higher than the 15% or 25% lowest corporate tax rates. For this reason, keeping money in a corporation often creates overall tax savings.

S Corporation Tax Status

This section covers a once highly popular tax election that still makes sense for some small corporations—the S corporation tax election. As noted above, if you elect S corporation tax status, all profits pass through the corporation and are taxed, one time only, on the individual income tax returns of the corporate shareholders.

TIP

Consider forming an LLC instead of an S corporation. The S corporation tax election is no longer the only way to simultaneously achieve limited personal liability for business debts and pass-through taxation of business profits. If you have not already incorporated (and most readers of this book probably haven't), you may be better off forming a limited liability company, especially if you do not need to raise money by giving equity investors a stake in your business.

Federal S Corporation Tax Election Requirements

To qualify for S corporation tax status with the IRS, a corporation must fall within the definition of a small business corporation under Subchapter S of the Internal Revenue Code. Only a corporation that meets these requirements qualifies:

- It must be a U.S. corporation, and its shareholders must be U.S. citizens or residents.
- There must be only one class of stock (all shares have equal rights, such as dividend and liquidation rights). However, differences as to voting rights are permitted.
- All shareholders must be individuals, estates, certain qualified trusts, or a

tax-exempt organization (including tax-exempt charities and pension funds).
- There must be no more than 100 shareholders. Shares that are jointly owned by members of the same family (as defined in the Internal Revenue Code) are considered owned by one person.

A corporation that meets these requirements can elect S corporation tax treatment by filing IRS Form 2553 with the IRS, which must be signed by all current shareholders and by anyone else who owned shares during the preceding corporate tax year. The election must be made on or before the 15th day of the third month of the corporation's tax year for which the S status is to be effective, or any time during the preceding tax year. A new corporation that wishes to start off as an S corporation must make the election before the 15th day of the third month after the date the corporation's first tax year begins. The corporation's first tax year begins, under the S corporation election rules, when it issues stock to shareholders, acquires assets, or begins doing business, whichever occurs first. Generally, your first tax year will begin on the date you file your articles of incorporation. Check with your tax adviser to ensure that you fully understand these election rules and make your election on time—if you miss the deadline, your election won't be valid. (See "S Corporation Tax Election" in Chapter 6.)

Once a corporation elects to become an S corporation, it will be treated as one until the status is revoked or terminated. To revoke S corporation status, you must file shareholder consents to the revocation. You must have the consent of shareholders who collectively own at least a majority of the stock in the corporation to make the revocation effective.

S corporation status can also be automatically terminated, if the corporation doesn't continue to meet all of the requirements listed above, and therefore no longer qualifies as a small business corporation. For example, if the corporation issues a second class of shares or issues shares to a noneligible individual, or partnership, corporate, or LLC shareholders, it will lose S corporation status. Such a termination will be effective as of the date on which the terminating event occurs (not retroactively to the beginning of the tax year).

CAUTION

You must wait at least five years between S corporation tax elections. Once its S status has been revoked or terminated, the corporation may not reelect S corporation tax status until five years after the termination or revocation.

Advantages and Disadvantages of S Corporation Tax Treatment

There are benefits and drawbacks to making an S corporation election with the IRS.

Advantages of S Corporation Tax Treatment

S corporation tax treatment offers these potential advantages, depending on the needs and nature of your business:

- **Self-employment tax break.** Corporate profits passed through to shareholders who work for the corporation are not subject to self-employment taxes, as long as the shareholder-employee also pays herself a reasonable salary.

EXAMPLE: Johanna is one of two shareholders of Moonlight Designs, Inc., a Web page design consulting firm, which has elected S corporation tax status. She runs the firm as president, together with fellow shareholder-employee Rafael, who is VP. Both work part-time for the corporation; their day jobs are with other Web page design firms. This year, net profits from Moonlight Designs are $150,000. Johanna and Rafael are each paid a reasonable salary of $50,000, on which both the corporation and the shareholder-employee must pay Social Security taxes. The remaining $50,000 in Moonlight profits passes to the shareholders as profits of the S corporation, and is not subject to corporate or individual Social Security taxes. By contrast, if Moonlight had not incorporated but instead operated as an LLC, the owners would have to pay self-employment tax on this extra allocation of $50,000 in profits.

- **Pass-through of corporate losses.** In start-up businesses that expect initial losses before the business begins to show a profit, S corporation tax status can pass these initial losses to the individual tax returns of the shareholders who actively participate in the business. This allows them to offset income from other sources with the losses of the corporation. (See "Requirements to Pass Through S Corporation Losses," below, for further information.)

  EXAMPLE: Will and Bruno decide to form and incorporate a part-time air charter business. They'll continue to work during the week at their salaried jobs until their new business gets off the ground. They project that in the first few years of corporate life, their business will generate substantial losses (modest receipts from flying weekend charters accompanied by large expenditures for the purchase of liability insurance and other expenses). Rather than operate as a regular C corporation and take these losses at the corporate level, they decide to elect S corporation tax status and deduct these losses immediately against their individual full-time salary income on their individual tax returns. In five years, they expect their corporation to turn a profit, and will revoke their S corporation election to take advantage of lower corporate tax rates on business profits.

- **No dissolution tax on appreciated assets.** As discussed in Chapter 1, regular corporations with assets that have gone up in value since their acquisition are subject to a corporate and shareholder level tax when the corporation dissolves. S corporations are not generally subject to this corporate level tax (unless they previously operated as a regular C corporation). S corporation shareholders pay just one level of tax on appreciated assets when the corporation dissolves. Especially for corporations that may dissolve and own appreciated assets, S corporation tax status may be the best way to go.

  EXAMPLE: Sam and his sister Terry decide to form a corporation to own real property. During the anticipated ten-year life of their corporation, they expect the property to appreciate considerably. In order to avoid a corporate level tax on this appreciation when the corporation is dissolved and the property sold, they decide to elect S corporation status prior to the purchase of any property by their corporation.

- **Legal and business benefits of the corporate form.** As an S corporation, you still enjoy the other advantages of incorporating—such as the built-in operating structure and limited liability.

Disadvantages of S Corporation Tax Treatment

Not surprisingly, there are also some potential disadvantages to electing S corporation status. The list below also includes information on LLCs. Because LLCs also allow owners to pass through profits and limit their legal liability, those considering forming an S corporation should compare the relative benefits and drawbacks of forming an LLC instead. As the list below demonstrates, LLCs often allow more flexibility and might provide better tax treatment:

- **Owners must be individual U.S. citizens or residents.** S corporation shareholders must be individuals who are U.S. citizens or residents, or special types of trusts. In contrast, LLCs can admit any person or entity, such as a corporation, partnership, or another LLC, as a member.
- **Limitations on allocations of profits and losses.** S corporations must allocate dividends, liquidation proceeds, and corporate losses in proportion to stockholdings. LLCs can allocate profits and losses among members disproportionately—these are called special allocations under the tax regulations.
- **Limitations on the pass-through of corporate losses.** The amount of losses that may be passed through to S corporation shareholders is limited to the total of each shareholder's basis in his or her stock, plus any amount each shareholder has personally loaned to the corporation. But an LLC owner may be able to count his or her pro rata share of all money borrowed by the LLC, not just loans made by the owner, in computing how much of any business loss the owner can deduct in a given year on his or her individual income tax return (subject to special rules).
- **Restrictions on employee benefits and perks.** S corporations cannot adopt an employee stock ownership plan (although they are permitted to adopt a stock bonus plan), and shareholder-employees owning more than 2% of the S corporation's stock are treated the same as partners for purposes of fringe benefits. LLCs and their owners are subject to the same restrictions.

Requirements to Pass Through S Corporation Losses

One reason to elect S corporation tax status is to pass corporate losses through to the tax returns of the business owners, where they can be treated as individual losses. But there can be a tax trap for the unwary—the amount of loss you are eligible to pass through to your individual tax return is limited by your basis in your stock (essentially, what you paid for it plus or minus later adjustments), plus any loans you personally make to your corporation.

> EXAMPLE: Jeremy paid $10,000 for his shares in his solely owned S corporation. He also personally lent his corporation $10,000. His S corporation loses $30,000 in its first year of operation. Jeremy potentially can show a loss of $20,000 on his individual tax return for the year—he may be able to deduct the remaining $10,000 S corporation loss in future years if his stock basis increases, or if he lends his S corporation additional funds.

Other tax rules limit the deductibility of S corporation losses. Ask your tax adviser for more information.

S Corporation Tax Election for State Income Tax Purposes

Once a corporation elects S corporation tax treatment with the IRS, it is automatically treated as an S corporation by the California Franchise Tax Board for state income tax purposes, unless the corporation opts out of California S corporation treatment. This means that the profits of your S corporation are not taxed at state income tax rates, but pass through the corporation and are taxed to your California shareholders at their California individual income tax rates. However, as explained in "California S Corporation Tax Treatment," above, California S corporations are still subject to a 1.5% franchise tax on net profits and, except during the first year of the corporation's existence, must pay the minimum corporate franchise tax each year (currently $800), regardless of profits.

Corporate Accounting Periods and Tax Years

The accounting period of the corporation is the period for which the corporation keeps its annual books and must correspond to the corporation's tax year. Generally, corporations can choose a calendar year from January 1 to December 31, or a fiscal year consisting of a 12-month period ending on the last day of any month other than December (for example, from July 1 to June 30). In special situations, a corporation may wish to choose a 52–53-week year. This is a period which ends on a particular day closest to the end of a month (for example, the last Friday of March or the Friday nearest to the end of March).

Most corporations will choose either a calendar year or a fiscal year as their accounting period. For most corporations, a calendar tax year will prove easier, because it will be the same year as that used by the individual shareholders. Some corporations, because of the particular business cycle of the corporation or simply because December is a hectic month, may wish to choose a different month to wind up their yearly affairs.

Tax Year Rules for S and Personal Service Corporations

If you plan to elect federal S corporation tax status or if your corporation meets the definition of a personal service corporation, you must choose a calendar year for your corporate tax year (and your accounting period) unless the IRS approves your application to use a fiscal year.

A personal service corporation is defined in the Internal Revenue Code as "... a corporation the principal activity of which is the performance of personal services ... [if] such services are substantially performed by employee-owners." This means that if you are incorporating a service-only business or profession (for example, lawyers, architects, consultants, and financial planners), you must adopt a calendar year as your corporate tax year unless you request and are granted permission to use a different year by the IRS.

Although federal S corporations are not considered personal service corporations, they must adopt a calendar year as their tax year unless they can show the IRS that they fall within an exception to the calendar year rule. A new corporation that plans to elect S corporation tax status can apply for a fiscal tax year, instead of the normal January 1 calendar tax year, on its S corporation election form (IRS Form 2553). Personal service corporations request a noncalendar tax year by filing IRS Form 1128 with the IRS.

If you want to adopt a fiscal tax year for your personal service corporation or S corporation, ask your tax adviser to explain the requirements and procedures.

Tax Concerns When Stock Is Sold

This section discusses two special tax provisions that apply to owners of small corporations when their corporation or its shares are sold. (Normally, both occur as part of the same transaction, but one owner may decide to sell his or her shares separately to the corporation, its remaining shareholders, or an outsider.) The first part of this section covers the gloomy situation of an owner selling shares for less than their original purchase price—that is, for less than what the owner paid for the shares when the corporation was founded. The second part covers the more pleasant situation of selling shares at a profit—as well as the less pleasant side effect of such a sale: paying taxes on the stock profits.

We cover only the general rules here. If these issues are of interest to you, make sure you review their requirements in more depth with your tax adviser.

Section 1244 Tax Treatment for Stock Losses

We know that you don't plan to sell your corporation or its stock at a loss. But if this happens, the sting will be lessened to some extent if your stock qualifies for what is called Section 1244 treatment. Although this sounds technical, the concept is fairly simple. Under Section 1244 of the Internal Revenue Code, many corporations can provide their shareholders with the benefit of treating losses from the sale, exchange, or worthlessness of their stock as ordinary rather than capital losses on their individual tax returns, up to a maximum of $50,000 (or $100,000 for a husband and wife filing a joint return) in each tax year. The advantage to this treatment is that you can fully deduct ordinary losses against individual income (thus lowering the total amount on which you have to pay taxes). In contrast, capital losses are only partially deductible—generally, you can use capital losses to offset a maximum of $3,000 of individual income per tax year.

To qualify for Section 1244 tax treatment, your loss on the sale of stock must meet the following requirements:

- You must be the original owner of the shares. If you sell your shares to another shareholder or give your shares to a family member, the person who received your shares is not entitled to claim a Section 1244 loss.
- You must have paid money or property (other than corporate securities) for your shares.
- More than 50% of the corporation's gross receipts during the five tax years preceding the year in which the loss occurred must have been derived from sources other than royalties, dividends, interest, rents, annuities, or gains from sales or exchanges of securities or stock. If the corporation has not been in existence for five tax years, this 50% rule applies to the total number of tax years for which the corporation has been in existence.
- The total amount of money or the value of property received by the corporation for stock, as a contribution to capital and as paid-in surplus, cannot exceed $1 million.
- At the time of the loss, you must submit a timely statement to the IRS electing to take an ordinary loss pursuant to Section 1244. There is no special form you have to use for this purpose; your tax adviser can draft a statement that contains the required information.

RELATED TOPIC

Prepare your Section 1244 resolution. The minutes you will prepare when you reach

Chapter 5, Step 6, include a Section 1244 resolution. You can use this as internal documentation of your intent to have future stock losses by your shareholders be eligible for Section 1244 tax treatment. Most, if not all, incorporators will want to include this resolution in their minutes and keep a copy in their corporate records book. If your corporation does not meet the Section 1244 requirements when a stock loss occurs, the loss will simply be treated as a capital loss rather than an ordinary loss.

Section 1202 Capital Gains Tax Exclusion

People who own shares that qualify as small business stock receive the benefit of lower capital gains tax rates when they report profits from the sale or other disposition of their corporate shares. An individual shareholder can exclude from taxation 50% of the gain on sales of small business stock, subject to a maximum exclusion of $10 million or ten times the shareholder's basis in the stock.

> EXAMPLE: Bob and Ken are 50-50 owners of Grass Roots Turf Supplies, Inc. Each founder paid $20,000 for his initial shares. Six years later, Bob decides to move on to greener pastures, and agrees to sell his shares to Ken for $50,000. Bob's capital gain on the sale of his shares is $30,000. If Bob's stock qualifies as small business stock (see below), he has to pay capital gains tax on only $15,000; he can exclude the other $15,000 on his income tax return. The Section 1202 capital gains tax rate applied to one-half of the stock sale proceeds is 28%, for an effective tax rate of 14% on the total sales amount. This is 1% less than the current 15% long-term capital gains rate that most taxpayers pay.

Stock qualifies as small business stock only if:

- You hold the shares for at least five years. However, if you are given shares or inherit them during the five-year period, you can add on the amount of time the shares were held by the person who gave or bequeathed them to you. Also, if you have held the shares for six months, you can defer paying taxes on 100% of the gain from a sale if you reinvest the sales proceeds into another small business corporation within 60 days. (The taxes on the gain from the first sale are deferred until you sell the second corporation's shares.)
- You purchased the stock with money or property (other than stock), or you received it as employee compensation.
- The corporation had gross assets of $50 million or less on the date the shares were issued to you.
- The corporation is engaged in the operation of an active business (not making money exclusively from investments, rents, and the like). However, the practice of an incorporated profession, such as a medical, accounting, or engineering practice and several other types of businesses (like hotels, farming, and mining) do not qualify under this tax provision.

You can use the standard IRS 1040 tax return to report and pay taxes on Section 1202 stock gains. To learn more about how to do this, see the IRS instructions that accompany Form 1040, or ask your tax adviser.

Tax Treatment When an Existing Business Is Incorporated

Here, we focus on the tax implications of incorporating an existing business—that is, of issuing shares of your new corporation in return for the assets of the existing unincorporated business. The rules in this area are quite complex, so be sure to talk them over with your tax adviser if they may apply to you.

SKIP AHEAD

If you are not incorporating an existing business, you can skip this section.

Tax-Free Exchanges Under Section 351

When you incorporate an existing business, you transfer its assets and liabilities to the new corporation in return for shares of stock. Under normal federal income tax rules, this sort of transfer of assets would be a sale. And as you know, any time you sell an asset to someone, you generally have to pay taxes on the profit you make from the transaction. In tax terms, the profit is the difference between the selling price and your tax basis in the property. Essentially, your tax basis in the property is the amount you paid for it minus depreciation plus capital improvements.

EXAMPLE: Assume that your business purchased a building at a cost of $180,000. In the years since purchase, the business has taken $90,000 depreciation on the property and made $20,000 in capital improvements to the property. This means the adjusted basis of the property is now $110,000 (cost of $180,000 – $90,000 depreciation + $20,000 improvements). If the property is sold for $210,000, the taxable gain (profit) is $100,000 ($210,000 – its $110,000 adjusted basis). To keep things simple, we are ignoring the cost, sales price, and basis of the land on which the building is located (land is not depreciable).

Naturally, most incorporators of an existing business prefer not to pay taxes on the sale of property to their corporation in return for shares of stock. This is particularly true if the property that is being transferred to the corporation has gone up substantially in value. Fortunately, this is where Section 351 of the Internal Revenue Code comes in: It allows incorporators to transfer property to their corporation in return for stock in a tax-free exchange without recognizing any gain or loss on the transfer. Instead, payment of tax on the gain is deferred until the shares are sold.

To qualify for Section 351, you must meet two control tests immediately after the transfer:

- The transferors, as a group, must own at least 80% of the total combined voting power of all classes of issued stock entitled to vote.
- The transferors must also own at least 80% of all other issued classes of stock of the corporation.

Most initial stock issuance transactions of small corporations should meet these control tests and therefore will be eligible for this tax-free exchange treatment. Because this is your first stock issuance involving one class of common voting shares, you don't need to worry about previously issued stock or other classes of stock.

EXAMPLE: Harvey, Frank, and Frances decide to form a corporation. The corporation will issue 500 shares of stock at a price of $100 per share. Harvey will receive 100 shares for a $10,000 cash payment; Frank and Frances will receive 200 shares apiece for their equal interests in the assets of their partnership valued at $40,000. The transaction qualifies for Section 351 tax-free exchange treatment, because at least 80% (in this case, 100%) of all shares in the corporation will be owned by the transferors of money and property after the transfer.

Of course, little is really free under tax statutes and regulations. A tax-free exchange simply defers the payment of taxes until you sell your shares or your corporation is sold or liquidated. At that time, your shares will have the same basis as the property you originally transferred to the corporation, plus or minus any adjustments made to your shares while you held them.

> EXAMPLE: You transfer property with a fair market value of $20,000 and an adjusted basis of $10,000 to the corporation in a Section 351 tax-free exchange for shares worth $20,000. Your shares will then have a basis of $10,000. If you sell the shares for $30,000, your taxable gain will be $20,000 ($30,000 selling price minus their basis of $10,000). The corporation's basis in the property received in a tax-free exchange will also generally be the same as the adjusted basis of the transferred property. In this example, the corporation's basis in the property will be $10,000.

Even in a tax-free transaction, the shareholders must pay tax on any money or property they receive in addition to stock. For example, if you transfer a truck worth $50,000 in a tax-free exchange to the corporation in return for $40,000 worth of shares and a $10,000 cash payment by the corporation, you will have to report the $10,000 as taxable income.

> CAUTION
>
> **The IRS requires information about Section 351 transactions.** Federal income tax regulations require the corporation and each shareholder to file statements with their income tax returns listing specific information about any Section 351 tax-free exchange. The corporation and the shareholders must also keep permanent records containing the information listed in these statements.

Potential Problems With Section 351 Tax-Free Exchanges

There are, of course, complexities that may arise when you attempt to exchange property for stock in your corporation under Section 351. Let's look at a few of the most common problem areas.

Issuing Shares in Return for the Performance of Services

Although California law allows stock to be issued for work (services) already performed for the corporation (see "Selling Stock," in Chapter 2), labor is not considered property for purposes of Section 351. Remember, stock must be issued in return for property to qualify for this tax-free exchange treatment.

What this means is that you cannot count shares issued to shareholders for work or services in calculating the 80% control requirement. Even if you are able to meet the control test (not counting the stock issued for services), any shareholder who receives stock for services will have to report the value of his or her shares as taxable income.

> EXAMPLE: Your corporation plans to issue $50,000 worth of shares upon its incorporation to you and the cofounder of your corporation, Fred. You will transfer property worth $35,000 for $35,000 in shares while Fred will receive $15,000 in shares in return for work, valued at $15,000, he has already performed for the corporation. The transfer will be taxable to both you and Fred, because the basic control test of Section 351 won't be met: You are the only person who will transfer property in return for stock, and you will only own 70% of the shares of the corporation.

If the facts in this example are changed so that you receive 80% of the stock in exchange for property—for example, if you transfer $40,000 worth of property and Fred contributes $10,000 in past services—the transfer will be tax-free under Section 351, but Fred will have to report his $10,000 in shares as taxable income.

TIP

Intangible property qualifies under Section 351. Unlike work and services, intangible property, such as the goodwill of a business or patents, is considered property for purposes of Section 351. Thus, if you, as a prior business owner, contribute a valuable copyright, trademark, patent, or know-how to a new corporation, it can qualify as property under Section 351, and the shares you are issued can be counted in determining whether your incorporation meets the 80% control requirements of Section 351.

Issuing Stock and a Promissory Note in Exchange for Transferred Business Assets

Section 351 applies to the transfer of property in exchange for stock, not promissory notes or other debt instruments. For example, if you transfer business assets to the corporation in return for shares of stock plus a promissory note from the corporation, you will have to report and pay taxes on the gain (technical rules determine the amount of gain that must be reported). See your tax adviser if you plan to incorporate an existing business and wish to receive a promissory note in addition to shares back from your corporation.

Agreeing to Pay Liabilities Associated With the Transferred Property

When an existing business is incorporated and the owners of the prior business transfer its assets and liabilities to the corporation in return for shares of stock, the prior business owners may have to pay taxes if the liabilities assumed by the corporation exceed the basis of the business assets transferred to the corporation.

For example, if you transfer business assets with a basis of $40,000 to your corporation, but your corporation also assumes $60,000 worth of debts of your unincorporated business, the difference of $20,000 is, as a general rule, taxable to you.

SEE AN EXPERT

Consult an expert about property transfer rules. Federal tax statutes and their associated regulations contain many technical rules and exceptions to rules about transferring property to a corporation in return for stock. If you will be transferring property to your corporation in return for shares of stock (and possibly notes or other evidences of debt to be repaid by the corporation), you will need to check with an accountant to ensure favorable tax results under Section 351.

Is a Section 351 Tax-Free Exchange Desirable?

Most incorporators want to qualify for a Section 351 tax-free exchange. But this isn't always the case. Some incorporators may wish to recognize a gain or loss on the transfer of assets of the prior business to the corporation. (You may need to plan in advance to accomplish this.) Here are some reasons why an incorporator might want to avoid a Section 351 exchange:

- Some incorporators may wish to recognize a taxable gain on the transfer of business assets to increase the corporation's basis in these assets (perhaps to allow the corporation to take more depreciation deductions against these assets).

EXAMPLE: Assume that you will transfer assets with a fair market value of $50,000 to your corporation. Your basis in these assets is $30,000. If you transfer these assets to the corporation for $50,000 worth of stock in a taxable exchange, you will recognize a taxable gain of $20,000. However, the corporation's basis in these assets will be your basis before the sale ($30,000) plus the amount of gain recognized by the transferor (your individual gain of $20,000). Consequently, the corporation's basis in these assets will be increased to $50,000. This will allow the corporation to take additional depreciation in these assets over time and will lower the gain the corporation will recognize upon a sale of these assets (if the corporation sells the assets for $60,000, the gain will be $10,000—the difference between the corporation's basis and the selling price).

- If the assets in the above example had been transferred to the corporation in a tax-free exchange, the corporation's basis would be the same as your pretransfer basis in the property ($30,000), and the gain recognized by the corporation from the sale of these assets would be the higher figure of $30,000 (the difference between the corporation's $30,000 basis and the $60,000 selling price).
- Some incorporators may wish to recognize a loss on the transfer of assets to their corporation. If you transfer assets to your corporation in a Section 351 tax-free exchange for stock, you cannot recognize either a gain or a loss on the transfer at the time of the transfer—you have to wait until your corporation is sold or liquidated or you sell your shares to take the loss on your individual tax return.

EXAMPLE: If your basis in a building is $75,000, and, because of market conditions, the current value of the building is now only $60,000, you will need to transfer the building to the corporation in a taxable exchange to recognize this loss of $15,000 on your current year individual tax return. This is not a typical situation, but it may be relevant to some incorporators.

Additional Tax Considerations When Incorporating an Existing Business

Here are a few additional tax and business issues to consider if you are incorporating an existing business.

When Is the Best Time to Incorporate the Prior Business?

When incorporating an existing business, you should pick an incorporation date that results in the lowest possible tax bill.

EXAMPLE: If you anticipate a loss this year and a healthy profit next year, you may wish to remain unincorporated now and take a personal loss on your individual tax return. Remember: Corporate losses stay in the corporation and do not pass through to the individual tax returns of the shareholders unless the corporation elects S corporation tax status (and other technical requirements are met). Next year, you can incorporate and split your business income between yourself and your corporation to reduce your overall tax liability.

Should You Transfer All Assets and Liabilities to the New Corporation?

When an existing business is incorporated, it generally transfers all assets and liabilities to the corporation. However, in special circumstances, incorporators may not wish to transfer all assets or liabilities of the prior business to the corporation.

Retaining Some of the Assets of the Prior Business

In some instances, the prior business owners may not wish to transfer some of the assets of the prior business to their new corporation. For example:

- You need to retain sufficient cash to pay liabilities not assumed by the corporation, such as payroll and other taxes.
- You want to retain ownership in some of the assets of the prior business. For example, you may wish to continue to own a building in your name and lease it to your corporation. By doing this, you can continue to personally deduct depreciation, mortgage interest payments, and other expenses associated with the property on your individual tax return. And, of course, your corporation can deduct rent payments made under the lease (a rent comparable to the top amounts that similar commercial space rents for in your geographical area should pass IRS muster).

Finally, don't forget that if property is transferred to your corporation and it later appreciates, both your corporation and its shareholders may have to pay tax on the appreciation. Incorporators may decide not to transfer real property to their corporation to avoid this double tax—ask your tax adviser for more information.

Retaining Some of the Liabilities of the Prior Business

You may not wish to transfer—that is, have your corporation assume—all of the liabilities of the existing business. Here are two reasons why this might make sense:

- Assuming the liabilities of the prior business sometimes results in the assessment of tax (the amount by which the liabilities exceed the basis of the transferred assets—see "Potential Problems With Section 351 Tax-Free Exchanges," above).
- Payment of expenses by the prior business owners, rather than by the corporation, allows the owners to deduct these expenses on their individual tax returns, which reduces their individual taxable incomes.

Liability for the Debts of the Unincorporated Business

Another consideration when incorporating an existing business is whether the owners of the unincorporated business remain personally liable for its debts after it is incorporated. These rules have little practical significance for many incorporators who, as a matter of course and good-faith business practice, will wish to promptly pay all the debts and liabilities passed on to the new corporation. But, in case a debt is contested or for some other reason you wish to extend the time for payment, here are the legal basics:

- Whether or not the corporation assumes the debts and liabilities of the prior business, the prior owners remain personally liable for these debts and liabilities.
- The new corporation is not liable for the debts and liabilities of the prior business unless it specifically agrees to assume them. If it does not assume them, the prior owners remain personally liable.
- If the transfer is fraudulent or done with the intent to frustrate or deceive creditors, the creditors of the prior business can file legal papers to seize the transferred business assets. Similarly, if

the corporation does not, in fact, pay the assumed liabilities of the prior business, the creditors of the prior business may be allowed to seize the transferred assets.

- If transferred assets are subject to recorded liens (for example, a mortgage on real estate), these liens will survive the transfer and the assets will continue to be subject to them.
- The former business owners can be personally liable for *postincorporation* debts if credit is extended to the corporation by a creditor who thinks that he or she is still dealing with the prior business (for example, a creditor who has not been notified of the incorporation). (See "Notify Creditors and Others of Dissolution of Prior Business" in Chapter 6 for the steps to take to notify creditors when you incorporate.)
- The corporation may be liable for delinquent sales, employment, or other taxes owed by the unincorporated business.

A corporation that specifically assumes all of the debts and liabilities of the unincorporated business is exempt from most of the provisions of the California bulk sales law. This results in a reduction in incorporation paperwork. (See Chapter 5, Step 9.)

Tax Treatment of Employee Compensation and Benefits

This section provides an overview of the tax treatment of corporate salaries and fringe benefits. This is a very general discussion—ask your tax adviser for the most current information. Also see IRS Publication 15B, *Employer's Tax Guide to Fringe Benefits.*

Salaries

A regular or C corporation may deduct amounts paid to employees as salaries (including bonuses) for corporate income tax purposes. To be deductible, salaries and bonuses must be reasonable and must be paid for services actually performed by the employees. Huge salary increases or large discretionary lump-sum bonuses paid to shareholder-employees of closely held corporations may be scrutinized by the IRS, since they can be, and sometimes are, used as a means of paying disguised dividends to the shareholders.

But don't worry too much about the IRS claiming that your corporation's salaries or bonuses are too high. In an age when top execs of publicly held corporations are notoriously overpaid, and entertainment and sports figures who only make $1,000,000 often feel miserably underpaid, higher levels of compensation can be considered reasonable. You may be able to successfully argue that the salary, bonuses, and benefits you receive as compensation from your corporation are reasonable given the amount earned by executives in similar businesses. In a sense, your argument boils down to this: If you are good enough to produce profits large enough to pay a huge salary, you reasonably deserve it.

In the unusual event that the IRS claims a salary is unreasonable, it will treat the excess amount as a dividend. This will not have an adverse effect on the shareholder-employee's tax liability, because the payment must be included on his or her individual tax return either way. In fact, dividends are taxed at 15% or less, which typically is less than the tax rate applied to other types of individual income. However, it will prevent the corporation from deducting the disallowed portion of compensation as an ordinary and necessary business expense. So the corporation will have to pay corporate taxes on the dividends amount too.

TIP

Ask your board of directors to state how valuable you are. If you are nervous about paying yourself a large salary and a generous fringe benefit package, especially if you only work for your corporation part-time, ask your board to adopt a resolution detailing your abilities, qualifications, and responsibilities, showing why you are entitled to the wages and benefits your corporation is paying you. You can find such a resolution in *The Corporate Records Handbook*, by Anthony Mancuso (Nolo).

Pension and Profit-Sharing Plans

Corporations may deduct payments made on behalf of employees to qualified pension or profit-sharing plans. Contributions and accumulated earnings under such plans are not taxed until they are distributed to the employee. This is advantageous because employees generally will be in a lower tax bracket at retirement age, and the funds, while they are held in trust, can be invested and allowed to accumulate with no tax due on investment income or gains prior to their distribution.

Generally speaking, there are two basic types of pension plans: defined-contribution and defined-benefit plans (there are some hybrid types as well). A defined-contribution plan guarantees a specified yearly contribution of no more than 25% of an employee's annual salary to each employee. A defined-benefit plan guarantees a specified benefit upon retirement, which can be as large as 100% of an employee's annual pay during his or her highest-paid years. These contribution ceilings are subject to maximum yearly contribution limits, dollar amounts that are tied to the federal cost of living index. Your contributions cannot exceed these limits, even if an employee's yearly pay otherwise justifies a large pension contribution.

For detailed information on employee pension plan contribution and benefit rules, see *Tax Savvy for Small Business*, by Frederick W. Daily (Nolo). Also see the following IRS publications (available from the IRS website at www.irs.gov):

334: *Tax Guide For Small Business*
560: *Retirement Plans for Small Business (SEP, SIMPLE, and Qualified Plans)*
575: *Pension and Annuity Income*
590: *Individual Retirement Arrangements.*

Medical Benefits

Tax-favored corporate medical benefits include deductible direct reimbursement plans, term life insurance, and other benefits. Let's look at each.

Medical Expense Reimbursement

Amounts paid by a corporation as part of a medical expense reimbursement plan to repay the medical expenses of employees, their spouses, and dependents, are deductible by the corporation and are not included in the employee's income for tax purposes.

Accident and Health Insurance

A corporation may deduct premiums paid by the corporation for accident and health insurance coverage for employees, their spouses, and dependents. The premiums paid by the corporation are not included in the employee's income for tax purposes. In addition, insurance proceeds and benefits are not normally taxable. Coverage need not be part of a group plan, such as Blue Cross. If you prefer, the employee may pick her own policy, pay for it, and obtain reimbursement from the corporation.

Unincorporated business owners (and S corporation shareholder-employees) also are allowed to deduct the premiums paid for themselves and their spouses for health insurance.

Life Insurance

A corporation can deduct premiums paid on behalf of employees for group term life insurance, as long as the corporation is not the beneficiary. This tax break is available only if the plan does not discriminate in favor of key employees. An employee covered by a qualified group term insurance plan is not taxed on premium payments by the corporation for up to $50,000 worth of insurance coverage. Death proceeds under such insurance are also generally not included in the employee's income for tax purposes.

Disability Insurance

Premiums paid by a corporation for disability insurance coverage for its employees are deductible by the corporation. Benefits paid under a disability insurance policy are generally taxable to the employee unless the employee paid the premiums or suffers a permanent injury.

CHAPTER

Steps to Form Your Corporation

This chapter will show you, step by step, how to form your California corporation by preparing and filing articles of incorporation, preparing bylaws, preparing minutes of, and holding, your first meeting of the board of directors, selling and issuing your initial shares of stock, and taking care of other essential organizational formalities. You'll see that these steps are not complicated. For the most part, you will simply have to fill in a small number of blanks on the forms provided. Take your time and relax; you'll be surprised at how easy it all is.

Although we provide you with standard forms and show you how to fill them in, we realize that some incorporators may have special needs dictated by the particular facts and circumstances of their incorporation. We can't customize these forms to fit the needs of all businesses, so some incorporators will need to check their papers with a lawyer and/or an accountant. (See Chapter 7.)

FORM

You can download any of the forms in this book, including the incorporation forms, from the Nolo website. To access the forms online, use the link provided in Appendix A. Hard copies of some of the forms are included in Appendix B.

CAUTION

Forms and fees may change. All the forms and fees mentioned in this chapter and in Appendix B are subject to change at any time. Filing fees often change on the first day of the year; franchise tax amounts can change at any time. New filing rules that went into effect on January 1, 2013 are covered in this book.

To make sure the forms, fee amounts, and addresses are current at the time of your incorporation, check the secretary of state's website at www.sos.ca.gov/business. Also check Nolo's website where we will post updates (see Appendix A for the link).

Step 1. Choose a Corporate Name

The first step in organizing your corporation is selecting a name for your corporation that meets the requirements of state law. Your corporate name is approved by the California Secretary of State when you file your articles of incorporation. You are not legally required to include a corporate designator in your corporate name such as "Corporation," "Incorporated," "Limited," or an abbreviation of one of these words ("Corp.," "Inc.," or "Ltd."), unless, as discussed below, your corporation will include the name of an individual. However, most incorporators will be anxious to use one of these designators precisely because they want others to know that their business is incorporated.

The Importance of Your Corporate Name

Before looking at the legal requirements for choosing a corporate name, let's briefly discuss the importance of choosing the right name for your new corporation. Your corporate name will, to a large degree, identify the goodwill of your business. We don't mean this in any strict legal, accounting, or tax sense, but simply that the people you do business with, including your customers, clients, other merchants, vendors, independent contractors, lenders, and the business community generally, will identify your business primarily by your name. For this reason, as well as a number of practical reasons (such as not wanting to print new stationery, change yellow pages or advertising copy, create new logos, purchase new signs, and so on), you will want to pick a name that you will be happy with for a long time. So pay particular attention to your choice of a corporate name. As a practical matter, it's likely to become one of your most important assets.

Of course, if you are incorporating an existing business, you'll probably wish to use your current name as your corporate name if it has become associated with your products, services, and so on. Many businesses do this by simply adding an "Inc." after their old name (for example, Really Good Widgets might incorporate as Really Good Widgets, Inc.). Using your old name is not required, however, and if you have been hankering after a new one, this is your chance to claim it.

Here are a couple of additional points to consider when you choose a name:

- **Filing your corporate name with the secretary of state does not guarantee your right to use it.** Contrary to what many people believe, having your name approved by the California Secretary of State when you file your articles of incorporation does not guarantee you the absolute right to use it (as explained below, an unincorporated business may already be using it as their trade name, or another business may be using it as a trademark or service mark). Consequently, you will probably want to do some checking on your own to be relatively sure that no one else has a prior claim to your proposed corporate name.
- **You can use a name other than your formal corporate name.** You can adopt a formal corporate name in your articles that is different from the one you have used, or plan to use, locally in your business. You accomplish this by filing a fictitious business name statement with the county clerk in the counties in which you plan to do business. (We explain how to prepare and file this statement in Chapter 6.)

Secretary of State Name Requirements

The California Secretary of State will not accept your corporate name (and will reject your articles of incorporation) unless it meets the following requirements:

- Your name must not be the same as, or confusingly similar to, a name already on file with the secretary of state. The secretary maintains a list of names of existing California corporations and out-of-state corporations qualified to do business in California, names that have been registered with the secretary of state by out-of-state corporations, and names that have been reserved for use by other corporations. If your name is the same as, or confusingly similar to, any of these, your name will be rejected. We can't give you an exact definition of the phrase "confusingly similar." For practical purposes, this restriction simply means that your proposed name cannot be so similar to that of an existing name already on the secretary of state's list that it will be rejected by this office. For example, if you wish to set up a wholesale house for computer equipment under the name "Compusell, Inc.," and a corporation is already on file with the secretary of state with the name "Compusel International, Inc.," your name may be rejected as too similar. (Remember, you don't normally have to add "Inc." to your name—we include this corporate designator here just for purposes of the example.)
- A regular profit corporation (the type you will organize) cannot use certain words in its name that are reserved for special types of corporations. These restricted words include:

bank	credit union	cooperative
trust	trustee	United States

- In the (unusual and unlikely) event that you decide to form a close corporation, your corporate name must include the word "corporation," "incorporated," or "limited," or an abbreviation of one of these words. Again, this book cannot be used to form this special (and unusual) type of California corporation—make sure to have a lawyer modify your forms and stock certificates if you wish to incorporate as a close corporation.

Go to the California Secretary of State's website to see the complete text of the name regulations and restrictions.

Check to See If Your Proposed Name Is Available

To make sure your articles of incorporation aren't rejected because the name you've chosen is not available, you may wish to check its availability or reserve it before submitting your articles to the secretary of state.

You can check the availability of up to three corporate names by mail by sending a Name Availability Inquiry Letter to the Secretary of State in Sacramento. (This form is available online at the California Secretary of State's website or you can download it from the Nolo website (see Appendix A for the link). We have also included a copy of the form in Appendix B. Provide your name and address, a list of up to three proposed corporate names, and a request that each name be checked to see if it is available for use as a corporate name. At the top of the form, use "Firm Name" to show the name of your existing unincorporated business that you are incorporating. If you are forming a corporation for a new business entity, simply insert "N/A" in this blank. The secretary will respond to your written request within approximately one month.

TIP

You can set up a prepaid account. You can check available names by phone if you establish a prepaid account. Call the secretary of state at 916-653-1233 for information.

CAUTION

Check and reserve a corporate name. Even if the secretary indicates by return mail that a corporate name is available, it may not be available when you file your articles (if someone else actually uses it before you file your papers). To avoid this problem, you can check and reserve a name for a small fee, as explained below.

If a particular name is unavailable. If the particular corporate name you desperately want to use is unavailable because it is too similar to an existing name already on file with the secretary of state, there are a few things you can do:

1. Submit a written request for a review of your name's acceptability to the legal counsel's office at the secretary of state. Whether a name is so similar to another so as to cause confusion to the public depends on a number of factors, including the nature of each trade name user's business (the term trade name simply means a name used in conjunction with the operation of a trade or business) and the geographical proximity of the two businesses. If you do get into this sort of squabble, you will probably want to see a lawyer who is versed in the complexities of trade name or trademark law, or do some additional reading on your own.
2. Ask the other corporation already using a similar corporate name to consent, in writing, to your use of your corporate name.

   Note: Make sure to call the secretary of state and ask a name availability clerk if this written consent procedure will work for you—even with the consent of the other corporation, the secretary's office will not allow you to use a similar name if they feel the public is likely to be misled. If you get the go-ahead to use this procedure, ask the name availability clerk for the address of the other corporation and send them your written request for consent. Include an explanatory letter (and/or a preliminary phone call) indicating why they should agree to your use of your similar name (for example, that you will be engaged in a different line of business in a different locale).

3. Decide that it's simpler (and less trouble all the way around) to pick another name for your business. We normally recommend this third approach.

Reserve Your Corporate Name

For a small fee, you can check the availability of up to three names at once and reserve the first available name. This can be done by mail to the Sacramento office (it takes about one month) or in person at the Sacramento or Los Angeles offices (same day). We think it makes sense to do this rather than simply checking to see if your name is available. If your name is available, it will be reserved exclusively for your use for a period of 60 days. If you cannot file your articles within this period, you can re-reserve the name and pay another fee. Note that the secretary of state must receive your second reservation letter at least one day after the first certificate expires—the law does not allow two consecutive reservations of corporate names, so the requests must be separated by at least one day.

The fee to reserve a name by mail for 60 days is $10. There is an additional nonrefundable $10 fee to reserve a name in person. You can obtain a copy of the Name Reservation Order Form online from the California Secretary of State's website at www.ss.ca.gov.

You also can download a copy of the form from the Nolo website (see Appendix A for the link) and a copy of the form is included in Appendix B.

CAUTION

Fees and forms are subject to change. Make sure the fee amount is still correct and the form has not changed by checking the California Secretary of State's website.

One of the persons who signs your articles of incorporation (one of your initial directors—see Step 2, below) must insert his or her name in the space provided at the top of the Name Reservation Form. Your corporate name will be reserved for use by the individual who submits this form.

You can establish a prepaid account with the secretary of state to reserve names by phone. Call the secretary of state's office at 916-653-1233 for more information.

Perform Your Own Name Search

As we've said, approval by the secretary of state's office of your corporate name doesn't necessarily mean that you have the legal right to use this name. It simply means that your name does not conflict with that of another corporation already on file with the secretary of state and that you are presumed to have the legal right to use this name for your corporation in California. However, other businesses (corporate and noncorporate) may already have the right to use this same name (or one similar to it) as a federal or state trademark or service mark used to identify their goods or services. The secretary of state does not even check the state trademark/service mark registration lists maintained in

Secretary of State
Business Programs Division

1500 11th Street, 3rd Floor
Sacramento, CA 95814

Business Entities
(916) 657-5448

Name Reservation Request Form

(Corporation, Limited Liability Company, or Limited Partnership Names)

The proposed name is being reserved for use by:

Your Name: *(Insert name of incorporator who will sign articles)* Phone #: ____________

Firm Name (if any): *(Insert existing unincorporated business name here, if applicable)* Fax #: ____________

Address: *(Insert business address)*

City/State/Zip: ____________

Type of Entity (Select the applicable entity type. Only one type may be selected. **Note:** If the "Limited Partnership" type is selected, see page 2 of this Name Reservation Request Form for an additional requirement.)

☐ Corporation ☐ Limited Liability Company ☐ Limited Partnership

Name To Be Reserved (Enter the name to be reserved. Only one reservation will be made per Name Reservation Request Form. You may list up to three names, in order of preference, and the first available name will be reserved for a period of 60 days. The remaining names will not be researched.)

1st Choice: *(Insert 1st, 2nd, and 3rd choices in this section. The first available name will be reserved.)*

____ *is available.* ____ *is available only with consent from:* ____ *is not available. We have:*

2nd Choice: ____________

____ *is available.* ____ *is available only with consent from:* ____ *is not available. We have:*

3rd Choice: ____________

____ *is available.* ____ *is available only with consent from:* ____ *is not available. We have:*

Suspended/Forfeited Entity *(Not applicable for new corporations.)*

☐ If the proposed name is being reserved for the purpose of reviving a suspended or forfeited entity, check the box and include the entity number.

____
Entity Number

Mail Back Response *(Check here if you reserve in person.)*

☐ If the Name Reservation Request Form is submitted in person **and** if you would like the reservation to be mailed back, check the box and include a self-addressed envelope.

Fees (Please make check(s) payable to the Secretary of State.)

Reservation Fee: The fee for reserving a corporation, limited liability company or limited partnership name is $10.00 (per reserved name).

Special Handling Fee:

- In addition to the reservation fee, a $10.00 special handling fee is applicable for processing each Name Reservation Request Form delivered in person (drop off) to the Secretary of State's office.
- The $10.00 special handling fee must be remitted by separate check and will be retained whether the proposed name is accepted or denied for reservation.
- The special handling fee does not apply to name reservation requests submitted by mail.

THE SPACE BELOW IS RESERVED FOR OFFICE USE ONLY

Date:	Amt Rec'd:	R #:	By:

NAME RESERVATION REQUEST FORM (REV 01/2010) PAGE 1 OF 2

the secretary of state's office when checking to see if your name is available. Also, another business (corporate or noncorporate) may already have the legal right to use your name in a particular county if they are using it as a trade name (as the name of their business) and have filed a fictitious business name or "dba" statement with their county clerk.

Without wading too far into the intricacies of federal and state trademark, service mark, and trade name law, the basic rule is that the ultimate right to use a particular business name belongs to whoever first used it in connection with a particular trade or business, service, or product. In deciding who has the right to a name, the similarity of the types of businesses and their geographical proximity are usually taken into account. For example, if you plan to operate the "Sears Bar & Grille, Inc.," you probably won't have a problem with the well-known retail chain, but you might run into trouble with another bar or restaurant using the same name in your area.

Also, in an age where a huge number of service businesses—muffler shops, smog checks, eyeglass stores, house cleanup services, and so on—are being purchased nationally by large franchise chains, service businesses should be careful that their local name doesn't conflict with a national name that may later move into their area. If you find out that your Ukiah car dealership, Bob's Buicks, Inc., is the same as that of a Los Angeles car dealer, you're probably on safe ground, since it is unlikely that the public would be deceived. However, you could be challenged (probably successfully) if, in these examples, you incorporated as "Sears Merchandising, Inc.," or operated your car dealership in Ventura. To simplify things, ask yourself whether you, as a hypothetical customer, might reasonably confuse your proposed name with another one that already exists, and thereby deal with the wrong business. If you're honest, you can make this determination just as well as any lawyer.

Using Your Individual Name in Your Corporate Name

Although the law generally gives individuals a preferential right to use their names in connection with their businesses, there is an exception to this rule. Even if you use your own surname in your corporate name and your products, services, and geographical area of operation and marketing are different from those of another business, the other business can sue you to stop you from using your name if it contains a word or phrase that is similar to the other business's mark. Without going into the technicalities, our best advice is to use common sense. If your proposed corporate name contains a word or phrase that is the same as a known mark, you may wish to add a word or phrase to your corporate name to make it clear that you are unaffiliated with the company that owns the mark. For example, Mr. Sears might decide to incorporate as "John P. Sears Bar & Grille, Inc." This issue will not arise for most incorporators. If it does, we suggest you check with a trademark lawyer.

It makes sense to do a little checking on your own before filing your articles to see if another business is already using your name as a trade name, service mark, or trademark, particularly in the geographical area in which you plan to operate. Obviously, you will not be able to be 100% certain, since you can't possibly check all names in use by other businesses. However, there are some obvious sources you can check:

- Call the California Secretary of State's trademark/service mark registration section at 916-653-3984 and see if your proposed name is already registered for use by another business. They will check up to two names over the phone at no charge. It may take persistence to get through by phone—the office is understaffed and busy.

- Check with the county clerk in the county or counties in which you plan to do business to see if your name has already been registered by another person or business as a fictitious business name. Most county clerks will require you to come in and check the files yourself—it takes just a few minutes to do this.
- Go to a public library or special business and government library in your area that carries the federal *Trademark Register*, a listing of trademark/service mark names broken into categories of goods and services. Or search the federal *Trademark Register* yourself for free by pointing your Internet browser at the United States Patent and Trademark Office's website at www.uspto.gov.
- To check unregistered trade names (which the majority of names used by unincorporated businesses are), use a commonsense approach. Check major metropolitan phone book listings, the Internet, business and trade directories, and other business listings, such as the *Dun & Bradstreet* business listing. Larger public libraries have phone directories for many major cities within and outside of California.

If you don't want to do it all yourself, you can pay a private records search company to check federal and state trademarks and service marks as well as local and statewide business listings. They can check your proposed name against the sources we've listed above.

Alternatively, or in conjunction with your own efforts or search procedures, you can pay a trademark lawyer to oversee or undertake these searches for you. They will take the responsibility of hiring a private search company. In addition, they may provide a legal opinion on the legal issues surrounding, and the relative legal safety of, your use of your proposed corporate name. This opinion isn't necessary, but it can be valuable if the search discovers several similar, but not identical, names.

Obviously, the amount of checking and consulting you should do depends on how much time and money you are willing to devote to the task and how safe you need to feel about your choice of a corporate name. In most situations, following the commonsense search tips listed above will be enough.

Protect Your Name

Once you have filed your articles of incorporation, you may wish to take additional steps to protect your name. For example, you may wish to register your corporate name with your local county clerk as a fictitious business name (see "A California Corporation Can Use and Register a Fictitious Name," below). This lets other businesses know that your name is not available for their use. If your name will be used to identify products that you sell or services you provide, you may wish to register it with the California Secretary of State and the United States Patent and Trademark Office as a trademark or service mark (registration in other states where you do business may also be appropriate). The application procedures, which are relatively simple and inexpensive, are fully explained in *Trademark: Legal Care for Your Business & Product Name*, by Stephen Elias (Nolo).

A California Corporation Can Use and Register a Fictitious Name

The official name of a corporation is the name stated in its articles of incorporation. But a California corporation can do business under a fictitious name—that is, a name different from the name stated in its articles. If you decide to adopt a fictitious name for your corporation, you should register it in the county or counties where you will use it—this filing gives rise to a legal presumption that your corporation has the right to use the name in that county. (We explain how to do this in Chapter 6.)

Step 2. Prepare Your Articles of Incorporation

The next step in organizing your corporation is preparing the articles of incorporation. You will file this form with the secretary of state. Below is a sample of the articles of incorporation.

- The parenthetical blanks, such as "(*information*)," indicate information that you must complete on the form.
- Each circled number (for example, (1)) refers to an instruction that provides the specific information you need to complete the item. The instructions immediately follow the sample form.
- You can download the articles of incorporation form from the Nolo website and fill it out on your computer as you follow the sample form and instructions below. (See Appendix A for the link to the online form.)

Converting an Existing Business Entity Into a Corporation

The California Secretary of State provides special articles of incorporation forms for converting an existing business (such as an LLC or partnership) into a new corporation. If you are doing a conversion, use the articles form provided by the California Secretary of State instead of the one in this book and explained in this chapter. Only use the articles form in this book to form a corporation for a new business.

It's simple to use the state's conversion forms. First, go to the California Secretary of State's website at www.sos.ca.gov. Select "Business Entities," then select "Forms, Samples & Fees" and scroll down and select "Conversions." Read through the list and select the conversion form that applies to you. The ones most likely to apply to readers of this book with an existing business are the articles conversion forms to convert a domestic (California) LLC, limited partnership, or a general partnership to a domestic (California) stock corporation. Print, fill in, and file the appropriate form according to the instructions with the form. The fee to file a conversion articles form is $150 (higher than the standard $100 articles fee).

The tax issues related to converting to a corporation can be complex and tricky. Always seek advice from a tax expert before converting your business to a corporation. For a general heads-up on the tax issues involved, see the author's blog article, "Converting an LLC to a Corporation—It's Not as Simple as It Seems," at www.llccorporationblog.com.

SEE AN EXPERT

If you need help finding a lawyer, you can check Nolo's Lawyer Directory at www.nolo.com/lawyers for information about lawyers by practice area and geographic location.

Sample

Articles of Incorporation

ONE: The name of this corporation is *(name of corporation)*. (1)

TWO: The purpose of the corporation is to engage in any lawful act or activity for which a corporation may be organized under the General Corporation Law of California other than the banking business, the trust company business, or the practice of a profession permitted to be incorporated by the California Corporations Code.

THREE: The name and street address in the State of California of this corporation's initial agent for service of process is *(name and street address of initial agent)*. (2)

FOUR: (a) The initial street address of the corporation is: *(street address of the corporation)*. (3)

(b) The initial mailing address of the corporation, if different from the initial street address, is: *(mailing address of the corporation, if different)*. (3)

FIVE: This corporation is authorized to issue only one class of shares of stock, which shall be designated common stock. The total number of shares which this corporation is authorized to issue is *(number of shares)* (4) shares.

SIX: The liability of the directors of the corporation for monetary damages shall be eliminated to the fullest extent permissible under California law. (5)

SEVEN: The corporation is authorized to indemnify the directors and officers of the corporation to the fullest extent permissible under California law. (5)

(signature of Incorporator) (6)

(*typed name*), Incorporator

Fill In Your Articles

Instructions

1 Type the name of the corporation in the blank in Article One. If you have reserved a corporate name, the name you specify here must exactly match your reserved name. If you have decided not to use your reserved corporate name, that's fine—just check the availability of the new name before you type it in here.

2 Insert the name and business or residence address of the corporation's initial agent for service of process. This address must be a street address within California. The initial agent for service of process is the person whom you wish to authorize to receive legal documents for the corporation. Most incorporators will give the name of one of the directors and the principal office (street address) of the corporation here as the name and address of the corporation's initial agent. Do not use a post office box address or abbreviate the city name, and don't use "in care of" or "c/o." Also, don't designate a corporation as agent unless you check the state's instructions first on how to do this.

3 (a) Insert the street address of the principal office of the corporation, which should be in California.

(b) If the mailing address of the corporation is different from the street address, insert the mailing address here. If the mailing address is the same as the street address, insert "Same as street address, above."

4 Indicate the number of authorized shares of the corporation. The traditional longhand method is to first spell out the number, then indicate the figure in parentheses; for example, "TWO HUNDRED THOUSAND (200,000)." There's no longer a sensible reason for this convention (it made sense in the days of the quill pen), so you can either spell out the number or type in a figure in this blank.

CAUTION

This articles form authorizes only one class of shares. This article authorizes the corporation to issue one class of common shares, with each share having equal voting, liquidation, dividend, and other rights. If you want to authorize more than one class of shares, you will need to see a lawyer.

Authorized shares are shares of stock that the corporation can later sell to shareholders, at which time they are referred to as issued shares. There is no magic formula for computing the exact number of authorized shares you should specify—you can authorize as many or as few shares as you wish. However, the number of authorized shares you specify must, of course, be large enough to cover your initial stock issuance. You may wish to skip ahead to the instructions for preparing the "Issuance of Shares" resolution in your minutes in Step 6 of this chapter. After determining how many shares you will issue and adding a little extra to allow for the future issuance of additional shares (for example, if 1,000 shares will actually be issued, it is sensible to authorize at least 2,000 shares in your articles), type the final number you come up with here.

TIP

You may want to authorize extra shares. Authorizing additional shares beyond the actual amount you plan to issue can be helpful if you want to implement a stock bonus or option plan in the future. If you don't authorize additional shares now and decide later to increase the authorized number of shares stated in your articles, you will have to prepare a special amendment to your articles of incorporation and file it with the secretary of state.

5 Article Six uses the language contained in Section 204.5 of the Corporations Code to eliminate the personal liability of directors for monetary damages to the fullest extent permissible under California law. However, this

provision applies only to shareholder derivative suits (suits brought by, or in the right of, the corporation for breach of a director's duty of care to the corporation or stockholders). It does not apply to third-party lawsuits (suits brought by individual shareholders or outsiders for individual wrongs).

Article Seven uses language contained in Section 317(g) of the Corporations Code to allow the corporation to provide indemnification for the directors and officers beyond the limits expressly permitted by other subsections of Section 317. This article authorizes the corporation to provide for additional indemnification elsewhere (for example, in the corporation's bylaws or in agreements entered into by the corporation and its directors and officers). We have included broad indemnification rights for directors and officers in Article VII of the bylaws (see Step 4, below).

6 The person who signs your articles is the incorporator. You can have more than one incorporator, but most small corporations have only one, and it's typically the corporation's founder. If you name initial directors in your articles (doing so is optional—our form does not), then each director also must sign and acknowledge the articles. The incorporator should sign on the line provided, just before the word "Incorporator." The name of the incorporator (and initial directors if you have added them) should be typed beneath the signature line. Use a black-ink pen when signing your articles—the secretary of state must be able to photocopy them.

Prepare Your Cover Letter

A cover letter for your articles is included with this book. If you plan to file your articles in person (in Sacramento or Los Angeles), you do not need to prepare this letter. However, most incorporators will wish to use this letter to file their articles by mail with the Sacramento office of the secretary of state.

1 If you have reserved a corporate name, include this optional bracketed sentence from the sample cover letter, specifying your corporate name reservation number in the blank.

2 The fee you must pay to file your articles is $100. (Check that the fee hasn't changed.) Include a check with your cover letter, payable to the "California Secretary of State," for this amount.

The California Secretary of State accepts only the original articles document and will not accept any copies. The office will make one free copy of the file-stamped articles and return it to you. This should be sufficient—you can make your own copies of the file-stamped articles to give to banks or for other purposes. If that is how you want to proceed, then you can follow the cover letter we provide in this book.

If you want your free copy of articles certified (the secretary of state includes a certification that the copy conforms to the filed original), you need to ask for a certified copy in your cover letter and enclose an additional $5 fee. If you want additional copies, you must ask for the copies in your cover letter and pay $1 for the first page of the articles and $.50 for each additional page. Those charges apply for each requested additional copy of your articles. If you want any additional copies certified, you must add an additional $5 per certification. Most readers will not need a certified copy or any additional copies. In such cases, our simple cover letter should work just fine.

The number of California corporations continues to increase and the secretary of state's office is understaffed. As a result, you can expect to wait longer for your articles to be filed and returned to you. The secretary of state's office posts expected filing dates for each service (name availability, corporate filings, and so on). Currently, if you file by mail, you can expect to wait up to two months before your articles are filed and returned to you. To eliminate this delay, you may want to trek over to the Sacramento or Los Angeles office of the secretary of state to file your articles in person. Or you can pay a commercial filing service to do this for you. There is a separate special handling fee of $15 for in-person drop off filings.

CAUTION

Check to see if online filing is available in California before mailing your articles to the secretary of state. The California Secretary of State has been charged with implementing an online filing service called "California Business Connect" by 2016. Go online to the corporate filing service to check progress on this initiative before you mail in your articles. You can also check Nolo's website (see Appendix A for the link) for updates and instructions on how to proceed if there are any significant changes for filing articles in California.

The secretary of state offers expedited filing services for a fee. Filing can be accomplished within 24 hours of receipt of the document (delivered in person to the Sacramento office of the secretary of state) for an extra $350 fee. Class A four-hour service (requires a preclearance of your articles) or Class B same-day service cost even more. These are whopping fees compared to the more modest expedited filing fees typically charged by other states ($25 to $50 seems to be the average). To find out more about these services (the secretary may suspend the service occasionally if the filing volume is too high), go to the California Secretary of State's website and check the "Forms, Samples & Fees" link in the "Business Entities" section.

3 One of your initial directors should sign here. If you have reserved your corporate name, the person who submitted your corporate name reservation letter should also sign this cover letter.

Delaying the filing of your articles. You may be able to incorporate on a specific date (to establish a particular tax year). California law allows you to request a delayed filing date for your articles as long as this date is no more than 90 days from the date of receipt of your articles by the secretary of state (the delayed date may be a weekend day or a holiday, but your articles must be received by the secretary of state at least one business day before the requested future filing date). If you wish to do this, you must add an extra statement to your articles, or a statement on an attachment page.

Here is an additional article eight you can add to the end of your articles to request a delayed filing date:

EIGHT: These Articles shall be withheld from filing until the following future date: *future date* .

Make Copies of Your Articles

After completing your articles of incorporation, make a copy. The original will be filed with the secretary of state's office; the copy is for your records (keep it until you receive a file-stamped copy from the secretary's office). Also make one copy of the completed cover letter to keep for your records. You will mail the original cover letter with your articles of incorporation to the Sacramento office of the secretary of state.

If your articles contain more than one page, staple the pages of each copy of your articles together (use one staple in the upper left corner of each copy).

If you retype your articles of incorporation, please be aware that articles of incorporation must be typed on one side of a standard 8½" × 11" (letter-sized) page.

File Your Articles of Incorporation

Filing your articles is a formality. The secretary of state will file your papers if they conform to law and the proper fees are paid. The articles are the only formal organizational document

Cover Letter for Filing Articles

(name of incorporator)
(address)
(telephone number)

Secretary of State
Document Filing Support Unit
P.O. Box 944260
Sacramento, CA 94244-2600

Re: *(name of corporation)*

Dear Secretary of State:

I enclose the proposed Articles of Incorporation of *(name of corporation)* ______________________.

["This corporate name was reserved with your office pursuant to Certificate of Reservation #(______________________)." (1)]

Also enclosed is a check/money order in payment of the following fees:

Filing Articles of Incorporation $100 (2)

Please file the Articles and return a copy to me at the above address.

Very truly yours,

(signature of incorporator) (3)
(*typed name*), Incorporator

that you must file with the secretary of state (the only other incorporation filing is your Notice of Stock Transaction with the department of corporations—see Step 8). You do not file your bylaws, minutes of your first meeting, or any of the other incorporation forms or documentation contained in this book with any state agency.

To file your articles, mail the original, the cover letter, and a check or money order for the total fees payable to the "California Secretary of State." *To expedite processing, also enclose a stamped, self-addressed envelope.* Send these papers to the Sacramento office of the secretary of state shown in the heading of the sample cover letter for filing articles.

It can take two months for your articles to be filed and returned to you by mail (it can take longer during busy filing periods, so you may need to be patient).

Filing your articles in person. You may also file your articles in person at the Sacramento or Los Angeles office of the secretary of state—the office addresses and telephone numbers are listed at the beginning of Appendix B. The processing time for articles dropped off in person is three to seven business days.

There is an additional $15 special handling fee, however, for filing your articles in person. You must write a separate check for this amount; it will not be refunded if your over-the-counter articles are not acceptable for filing. You must provide the Los Angeles office with an extra signed copy of your articles of incorporation. Articles for converting an existing business to a corporation cannot be filed in person at the Los Angeles office.

Step 3. Set Up a Corporate Records Book (or Order a Corporate Kit)

Creating a corporate records book is an essential part of setting up a corporation. Your records book will help you keep important corporate papers in good order.

Set Up a Corporate Records Book

You will need a corporate records book to keep all your documents in an orderly fashion, including your articles, bylaws, minutes of your first board meeting and ongoing director and shareholder meetings, stock certificates, and stubs. Setting up and maintaining a neat, well-organized records book is one of your most important tasks—it will serve as a repository for corporate documents and as a formal paper trail documenting organizational and ongoing corporate formalities. You should keep your corporate records book at the principal office of your corporation.

To set up a corporate records book, you can simply place all your incorporation documents in a three-ring binder. If you prefer, however, you can order a corporate records kit through a legal stationery store.

A corporate kit typically includes:

- a three-ring binder corporate records book with the corporate name engraved on the book
- lithographed stock certificates with the name and state of formation of the corporation printed on the face of each certificate
- share register and transfer ledger pages, and
- a metal corporate seal to emboss your corporate name and year of incorporation on corporate documents.

The standard corporate kits sold by legal stationers and suppliers also contain bylaws, minutes of the first meeting, and printed stock certificates. These forms contain blanks that you must type in yourself. The bylaws and minutes contained in these other kits are often generic or minimal in nature and will not correspond to our forms or the specific instructions contained in this book.

Corporate Seals

A corporation is not legally required to have or use a corporate seal, but many find it handy to do so. A corporate seal is a formal way of indicating that a given document is the duly authorized act of the corporation. It is not normally used on everyday business papers (invoices, purchase orders, and the like) but is commonly employed for more formal documents such as leases, stock certificates, deeds of trust, and certifications of board resolutions. Most seals are circular in form and contain the name of the corporation, the state, and the year of incorporation. Embossed and stamped seals are also available separately through legal stationers.

Stock Certificates

This book contains black-and-white stock certificates intended for use by corporations issuing shares under the California limited offering exemption.

The book certificates contain a special legend noting that the shares have not been registered under state or federal securities laws (as discussed in Chapter 3). This legend is not legally required under the California limited offering exemption, however.

CAUTION

You can't use the stock certificates in this book if you form a close corporation or don't use the limited offering exemption. In the unusual event that you have decided to set up your corporation as a close corporation, or if you will not be relying on the California limited offering exemption when offering and issuing your shares, you cannot use the stock certificates contained in this book. In either of these special situations, you will need to order special certificates with different stock certificate legends printed on their face. Ask the lawyer who helps you in these situations to order the proper certificates for you.

TIP

Wait before ordering stock certificates or a seal. We suggest you wait until you have received the certified copies of your filed articles back from the secretary of state's office before you order a corporate kit, printed certificates, or a seal. This way, you'll be sure that you really have set up a corporation before you pay for these materials. However, if you are committed to forming your corporation and you have reserved your proposed corporate name for your use, then it's probably safe to order these corporate materials ahead of time.

Step 4. Prepare Your Bylaws

Your next step is to prepare the corporate bylaws included with this book. Bylaws are an internal corporate document that set out the basic ground rules for operating your corporation. They are not filed with the state.

The Bylaws Form

After you have received the copies of your articles from the secretary of state (and ordered a corporate kit if you decide to do so), your next incorporation task is to prepare your bylaws. You can download the bylaws from the Nolo website and fill them out on your computer following the instructions provided below. (See Appendix A for the link to the online bylaws form.) A hard copy of the bylaws is also available in Appendix B.

Be sure to read the provisions in the bylaws carefully to understand their purpose and effect. Many provisions relating to the duties and responsibilities of your corporation's directors, officers, and shareholders and the legal rules for operating your corporation have already been discussed in Chapter 2 of this book.

These general bylaws have been drafted and compiled to serve a number of purposes. First, they include specific information central to the organization and operation of your corporation (for example, the number of directors, quorum requirements for meetings, and dates of meetings). Second, they restate the most significant provisions of the California Corporations Code that apply to the organization and operation of your corporation. Third, they provide a practical yet formal set of rules for the operation of the corporation.

For example, we include certain minimum requirements such as the holding of an annual meeting of the board of directors, a majority quorum requirement for shareholders' meetings, and standard notice of meeting requirements, even though these are not absolutely required by law. On the other hand, they do not require other formal rules (such as special qualifications for directors and requiring an annual report to be prepared and sent to all shareholders each year), because we believe that most people who run small and moderate-sized businesses don't want additional layers of formal operating rules. If you wish to add to, or otherwise modify, the bylaws—especially if you want to dispense with the level of formality we provide—please have a lawyer help you.

We have included very broad indemnification provisions in Article VII of the bylaws, which require the corporation to indemnify (pay back) all directors and officers in all circumstances (that is, in both derivative and third-party suits) and for all amounts not prohibited by the Corporations Code. We feel these general provisions will be appropriate for most small corporations. However, you may want to make them broader or limit indemnification to particular amounts and circumstances. The point is, of course, as with most other legal documents, an almost infinite amount of fine tuning and customization is possible. While we do not believe that this type of customization will normally be needed, if you are interested in changing the indemnification provisions, please see Corporations Code Sections 204(a)(11) and 317, and consult an experienced corporate lawyer.

Prepare Your Bylaws

Although the bylaws will be your longest corporate document, you only have to fill in four blanks:

- Heading—the name of your corporation in the heading of the bylaws
- Article II, Section 2—the date and time of your annual shareholder meeting
- Article III, Section 2—the number of directors who must serve on your board, and
- Article III, Section 8—the number of directors (out of the total number of directors) who will be required to hold a meeting of your board (this number is called a quorum).

Below is a partial sample of the bylaws showing these four sections.

Instructions

(1) **Title:** Name of Corporation. Type your corporate name in the heading of the bylaws. Make sure the name shown here is the same as the name in the certified copies of your articles.

(2) **Article II, Section 2:** Date and Time of Annual Shareholders' Meeting. Indicate the date and time of your annual shareholders' meeting (for example, "the last Friday in December at 9 a.m." or "June 15 at 1 o'clock p.m.").

Your annual director meeting is automatically scheduled to be held immediately after this shareholders' meeting (see Article III, Section 7). The shareholder meeting is commonly held shortly before or after the close of the corporation's tax year (or tax return filing date), so that the shareholders can review the prior year's business and discuss and plan the coming year's business. Some incorporators schedule the meeting during the last month of the corporation's tax year so that the board of directors may, immediately following the shareholder meeting, make important year-end

Bylaws

(name of corporation) (1)

ARTICLE II
SHAREHOLDERS' MEETINGS

SECTION 1. PLACE OF MEETINGS

All meetings of the shareholders shall be held at the principal executive office of the corporation or at such other place as may be determined by the board of directors.

SECTION 2. ANNUAL MEETINGS

The annual meeting of the shareholders shall be held each year on *(day, month, and time of annual shareholders' meeting)* (2) ______________, at which time the shareholders shall elect a board of directors and transact any other proper business. If this date falls on a legal holiday, then the meeting shall be held on the following business day at the same hour.

ARTICLE III
DIRECTORS

SECTION 1. POWERS

Subject to any limitations in the articles of incorporation and to the provisions of the California Corporations Code, the business and affairs of the corporation shall be managed and all corporate powers shall be exercised by, or under the direction of, the board of directors.

SECTION 2. NUMBER

The authorized number of directors shall be *(total number of directors who will serve on your board)* (3).

After issuance of shares, this bylaw may only be amended by approval of a majority of the outstanding shares entitled to vote; provided, moreover, that a bylaw reducing the fixed number of directors to a number less than five (5) cannot be adopted unless in accordance with the additional requirements of Article IX of these bylaws.

SECTION 8. QUORUM AND BOARD ACTION

A quorum for all meetings of the board of directors shall consist of *(number—or percentage of total number—of directors representing a quorum)* (4) of the authorized number of directors until changed by amendment to this article of these bylaws.

Every act or decision done or made by a majority of the directors present at a meeting duly held at which a quorum is present is the act of the board, subject to the provisions of Section 310 (relating to the approval of contracts and transactions in which a director has a material financial interest); the provisions of Section 311 (designation of committees); and Section 317(e) (indemnification of directors) of the California Corporations Code. A meeting at which a quorum is initially present may continue to transact business notwithstanding the withdrawal of directors, if any action taken is approved by at least a majority of the required quorum for such meeting.

A majority of the directors present at a meeting may adjourn any meeting to another time and place, whether or not a quorum is present at the meeting.

CERTIFICATE

This is to certify that the foregoing is a true and correct copy of the bylaws of the corporation named in the title thereto and that such bylaws were duly adopted by the board of directors of the corporation on the date set forth below.

Dated: *(date of secretary's signature)* *(secretary's signature)* (5)

(*typed name*), Secretary

(impress corporate seal here) (5)

tax decisions such as fixing the corporation's liability for employee bonuses that they wish to deduct in the current year and pay after the start of the next corporate tax year. It's usually best to designate a fixed day (for example, the second Monday of a particular month) rather than a date to avoid having the meetings fall on a weekend. The Corporations Code requires you to hold this annual shareholder meeting.

3 **Article III, Section 2:** Number of Directors. Indicate the authorized number of directors of your corporation—this is the total number of directors who will serve on your board. Make sure you meet the minimum requirements of the Corporations Code set out in "How Many People May Organize the Corporation?" in Chapter 2.

4 **Article III, Section 8:** Quorum for Director Meetings. Indicate the number, or percentage of the total number, of directors who must be present at a director meeting to constitute a quorum that can conduct business (for example, by specifying "a majority," "one-third," or "two"). Although the usual practice is to indicate a majority here, under California law a quorum may be as few as one-third the number of authorized directors or two people, whichever is larger. A one-person corporation, however, may (and will) provide for a one-director quorum.

Under the above minimum rules, a four-director corporation may provide for a quorum of two, rather than a majority of three. Applying these rules to a three-director corporation, however, results in a majority quorum of two.

Whatever you decide, you should realize that this section of the bylaws concerns a quorum, not a vote requirement. Action can be taken by a majority of directors at a meeting at which a quorum is present. For example, if a six-director corporation requires a majority quorum and a meeting is held at which a minimum quorum (four) is present, action can be taken by the vote of three directors, a majority of those present at the meeting.

5 Do not date, sign, or seal your bylaws at the bottom of the last page now. The corporate secretary will do this after you hold your first meeting of directors (as explained immediately below, in Step 6).

Step 5. Appoint Initial Corporate Directors

Your next step is to have your incorporator, who is the person who signed your articles in Step 2, appoint initial corporate directors. This is an extremely simple step. The incorporator fills in an "Incorporator's Statement" to show the names and addresses of the initial directors who will serve on the board until the first annual meeting of shareholders (when the board members who will serve for the next term are elected by the shareholders). The incorporator dates and signs the statement, types his name in the blank under his signature at the bottom of the statement, and places a copy in the corporate records book.

To complete this step, have your incorporator complete the Incorporator's Statement following the sample form and instructions below. You can download the form from the Nolo website (see Appendix A for the link to the form) and a hard copy is available in Appendix B.

Instructions

1 Indicate the full names and business or residence addresses of your initial director(s). Remember: The general rule is that a California corporation must have at least three directors. However, if you will have only two shareholders, you may have only two directors; if you will have only one shareholder, you can have only one director. Of course, you can provide for additional directors above these

Incorporator's Statement

The undersigned, the incorporator of ______________________________________,
who signed and filed its Articles of Incorporation with the California Secretary of State, appoints the following individuals to serve as the initial directors of the corporation, who shall serve as directors until the first meeting of shareholders for the election of directors and until their successors are elected and agree to serve on the board:

Initial Directors' Names and Addresses:

______________________ (1) ______________________

____

____

____

____

____

____

Date: ______________________ (2)

Signature: ______________________________, Incorporator

Typed Name of Incorporator: ______________________

minimum limits if you wish (see "How Many People May Organize the Corporation?" in Chapter 2 for further information).

Article 3, Section 2, of your bylaws (prepared in Step 4, above) shows the full number of members on your board. The incorporator should appoint this number of board members if possible. If you must leave a seat open because you have not yet found all the right people to serve on your board, that's okay. Just make sure that you appoint enough directors to meet your bylaws' quorum requirement. Article 3, Section 8, defines your corporation's director-quorum requirement (typically, a majority of the full authorized number of directors is specified).

(2) Have the incorporator date and sign the form, insert his typed name under his signature, then place a copy in the corporate records book.

Step 6. Prepare Minutes of the First Meeting of the Board of Directors

The next step, now that you have filed your articles and prepared your bylaws, is to prepare the minutes of the first meeting of your board of directors. After preparing your minutes, you will actually hold a meeting. You should also prepare a waiver of notice and consent to holding of the first meeting of the board of directors (see below).

Fill In the Minutes of the First Meeting of the Board of Directors

The purpose of your minutes is to document essential organizational actions taken by your board of directors, including:

- specifying the principal executive office of the corporation
- adopting the bylaws
- electing officers
- adopting an accounting period (tax year) for your corporation
- authorizing the issuance of the initial shares of stock of the corporation, and
- if federal S corporation tax status is desired, approving this election.

Prepare your minutes by filling in the blanks in the Minutes of the First Meeting of the Board of Directors form. There is nothing difficult here, but there are a number of questions that you must answer.

Below is a sample of the minutes of the first meeting of directors form. The first page of the minutes form is a Waiver of Notice and Consent to Holding of First Meeting of Directors form. You can download the forms from the Nolo website (see Appendix A for the link to the forms) and a hard copy of the forms is available in Appendix B.

Instructions

Waiver of Notice and Consent to Holding of First Meeting of Board of Directors

This form is included as the first page of the meeting minutes form. It is necessary in order to dispense with formal director notice requirements that apply to special board meetings (see Article III, Section 7, of your bylaws). Here are the special instructions associated with this waiver of notice and consent:

(1) Name of Corporation

Type the name of your corporation in the heading to this page and in the first blank of the first paragraph.

(2) Address, Date, and Time of Meeting

Insert the address, date, and time of your first directors' meeting. Normally, you will show the address of the corporation here as the place of your board meeting. As you'll see below, we think it's wise for your first meeting to be more than just a paper meeting. In other words, if you have more than one director, you should

Waiver of Notice and Consent to Holding of First Meeting of Board of Directors

of

(name of corporation) (1)

We, the undersigned, being all the directors of *(name of corporation)* (1) ______, a California corporation, hereby waive notice of the first meeting of the board of directors of the corporation and consent to the holding of said meeting at *(address of meeting)* ______, on *(date of meeting)* ______, at *(time of meeting)* ______, (2) and consent to the transaction of any and all business by the directors at the meeting including, without limitation, the adoption of bylaws, the election of officers, the selection of the corporation's accounting period, the designation of the principal executive office of the corporation, the selection of the place where the corporation's bank account will be maintained, and the authorization of the sale and issuance of the initial shares of stock of the corporation.

Dated: *(date of signing of waiver)*

(signature of director)
(print or type name below signature line)

(signature of director)
(print or type name below signature line)

(signature of director)
(print or type name below signature line)

Minutes of First Meeting of the Board of Directors

of

(name of corporation) (1)

The board of directors of *(name of corporation)* (1) held its first meeting at *(address of meeting)*, on *(date of meeting)*, at *(time of meeting)*. (2)

The following directors, marked as present next to their names, were in attendance at the meeting and constituted a quorum of the full board:

(name of director) ☐ Present ☐ Absent (4)

(name of director) ☐ Present ☐ Absent

(name of director) ☐ Present ☐ Absent

On motion and by unanimous vote, *(name of director)* (5) was elected temporary chairperson and then presided over the meeting. *(name of director)* (5) was elected temporary secretary of the meeting.

The chairperson announced that the meeting was held pursuant to written waiver of notice and consent to holding of the meeting signed by each of the directors. Upon a motion duly made, seconded, and unanimously carried, it was resolved that the written waiver of notice and consent to holding of the meeting be made a part of the minutes of the meeting and placed in the corporation's minute book.

ARTICLES OF INCORPORATION

The chairperson announced that the articles of incorporation of the corporation had been filed with the California Secretary of State's office on *(date of filing of articles)*. (6) The chairperson then presented to the meeting a certified copy of the articles showing such filing, and the secretary was instructed to insert this copy in the corporation's minute book.

BYLAWS

A proposed set of bylaws of the corporation was then presented to the meeting for adoption. The bylaws were considered and discussed and, upon motion duly made and seconded, it was unanimously

RESOLVED, that the bylaws presented to this meeting be and hereby are adopted as the bylaws of this corporation;

RESOLVED FURTHER, that the secretary of this corporation be and hereby is directed to execute a certificate of adoption of the bylaws, to insert the bylaws as so certified in the corporation's minute book, and to see that a copy of the bylaws, similarly certified, is kept at the corporation's principal executive office, as required by law.

ELECTION OF OFFICERS

The chairperson then announced that the next item of business was the election of officers. Upon motion, the following persons were unanimously elected to the following offices, at the annual salaries, if any as determined at the meeting, shown to the right of their names:

	Name	**Salary**
President:	*(name of officer)*	$ *(salary)* 7
Vice President:	*(name of officer)*	$ *(salary)*
Secretary:	*(name of officer)*	$ *(salary)*
Treasurer: (Chief Financial Officer)	*(name of officer)*	$ *(salary)*

Each officer who was present accepted his or her office. Thereafter, the president presided at the meeting as chairperson, and the secretary acted as secretary.

CORPORATE SEAL

The secretary presented to the meeting for adoption a proposed form of seal of the corporation. Upon motion duly made and seconded, it was

RESOLVED, that the form of the corporate seal presented to this meeting be and hereby is adopted as the corporate seal of this corporation, and the secretary of this corporation is directed to place an impression thereof in the space directly next to this resolution.

8 *(impress corporate seal here)*

STOCK CERTIFICATE

The secretary then presented to the meeting for adoption a proposed form of stock certificate for the corporation. Upon motion duly made and seconded, it was

RESOLVED, that the form of stock certificate presented to this meeting be and hereby is adopted for use by this corporation, and the secretary of this corporation is directed to annex a copy thereof to the minutes of this meeting.

ACCOUNTING PERIOD

The chairperson informed the board that the next order of business was the selection of the accounting period of the corporation. After discussion and upon motion duly made and seconded, it was

RESOLVED, that the accounting period of this corporation shall end on *(ending date of the accounting period of the corporation)* (9) of each year.

PRINCIPAL EXECUTIVE OFFICE

After discussion as to the exact location of the corporation's principal executive office, upon motion duly made and seconded, it was

RESOLVED, that the principal executive office of this corporation shall be located at *(address, including city, county, and state of principal executive office)*. (10)

BANK ACCOUNT

The chairperson recommended that the corporation open a bank account with *(name of bank(s) and branch office(s))*. (11) Upon motion duly made and seconded, it was

RESOLVED, that the funds of this corporation shall be deposited with the bank and branch office indicated just above.

RESOLVED FURTHER, that the treasurer of this corporation is hereby authorized and directed to establish an account with said bank and to deposit the funds of this corporation therein.

RESOLVED FURTHER, that any officer, employee, or agent of this corporation is hereby authorized to endorse checks, drafts, or other evidences of indebtedness made payable to this corporation, but only for the purpose of deposit.

RESOLVED FURTHER, that all checks, drafts, and other instruments obligating this corporation to pay money shall be signed on behalf of this corporation by any ____*(number)*____ (12) of the following:

____*(name of person authorized to sign checks)*____ (13)

____*(name of person authorized to sign checks)*____

____*(name of person authorized to sign checks)*____

RESOLVED FURTHER, that said bank is hereby authorized to honor and pay any and all checks and drafts of this corporation signed as provided herein.

RESOLVED FURTHER, that the authority hereby conferred shall remain in force until revoked by the board of directors of this corporation and until written notice of such revocation shall have been received by said bank.

RESOLVED FURTHER, that the secretary of this corporation be and is hereby authorized to certify as to the continuing authority of these resolutions, the persons authorized to sign on behalf of this corporation, and the adoption of said bank's standard form of resolution, provided that said form does not vary materially from the terms of the foregoing resolutions.

PAYMENT, DEDUCTION, AND AMORTIZATION
OF ORGANIZATIONAL EXPENSES (14)

The board next considered the question of paying the expenses incurred in the formation of this corporation. A motion was made, seconded, and unanimously approved, and it was

RESOLVED, that the president and the treasurer of this corporation are authorized and empowered to pay all reasonable and proper expenses incurred in connection with the organization of the corporation, including, among others, filing, licensing, and attorney's and accountant's fees, and to reimburse any persons making any such disbursements for the corporation, and it was

FURTHER RESOLVED, that the treasurer is authorized to elect to deduct and amortize the foregoing expenditures pursuant to, and as permitted by, Section 248 of the Internal Revenue Code of 1986, as amended.

FEDERAL S CORPORATION TAX TREATMENT (15)

The board of directors next considered the advantages of electing to be taxed under the provisions of Subchapter S of the Internal Revenue Code of 1986, as amended. After discussion, upon motion duly made and seconded, it was unanimously

RESOLVED, that this corporation hereby elects to be treated as a Small Business Corporation for federal income tax purposes under Subchapter S of the Internal Revenue Code of 1986, as amended.

RESOLVED FURTHER, that the officers of this corporation take all actions necessary and proper to effectuate the foregoing resolution, including, among other things, obtaining the requisite consents from the shareholders of this corporation and executing and filing the appropriate forms with the Internal Revenue Service within the time limits specified by law.

QUALIFICATION OF STOCK AS SECTION 1244 STOCK (16)

The board next considered the advisability of qualifying the stock of this corporation as Section 1244 Stock as defined in Section 1244 of the Internal Revenue Code of 1986, as amended, and of organizing and managing the corporation so that it is a Small Business Corporation as defined in that section. Upon motion duly made and seconded, it was unanimously

RESOLVED, that the proper officers of the corporation are, subject to the requirements and restrictions of federal, California, and any other applicable securities laws, authorized to sell and issue shares of stock in return for the receipt of an aggregate amount of money and other property, as a contribution to capital and as paid-in surplus, which does not exceed $1,000,000.

RESOLVED FURTHER, that the sale and issuance of shares shall be conducted in compliance with Section 1244 so that the corporation and its shareholders may obtain the benefits of that section.

RESOLVED FURTHER, that the proper officers of the corporation are directed to maintain such records as are necessary pursuant to Section 1244 so that any shareholder who experiences a loss on the transfer of shares of stock of the corporation may determine whether he or she qualifies for ordinary loss deduction treatment on his or her individual income tax return.

AUTHORIZATION OF ISSUANCE OF SHARES (17)

The board of directors next took up the matter of the sale and issuance of stock to provide capital for the corporation. Upon motion duly made and seconded, it was unanimously

RESOLVED, that the corporation sell and issue the following number of its authorized common shares to the following persons, in the amounts and for the consideration set forth under their names below. The board also hereby determines that the fair value to the corporation of any consideration for such shares issued other than for money is as set forth below:

Name	Number of Shares	Consideration	Fair Value
______________________	________	____________	$ __________
______________________	________	____________	$ __________
______________________	________	____________	$ __________
______________________	________	____________	$ __________
______________________	________	____________	$ __________
______________________	________	____________	$ __________
______________________	________	____________	$ __________

RESOLVED FURTHER, that these shares shall be sold and issued by this corporation strictly in accordance with the terms of the exemption from qualification of these shares as provided for in Section 25102(f) of the California Corporations Code.

RESOLVED FURTHER, that the appropriate officers of this corporation are hereby authorized and directed to take such actions and execute such documents as they may deem necessary or appropriate to effectuate the sale and issuance of such shares for such consideration.

Since there was no further business to come before the meeting, upon motion duly made and seconded, the meeting was adjourned.

(signature of secretary) ____________
(typed name of secretary), Secretary **18**

actually sit down with the other directors at the place, date, and time indicated here to review and agree to the provisions in your completed minutes.

(3) Signatures of All Directors and Date of Waiver

Complete the date line on the waiver of notice page and have each director sign his or her name. If you have more than one director, the date shown can be the date the first director signs the form.

Title Page

The next page of your meeting minutes form (page 2) contains the title of the document and begins by reciting the facts necessary for you to hold your meeting, repeating the name of your corporation and the address, date, and time of the meeting given above. Fill in these blanks as explained just above.

(4) Present and Absent Directors

List the names of all your directors in these blanks. You will check the appropriate box to the right of each name when you hold your first board meeting to show whether each director is present or absent. Although we suggest that all of your directors be present at your first meeting, only a quorum of the board (as specified in Article III, Section 8, of your bylaws) actually need attend the meeting.

(5) Temporary Chairperson and Secretary

These blanks relate to a minor, but logically necessary, formality. You have not yet elected officers, but someone has to preside over the meeting and keep track of what happens. Type (or print) the name of one of your directors as your temporary chairperson in the first blank and another director as your temporary secretary in the second. If your corporation has only one director, you can enter this person's name in both these blanks.

Articles of Incorporation Resolution

This is the first resolution of your minutes and appears just after the introductory material on your title page. This resolution serves as a formal record of the date of filing of your articles of incorporation and indicates the first day of the legal existence of your corporation.

(6) Date of Filing of Articles

Type the date on which your articles were filed by the secretary of state—this is the "endorsed-filed" date stamped on the back of the last page of the certified copies of your articles of incorporation (see Step 2, above, for further information on filing your articles).

Bylaws Resolution

This resolution shows the formal adoption of your bylaws by the directors. The bylaws require you to keep your corporate records book (and a copy of your bylaws) at the principal executive office of the corporation. You will establish the location of this office in a separate minute resolution discussed below.

Election of Officers Resolution

This resolution allows you to elect the officers of your corporation and to authorize any officer salaries you feel appropriate.

When filling in these blanks, remember the following points (for a further discussion, see "How Many People May Organize the Corporation?" in Chapter 2):

- Under California law you must fill the offices of president, secretary, and treasurer (referred to in the California Corporations Code as the chief financial officer).
- You are not required to elect a vice president, although many incorporators will wish to do so.
- One person may be elected to all, or any number of, these officer positions. For example, in a one-person corporation, this individual will be elected as president,

secretary, and treasurer (and vice president, if this person wants to add this optional title to her name). Although less common, the same rule applies if you have more than one person in your corporation.

EXAMPLE: Joan, Gary, and Matthew form their own corporation. Because it's really Joan's business (her spouse Gary and her brother Matthew are simply investing as shareholders), Joan fills the officer positions of president, secretary, and treasurer.

- An officer need not be a director or shareholder in your corporation (although, for small corporations, the officer usually will be both).

7 Election of Officers and Optional Officers' Salaries

List the name of your president, secretary, and treasurer (chief financial officer) and any salary you wish to authorize for each officer. If you wish to fill the optional officer position of vice president, list the name of the person who will fill this office.

Filling in the salary blank is optional. Many corporations will not wish to provide for officer salaries (and will not fill in these blanks) because the individuals who will actively work for the corporation, whether they are also directors, officers, or shareholders, will not be paid a salary for their duties as an officer but will be paid in some other capacity.

EXAMPLE: Betty Bidecker is a 75% shareholder and the president and treasurer of her incorporated software publishing company. Bix Bidecker, her spouse, is a 25% shareholder and the vice president and secretary of the corporation. Rather than being paid for serving in any officer capacity, both are paid annual salaries as executive employees of the corporation: Betty as the publisher, and Bix as the associate publisher.

If you do provide for officer salaries, remember that these salaries must be reasonable in view of the actual duties performed by the officer and to compensation paid to others with similar skills in similar businesses. (See "Officers" in Chapter 2 for a further discussion of this issue.) But don't worry too much about overpayment. If you are active in your business and can afford to pay yourself a large salary because of the profitability of your corporation, your salary will most likely be reasonable in view of your success and, generally, in view of the trend toward paying higher corporate salaries these days.

Corporate Seal Resolution

This resolution is included in your minutes in case you wish to order and use a corporate seal. If you don't order and use one, just leave the space to the right of this resolution blank.

8 Impression of Corporate Seal

Stamp or impress the corporate seal in the space provided to the right of this resolution. If you don't buy a corporate seal, just leave this space blank.

Stock Certificate Resolution

This resolution is included in your minutes to adopt the form of stock certificate you will use (either the certificates included in Appendix B of this book or those which you have purchased on your own).

Accounting Period Resolution

This resolution allows you to specify the accounting period of your corporation. You should normally select this period with the help of your corporate tax advisor. (See Chapter 4 for a discussion of the rules that apply to selecting a corporate accounting period and tax year.)

9 Ending Date of Corporate Accounting Period

Indicate the date (month and day) of the end of your corporation's accounting period in this blank. For example, if you choose a calendar year accounting period for your corporation, the ending date is "December 31."

The California Franchise Tax Board and the IRS will look to your initial tax returns (not your bylaws) to determine the ending date of your corporate accounting period and tax year. For example, if your first corporate tax returns are submitted for a period ending on July 30, this date will be taken as the end date of your corporate tax year. In other words, you are not bound by this initial minute resolution, although your answer here should reflect your reasonable expectations for your ultimate accounting period and tax year.

After you file your initial returns, you may need the consent of the IRS and the California Franchise Tax Board to change your tax year. For further information on filing your initial returns and fixing your corporate tax year, see Chapter 4 and "Corporate Income Tax Return" in Chapter 6.

Principal Executive Office Resolution

This resolution allows you to formally specify the principal executive office of your corporation. This is a term used in the Corporations Code to indicate the legal address of the corporation. Most corporations will use their principal place of business (the active address where all or most of its business is carried out) as its legal principal executive office. Although not required, most incorporators will have a principal executive office within California (see Article I, Section 1, of the bylaws).

10 Full Address of Principal Executive Office

Type the street address, including the city, county, and state (California), of the principal executive office of your corporation (for example, "1212 Market Street, River City, Humboldt County, California"). Do not use a post office box.

Bank Account Resolution

This resolution authorizes the opening of the corporation's bank account(s) with one or more banks, showing the names of individuals authorized to sign checks and the number of signatures required on corporate checks. Typically, you will also have to fill out, and impress the corporate seal on, a separate bank account authorization form provided by your bank. Banks customarily require your corporation to have a federal Employer Identification Number. You can obtain this number by filing Form SS-4 with the IRS (see "Federal Employer Identification Number" in Chapter 6). All corporations will also need to obtain a state employer number and make deposits of state and federal withholding and employment taxes with an authorized bank, as explained more fully in Chapter 6.

11 Name of Bank(s) and Branch Office(s)

Type the name(s) of the bank(s) and branch office(s) where the corporation will maintain its accounts (for example, "Second Multistate Savings; West Covina branch").

12 Number of Signatures on Corporate Checks

State how many individual signatures will be required on each corporate check. For example, if you wish to have your president and secretary sign all corporate checks, type "two" in this blank.

13 Names of Individuals Who May Sign Checks

List the names of all individuals who are authorized to sign checks on behalf of your corporation. For example, although you may only require one authorized signature on corporate checks, you may wish to allow both your corporate treasurer and your president to sign corporate checks. Generally, you will list the name of one or more officers or key employees here (such as your salaried in-house bookkeeper).

14 Payment and Deduction of Organizational Expenses Resolution (Optional)

This resolution is optional. If you do not wish to use this resolution, do not include this page in your completed minutes.

Whether to Include This Resolution in Your Minutes

Many incorporators will wish to use this resolution to allow the corporation to reimburse the incorporators for, and have the corporation pay and deduct over a period of time, the expenses incurred in organizing the corporation under Section 248 of the Internal Revenue Code. This resolution is simply a statement that you intend to make the tax return election. Without a specific election to deduct these expenses over a specified period of time, such a deduction is normally not possible. To make this election, you attach a statement to your first federal corporate income tax return indicating that you are choosing to deduct and amortize organization expenses and you provide a description of the expenses together with other required details. Check with your tax advisor for help in deciding whether to use this resolution (and for help in preparing the statement to send to the IRS).

A corporation can deduct up to $5,000 of organizational (plus up to $5,000 of start-up) expenses in its first corporate tax year. You can amortize and deduct remaining organizational (and start-up) expenses over the next 15 years. Ask your tax adviser for more information.

15 Federal S Corporation Tax Treatment Resolution (Optional)

This resolution is optional. If you do not wish to elect S corporation status, do not include this page in your completed minutes.

Whether to Include This Resolution in Your Minutes

To decide whether to include this resolution in your minutes, you'll have to consider the tax factors discussed in "S Corporation Tax Status" in Chapter 4. If you decide to elect federal S corporation tax status, include this resolution in your minutes.

As discussed in "S Corporation Tax Status" in Chapter 4, many entrepreneurs that want pass-through taxation and limited liability prefer to form an LLC instead of an S corporation when creating a new business entity.

16 Section 1244 Stock Resolution (Optional)

This resolution is optional. If you do not wish to use this resolution, do not include this page in your completed minutes.

Whether to Include This Resolution in Your Minutes

Most incorporators will wish to have their stock treated as Section 1244 stock (so that any future stock losses may be deductible as "ordinary losses"—see Chapter 4 for a further discussion). If you do wish this tax treatment, we recommend you include this resolution in your minutes. Although not required under Section 1244, it documents your intentions if you later want to rely on Section 1244 due to future stock loss. You will have to keep ongoing records to ensure that you will be able to meet the requirements of Section 1244—your tax adviser can help you maintain these records.

Authorization of Issuance of Shares Resolution

This resolution authorizes your corporation to issue its initial shares to your shareholders after the meeting of your board. Throughout the book, we refer to this resolution as your "stock issuance resolution."

This resolution in your minutes does not result in the issuance of shares—it simply authorizes the appropriate corporate officers to issue shares to the shareholders after the meeting. You will actually issue shares as part of Step 9, below.

17 Share Issuance Information

In this resolution, you provide information relating to your initial stock issuance. For each shareholder you should indicate:

- the name of the shareholder
- the number of shares to be issued to this person
- the payment the shareholder will make for the shares (legally this payment is referred to as the "consideration" for the shares—we use this legal term in this column of the stock issuance resolution), and
- the fair value of the payment for shares to be made by the shareholder (either the amount of cash paid or the fair market value of any noncash payment). Section 409(e) of the California Corporations Code requires the board to make this determination of fair value to the corporation for all noncash consideration for which shares are issued.

Read "Issuing Shares: A Quick Review," below, before filling in the blanks for each of these items.

Joint shareholder note. As we explain in Step 9, below, many incorporators (particularly spouses) will purchase their shares jointly. If you plan to own shares jointly with your spouse or another person, list both names in the shareholder name blank for these shares.

> EXAMPLE: If Steve Marconi and Katherine Marconi will jointly purchase 1,000 shares for $1,000, they would fill in the blanks in the stock issuance resolution as shown below.

You do not need to indicate here how the joint owners will take title to their shares (for example, as community property—see Step 9, below). You will do this when you fill out your stock certificates.

Stock Issuance Examples

Here are some examples to help you fill in the blanks on your stock issuance resolution:

Issuance of shares for cash. If a shareholder will pay cash for his or her shares, simply type "Cash" for the consideration and the dollar amount as the fair value of the payment.

Issuance of shares for specific items of property. If a shareholder will purchase shares by transferring property to the corporation (we are referring to specific items of property here such as a computer system, a truck, a patent,

Authorization of Issuance of Shares

Name	Number of Shares	Consideration	Fair Value
Steve Marconi and Katherine Marconi	1,000	Cash	$1,000

or a copyright; not the complete assets of a business—this latter situation is dealt with in the next example), be as specific as you can when entering the consideration (for example, "2010 Ford pickup, vehicle ID #______"), and show the fair market value of the property as the fair value of the payment. (In the case of a vehicle, *Kelley Blue Book* value is a good measure.)

Issuance of shares for assets of a prior business. If you are incorporating a prior business, and a shareholder will transfer his or her part, or full, interest in the prior business to the corporation in return for shares, describe the interest in the prior business which will be transferred by each owner—not the specific assets of the business.

EXAMPLE: If two business owners will be incorporating their preexisting partnership, "Just Partners," the following simple description in the consideration blank would be appropriate for each shareholder

Issuing Shares: A Quick Review

Chapter 3 explains how to issue shares in compliance with the California limited offering exemption and federal securities laws. Here's a quick review of a few additional points made in other chapters:

- Make sure that the total number of shares to be issued to all shareholders is not greater than the number of shares authorized to be issued in Article Four of your articles of incorporation. Article Four places an upper limit on the number of shares which you can actually issue. (See Step 3, Instruction 3.)
- You may issue shares for cash, tangible or intangible property actually received by the corporation, debts cancelled, and labor done or services actually rendered to the corporation, or for its benefit, or in its formation. However, you cannot issue shares in return for the performance of future services by a shareholder or for promissory notes (a promise by the shareholder to pay for the shares later) unless certain conditions are met. (See "Selling Stock" in Chapter 2.)
- As a matter of common sense, and to avoid unfairness or fraud, issue your shares for the same price per share to all initial shareholders. Make sure to place a fair value on the assets or other property or services received in return for the shares. If you are transferring the assets of an existing business to your corporation in return for shares (that is, if you are incorporating a prior business), we suggest that you have an accountant or other qualified appraiser determine the value of these assets in writing. You may also wish to have a balance sheet prepared for the prior business, showing the assets and liabilities being transferred to your corporation (you can attach this balance sheet to the bill of sale, which you can prepare as part of Step 9, below, to document this type of transfer). Be realistic in your determination of fair value of all noncash payments for shares, particularly if you will be issuing shares in return for speculative or intangible property such as the goodwill of a business, copyrights, patents, and the like. You don't want to shortchange other shareholders who have put up cash or tangible property of easily determined value.

Don't forget to ask your tax adviser if you qualify for tax-free treatment of your stock issuance under Internal Revenue Code Section 351 (see "Tax Treatment When an Existing Business Is Incorporated" in Chapter 4).

(each prior business owner): "One-half interest in assets of the partnership 'Just Partners,' as more fully described in a bill of sale to be prepared and attached to these minutes."

You can prepare this bill of sale as part of Step 9, below. Each partner can list one-half of the dollar value of these assets (that is, one-half of their book value as reflected on a current balance sheet) as the fair value of the payment to be made by each shareholder.

Issuance of shares for cancellation of indebtedness. If shares will be issued for the cancellation of all debt the corporation owes to a shareholder, a description of the debt should be given as the consideration for the shares (for example, "cancellation of a promissory note dated ____________________"). The fair value of the payment is the dollar amount of the remaining unpaid principal amount due on the debt plus any unpaid accrued interest. Ideally, you should attach a copy of the note or other written evidence of the debt to your minutes.

This type of transaction is unusual, since a newly formed corporation will not normally owe shareholders any amounts except, perhaps, small advances for the costs of organizing the corporation, which will be reimbursed by the corporation directly. (See "Payment and Deduction of Organizational Expenses Resolution," above.)

Issuance of shares for past services. If you will be issuing shares to a shareholder in return for past services actually rendered the corporation, indicate the date and name of the person who has provided the services as the consideration to be paid by this shareholder (for example, "Services rendered the corporation by Bob Beamer, January 5 to February 15, 20___").

The fair value of the payment is the fair market value of the services performed by this shareholder. A bill from the shareholder to the corporation showing the amount due for these services should be attached to your minutes. Remember, you cannot issue shares for services which have not yet been performed.

We are also referring here to shares issued in return for labor done, another category of consideration for shares specified in the Corporations Code (see "Selling Stock" in Chapter 2). Our guess is that labor done is meant to distinguish contracting-type services performed for the corporation (construction of a building and so on) from organizational or administrative type services. Since we see no real distinction between these types of services, we include this type of labor in our discussion here. It is unlikely that you will issue shares to persons who have performed work for the corporation (unless they are close friends or business associates who will be active participants in your corporation)—contractors prefer money, not shares, as payment for services rendered.

Shares issued for services do not qualify as shares issued for property under Section 351 of the Internal Revenue Code (see "Potential Problems With Section 351 Tax-Free Exchanges" in Chapter 4).

18 Signature of Secretary

Have your corporate secretary sign at the bottom of the last page of the minutes and type his or her name just under the signature line.

Hold the First Meeting of the Board of Directors

After preparing your minutes, we suggest you actually hold a meeting with all your directors present (although only a quorum is required to attend, we think it is sensible to have as many directors present as possible). Each director should review and agree to the resolutions contained in your minutes. As a reminder, make sure to do the following:

1. Date, and have each director sign, the Waiver of Notice Form (Instruction 3 to "Fill In the Minutes of the First Meeting of the Board of Directors," above).
2. Indicate which directors were present and absent by checking the appropriate box to the right of each director's name in your printed minutes (Instruction 4 to "Fill In the Minutes of the First Meeting of the Board of Directors," above).
3. Have the corporate secretary sign the last page of the minutes (Instruction 18 to "Fill In the Minutes of the First Meeting of the Board of Directors," above).

Consolidate Your Papers

After printing your minutes, make sure to do the following before going on to Step 7, below:

- Have your secretary sign, date, and seal the "Certificate" section at the end of your bylaws.
- Set up a corporate records book with (at least) the following four sections:
  - articles of incorporation
  - bylaws
  - minutes of meetings, and
  - stock certificates.

  You can use a simple three-ring binder for this purpose.
- Place your minutes and attachments (copies of your articles endorsed-filed by the California Secretary of State, bylaws certified by your corporate secretary, a sample stock certificate, any copies of notes cancelled, bills for services rendered, balance sheet for a prior business, and so on) in your corporate records book.
- Keep your corporate records book at the corporation's principal executive office. Remember to document future corporate transactions (by preparing standard minutes of annual director and shareholder meetings) and place copies of corporate minutes and other documents in your corporate records book.

Congratulations! You have now completed the minutes of your first meeting. Next, we explain how to accomplish your last major organizational task, complying with the formalities of the California limited offering stock exemption and issuing your shares, in Steps 7, 8, and 9. Stay with us—you're just a few steps away from completing your incorporation.

Step 7. Prepare Shareholder Representation Letters

Here, we show you how to prepare shareholder representation letters to document your compliance with the California limited offering exemption when issuing your initial shares. This step, with Steps 8 and 9 of this chapter, are the formal steps you must take to issue your shares. You will not receive the consideration (payment) for shares or issue them to your shareholders until Step 9, below.

Take a moment to review the requirements of the limited offering exemption in Chapter 3. If you have any questions concerning your eligibility for this exemption or how to fill in any of the blanks associated with this form after reviewing Chapter 3 and the instructions below, consult a lawyer.

Steps You Should Have Already Taken

Before preparing shareholder representation letters, make sure that you have done the following:

- made a reasonable inquiry to make sure each shareholder will be purchasing shares for his or her own account. If someone will be buying the shares for resale or for someone else's account, you will not want to issue shares to this person. A shareholder's written statement that he or she is buying for his or her own account may not be enough—the corporation should take steps to make sure this statement is true.

- disclosed all facts concerning the finances and business of the corporation and the terms and conditions of your proposed stock issuance to all prospective shareholders. You should provide this disclosure in writing so you can prove that full disclosure was made to all shareholders—remember, state and federal securities laws require you to disclose all material facts. (See "The Limited Offering Exemption" and "Federal Securities Act" in Chapter 3.)

Prepare Shareholder Representation Letters

You need to prepare a shareholder representation letter for each of your initial shareholders (this includes each person, such as a spouse, who will jointly own shares in your corporation). To get started, make a copy of the shareholder representation letter to fill out for each of your prospective shareholders (the persons you listed in the stock issuance resolution in your minutes, prepared as part of Step 7, above).

If any of your shares will be owned jointly (for example, if a husband and wife will take ownership to their shares jointly as community property or in joint tenancy—see "Taking Title to Stock" in Step 9, below), you will need to complete a separate shareholder representation letter for each of the joint owners.

Below is a sample shareholder representation letter and instructions for filling in the blanks.

Instructions

(1) Insert the name of your corporation and street address of the principal executive office of the corporation in these blanks.

(2) Print or type the name of the shareholder in the first blank in this paragraph. In the second blank, indicate the percentage of interest the shareholder will receive in the shares (in most cases, you will simply show a "full" interest here—see the next paragraph if the shares will be co-owned). In the third blank, insert the number of shares that will be issued individually or jointly to the shareholder.

If the shareholder will be taking title to his or her shares individually (without any co-owners), insert "full" here to show that the shareholder will receive a full interest in the shares. If you are issuing a block of shares jointly to two shareholders (whether in joint tenancy or tenancy in common or as part of a business partnership), then you will insert "undivided half" interest here to indicate that the shareholder for whom you are preparing the letter will receive a half-interest in the block of shares together with another co-owner. (For a discussion of ways to take title to shares and the basic characteristics of each type of ownership, see "Taking Title to Stock" in Step 9, below.)

> **EXAMPLE:** Gregg Walker and his friend and business associate Frank Federman form their own corporation. Gregg will own 500 shares individually. Frank will take title to his 500 shares jointly with his wife, Tracy Federman (for legal and tax reasons, the Federmans will take title to their shares in joint tenancy—see "Taking Title to Stock" in Step 9, below). In this instance, the corporation would prepare three shareholder representation letters: one for Gregg, one for Frank, and one for

Tracy. Here's how this paragraph would be prepared for each shareholder:

Shareholder Letter 1 (Gregg Walker)

> I, ___Gregg Walker___, in connection with my purchase of a/~~an~~ ___full___ interest in ___500___ common shares of the corporation named above, hereby make the following representations:

Shareholder Letter 2 (Frank Federman)

> I, ___Frank Federman___, in connection with my purchase of ~~a~~/an ___undivided half___ interest in ___500___ common shares of the corporation named above, hereby make the following representations:

Shareholder Letter 3 (Tracy Federman)

> I, ___Tracy Federman___, in connection with my purchase of ~~a~~/an ___undivided half___ interest in ___500___ common shares of the corporation named above, hereby make the following representations

③ Complete Section A of the letter. The purpose of this section is to indicate that the shareholder fits within one of the shareholder suitability categories of the limited offering exemption. Check the box to the left of one of the six suitability clauses in this section to show which requirement the shareholder meets.

> **EXAMPLE:** If you are preparing a letter for a director or officer of your corporation, check Box 1 to show that the shareholder fits within the exemption as an Inside Shareholder (Category 1).
>
> If you are preparing a letter for a spouse of one of these directors or officers (and the spouse shares the same principal residence as the director or officer), check the box next to Category 6 to show that this shareholder is a Relative of Another Suitable Shareholder (Category 6).

You only need to check one box for each shareholder. However, if a shareholder fits within more than one suitability category, you can check each box that applies, if you wish. A shareholder can meet the requirements of Category 4 by checking either or both Boxes 4(a) and/or 4(b) in the shareholder representation letter.

Check Box 5(a) for a shareholder who is relying on the financial or business experience of a professional adviser to protect his or her interests in the stock purchase transaction. In this case, you and your professional adviser need to complete the separate page in the shareholder representation letter that contains Sections 5(a) and 5(b). To do this, check Box 5(a) and indicate the name of the professional adviser on the blank line in this paragraph. Then complete Section 5(b) by typing the name of the shareholder who is being represented, the number of shares the shareholder will purchase, and the name of the corporation in the appropriate blanks in Paragraph 1 of 5(b). The adviser should state his or her profession in Paragraph 2 of 5(b) (see "Who Can Be a Professional Adviser?" below) and sign and date the adviser representation at the bottom of Section 5(b) (type the adviser's name directly under the signature line).

④ Paragraphs B, C, and D of each shareholder letter contain important representations and disclosures that each shareholder must make. Make sure each shareholder reads these paragraphs and understands their effect before

Shareholder Representation Letter

To: *(name of corporation)* (1)

(address)

(city, state, zip)

I, *(name of shareholder)*, (2) in connection with my purchase of a/an ______________________ (2) interest in *(number of shares)* (2) common shares of the corporation named above, hereby make the following representations:

A. I am a suitable purchaser of these shares under the California limited offering exemption because:

[Check the box to the left of one of the following clauses which describes how you qualify as a suitable purchaser of shares under the California limited offering exemption. The number and name of the limited offering suitability category associated with each clause is indicated above each clause in the sample below.] (3)

Category 1. Inside Shareholder:

☐ 1. I am a director, officer, or promoter of the corporation, or because I occupy a position with the corporation with duties and authority substantially similar to those of an executive officer of the corporation.

Category 2. Existing Relationship:

☐ 2. I have a preexisting personal and/or business relationship with the corporation, or one or more of its directors, officers, or controlling persons, consisting of personal or business contacts of a nature and duration which enables me to be aware of the character, business acumen, and general business and financial circumstances of the person (including the corporation) with whom such relationship exists.

Category 3. Sophisticated Shareholder:

☐ 3. I have the capacity to protect my own interests in connection with my purchase of the above shares by reason of my own business and/or financial experience.

Category 4. Major Shareholders:

(Check box 4(a) or box 4(b) below: check both if both apply)

☐ 4(a). Pursuant to Section 260.102.13(e) of Title 10 of the California Code of Regulations, I am purchasing $150,000 or more of the corporation's shares, and either (1) my investment (including mandatory assessments) does not exceed 10% of my net worth or joint net worth with my spouse, or (2) by reason of my own business and/or financial experience, or the business and/or financial experience of my professional adviser (who is unaffiliated with and not compen-sated by the corporation or any of its affiliates or selling agents), I have, or my professional adviser has, the capacity to protect my own interests in connection with the purchase of these shares.

☐ 4(b). Pursuant to Section 260.102.13(g) of Title 10 of the California Code of Regulations, I am an "accredited investor" under Rule 501(a) of Regulation D adopted by the Securities and Exchange Commission under the Securities Act of 1933. This means either (1) my individual net worth, or joint net worth with my spouse, at the time of the purchase of these shares, exceeds $1,000,000; (2) my individual income is in excess of $200,000 in each of the two most recent years or my joint income with my spouse is in excess of $300,000 in each of those years, and I have a reasonable expectation of reaching the same income level in the current year; or (3) I qualify under one of the other accredited investor categories of Rule 501(a) of SEC Regulation D.

Category 5. Reliance on Professional Adviser:

☐ 5(a). I have the capacity to protect my own interests in connection with my purchase of the above shares by reason of the business and/or financial experience of *(name of professional adviser)* , (3) whom I have engaged and hereby designate as my professional adviser in connection with my purchase of the above shares.

☐ 5(b). REPRESENTATION OF PROFESSIONAL ADVISER
(Name of professional adviser) (3) hereby represents:

(1) I have been engaged as the professional adviser of *(name of shareholder)* (3) and have provided him or her with investment advice in connection with the purchase of *(number of shares)* (3) common shares in *(name of corporation)* (3).

(2) As a regular part of my business as a/an *(profession)* (3), I am customarily relied upon by others for investment recommendations or decisions and I am customarily compensated for such services, either specifically or by way of compensation for related professional services.

(3) I am unaffiliated with and am not compensated by the corporation or any affiliate or selling agent of the corporation, directly or indirectly. I do not have, nor will I have (a) a relationship of employment with the corporation, either as an employee, employer, independent contractor, or principal; (b) the beneficial ownership of securities of the corporation, its affiliates, or selling agents, in excess of 1% of its securities; or (c) a relationship with the

corporation such that I control, am controlled by, or am under common control with the corporation, and, more specifically, a relationship by which I possess, directly or indirectly, the power to direct, or cause the direction, of the management, policies, or actions of the corporation.

Dated: *(date of signing)* (3) *(signature of professional adviser)*
(typed name of adviser)

Category 6. Relative of Another Suitable Shareholder:

I am the spouse, relative, or relative of the spouse of another purchaser of shares and I have the same principal residence as this purchaser. (3)

(4) B. I represent that I am purchasing these shares for investment for my own account and not with a view to, or for, sale in connection with any distribution of the shares. I understand that these shares have not been qualified or registered under any state or federal securities law and that they may not be transferred or otherwise disposed of without such qualification or registration pursuant to such laws or an opinion of legal counsel satisfactory to the corporation that such qualification or registration is not required. (5)

(4) C. I have not received any advertisement or general solicitation with respect to the sale of the shares of the above-named corporation.

(4) D. I represent that, before signing this document, I have been provided access to, or been given, all material facts relevant to the purchase of my shares, including all financial and written information about the corporation and the terms and conditions of the stock offering and that I have been given the opportunity to ask questions and receive answers concerning any additional terms and conditions of the stock offering or other information which I, or my professional adviser if I have designated one, felt necessary to protect my interests in connection with the stock purchase transaction.

Dated: *(date of signing)* (6) *(signature of shareholder)* (6)
(typed name of shareholder)

Why You Need to Prepare Shareholder Representation Letters

Here are the most important reasons for preparing a representation letter for each prospective shareholder:

- The California limited offering exemption requires each purchaser of shares to represent, in writing, that he or she is purchasing the shares for his or her own account and not for resale.
- Each purchaser of California limited offering shares should document, in writing, that he or she fits within one of the six shareholder suitability categories discussed in "Special Shareholder Suitability Rules" in Chapter 3.
- If a purchaser relying on the limited offering exemption cannot meet one of the tests based on his or her own relationship to the corporation, its directors, or officers, or because of his or her financial savvy or qualifications (see Categories 1–4 and Category 6 in "Special Shareholder Suitability Rules" in Chapter 3), then he or she should designate, in writing, a professional adviser who has sufficient business or financial experience to protect the shareholder's interests (Category 5).
- In addition to California law, your corporation must comply with federal securities law. Most small, closely held corporations will wish to rely on the federal "private offering" stock exemption when issuing their initial shares. (See "Federal Securities Act" in Chapter 3.) It will be safer to rely on this exemption if you document that the shareholders have received a full disclosure of all material facts and have had an opportunity to ask questions and receive answers concerning the terms and conditions of the stock issuance. The shareholder representation letter takes care of this.

he or she signs the letter. (See "The Limited Offering Exemption" and "Federal Securities Act" in Chapter 3 for further information on these representations.)

5 The stock certificates in Appendix B of this book contain a legend that alerts your shareholders to the restrictions contained in this paragraph. If you order other stock certificates, you can type this legend on the face of your printed certificates. (See the tear-out certificates at the back of this book for the language to use for this legend.)

6 Each shareholder should sign and date his or her representation letter. Remember, if you have checked Category 5 for any shareholder, make sure the shareholder has his or her professional adviser date and sign the Representation of Professional Adviser section of the letter. Make a copy of each completed letter to place in your corporate records book, and give each shareholder the completed original.

CAUTION

Check the shareholder representation letter. This letter is an important legal document, in which the shareholder makes a number of important statements. We suggest that you advise your shareholders to check with their lawyer before signing it.

CAUTION

Don't miss this filing deadline. If you intentionally disregard the timely filing of the Notice of Stock Transaction form, the Commissioner of Corporations can make you pay the full filing fee that would have been owed if you had qualified your stock issuance. This can be a very hefty fee so make sure to file your notice on time. If you have any questions, see a lawyer immediately.

Step 8. Prepare and File Notice of Stock Transaction Form

When issuing your initial shares under the California limited offering exemption, you must prepare and file a Notice of Transaction Pursuant to Corporations Code Section 25102(f). The notice form must be filed within 15 calendar days "after the first sale of the securities in the transaction in this state." Make sure to file on time. If you don't, the department can make you pay the fees that would normally be due if you issued your shares under a permit (ouch!). Your first sale of shares happens when the corporation first receives payment from any shareholder for any of your initial shares.

Legally, the first sale occurs "when the issuer [corporation] has obtained a contractual commitment in this state to purchase one or more of the securities [shares] the issuer intends to sell in connection with the transaction." We assume that you have not entered into any such preissuance commitment (such as a shareholder's subscription agreement). If you follow the steps in this chapter in sequence, you will receive all of the payments for your shares (consideration) in return for the issuance of all of your shares as part of Step 9, below. To be absolutely sure, however, you should prepare and file the Notice of Stock Transaction form now, before you sell your shares. This way you will be certain your notice form is filed with the department of corporations in advance of the 15-day deadline.

Who Can Be a Professional Adviser?

Attorneys, certified public accountants (CPAs), persons licensed or registered as broker-dealers, agents, investment advisers, and banks and savings and loan associations have been specifically designated by the regulations to the limited offering exemption as qualified to act as professional advisers. This list is not exhaustive, however. You may also rely on and designate a person "who, as a regular part of such person's business, is customarily relied upon by others for investment recommendations or decisions, and who is customarily compensated for such services, either specifically or by way of compensation for related professional services."

Professional advisers must not be affiliated with, or compensated by, the corporation or by any of the corporation's affiliates or selling agents. Paragraph 3 of Section 5(b) of the professional adviser's representation repeats the specific language of the regulations related to these requirements and asks the professional adviser to represent that he or she meets these requirements. (For a further discussion of this category under the limited offering exemption, see "Special Shareholder Suitability Rules" in Chapter 3.)

A few additional points before you do your notice form:

- Prepare and file this form after you have pinned down all of the details of your initial stock issuance (who will purchase your shares, the type and amount of payment to be received, and so on). These details should be contained in the stock issuance resolution of your minutes, prepared as part of Step 6 of this chapter. (Your stock issuance information is also contained in your shareholder representation letters, prepared as part of Step 7, above.)

Notice of Stock Transaction

(Department of Corporations Use Only)
Fee paid $ *(leave these lines blank)* (1)
Receipt No. ______________

DEPARTMENT OF CORPORATIONS FILE NO., if any:
(leave this line blank) (1)

Insert File number(s) of Previous Filings Before the Department, if any.

(2)

Fee: $25.00 $35.00 $50.00 $150.00 $300.00
(Circle the appropriate amount of fee. See Corporations Code Section 25608(c))

COMMISSIONER OF CORPORATIONS
STATE OF CALIFORNIA

NOTICE OF TRANSACTION PURSUANT TO CORPORATIONS CODE SECTION 25102(f)
A. Check one: Transaction under (X) Section 25102(f) ( ) Rule 260.103. (3)

ELECTRONIC FILING REQUIREMENT AND HARDSHIP EXCEPTION:
This notice must be filed electronically through the Internet process made available by the Department of Corporations on www.corp.ca.gov, unless the issuer claims the hardship exception as described in Number 8 below.

1. Name of Issuer:
   (name of corporation) (4)

2. Address of Issuer:
   (address of principal executive office) (5)
   Street City State Zip
   Mailing Address:
   (mailing address, if different) (5)
   Street City State Zip

3. Area Code and Telephone Number: *(telephone number of corporation)* (6)

4. Issuer's state (or other jurisdiction) of incorporation or organization:
   California (7)

5. Title of class or classes of securities sold in transaction:
   Common Stock (8)

6. The value of the securities sold or proposed to be sold in the transaction, determined in accordance with Corporations Code Sec. 25608(g) in connection with the fee required upon filing this notice, is (fee based on amount shown in line (iii) under "Total Offering"):

	California	*Total Offering*
(9) (a)(i) in money	$__________	$__________
(ii) in consideration other than money	$__________	$__________
(10) (iii) total of (i) and (ii)	$__________	$__________

(b) ( ) Change in rights, preferences, privileges or restrictions of or on outstanding securities ($25.00 fee.) (See Rule 260.103.)

7. Type of filing under Securities Act of 1933, if applicable: ______________________

None (11)

8. **Hardship Exception for electronic filing.** An issuer may file this paper notice in person or by mail only if either of the following exceptions apply. The issuer shall check applicable box and include the reason(s) and description(s) for the hardship exception in the space provided.

(12) ☐ Computer equipment including hardware and software is unavailable to the issuer without unreasonable burden or expense. If this is the case, describe below both of the following; the reason(s) that the computer equipment including hardware and software is unavailable without unreasonable burden or expense, and the description(s) of the unreasonable burden or expense.

(12) ☐ The issuer cannot obtain and provide information (including credit card or other identifying information) requested on the Department's electronic notice or through the Internet filing process. If this is the case, describe below both of the following: the reason(s) that the issuer cannot obtain and provide the requested information on the electronic notice or through the Internet filing process without unreasonable burden or expense, and the description(s) of the unreasonable burden or expense to the issuer to make the electronic filing.

After checking the applicable hardship exception above, the issuer shall describe below the reason(s) and description(s) for that hardship exception. (If additional space is needed, attach a separate sheet to this notice.)

(13) 9. ( ) Check if issuer already has a consent to service of process on file with the Commissioner. (Instruction: Each issuer (other than a California Corporation) filing a notice under Section 25102(f) must file a consent to service of process (Form 260.165), unless it already has a consent to service on file with the Commissioner. If no consent to service of process is on file with the Commissioner, attach the consent to this notice.)

10. *(signature of officer or director)* (14)
Authorized Signature on behalf of issuer

(typed name of officer or director) (14)
Print name and title of signatory

(date of signing)
Date

Name, Address and Phone number of contact person:

(typed name, address, and telephone number of signer, above) (14)

260.102.14(c) (8-05) 2

- You will need to have your federal Employer Identification Number (EIN) before you do your notice form online. (See "Federal Employer Identification Number" in Chapter 6 for instructions on how to get your federal EIN.)
- The information provided in this notice form should relate to your entire initial stock issuance transaction. No subsequent notices need to be filed with the state for sales of shares in connection with the same transaction. Remember, you will need to obtain a permit or seek another exemption (file another notice with the help of a lawyer) for any subsequent issuances of shares.
- If you decide to file a federal notice form notifying the SEC of your initial stock offering under one of the rules of Regulation D or Section 4(6) of the federal Securities Act, you can dispense with the notice form shown here and send the Department of Corporations a copy of your federal notice form instead, together with a cover letter and the proper filing fee. (See Section 260.102.14 of Title 10 of the California Code of Regulations for further information.) As we indicate in "Federal Securities Act" in Chapter 3, we don't expect most small, closely held corporations to make this federal filing, and we therefore assume that you will have to file the California notice form discussed in this section.
- This California notice form is not required if none of your shares are purchased in California. We assume, however, that all or most of your shares will be purchased in this state by California residents. (See "Securities Laws and Exemptions" in Chapter 3, for a brief discussion of some of the technicalities involved with out-of-state sales of shares.)

Prepare Your Notice of Stock Transaction Form

You must file your Notice of Transaction Pursuant to Corporations Code Section 25102(f) online, unless you qualify for a hardship exception (for example, you cannot gain access to a computer or are otherwise unable to answer the online questions). To file online, go to the California Department of Corporations' website at www.corp.ca.gov. In the search box, type "Notice of Transaction." In the results page, you should see a link to the Notice of Transaction Pursuant to Corporations Code Section 25102(f). Follow the online instructions for completing and filing the notice form. To get started, you will need your federal Employer Identification Number (EIN). (See "Federal Employer Identification Number" in Chapter 6 for instructions on how to obtain your federal EIN.) You will also need a credit card to pay your filing fee online.

You can refer to the sample Notice of Transaction form and instructions below for help with filling out the form. These instructions assume that you qualify for the hardship exception and will be completing and mailing the paper form of the notice. We have included a blank copy of the Notice of Transaction Pursuant to Corporations Code Section 25102(f) in Appendix B or you can download a copy of the form from the Nolo website (see Appendix A for the link). If you do file a paper copy of the notice, make sure you use the most recent version of the notice form. You can check online at the Department of Corporations website (www.corp.ca.gov) or call one of the offices of the department listed in Appendix B and ask them to send you the most recent version of the form.

Instructions

1 **Top of Form:** Ignore the blanks at the upper left and right portions of the form. The blanks at the upper left will be filled out by the Department of Corporations. The blank at the upper right is only for corporations that have previously qualified securities with the department and have been issued a department file number.

2 **Heading:** Circle or mark the amount of the filing fee (see "Your Notice Form Filing Fee," below).

3 **Item A:** Check the box titled "Section 25102(f)"—this means that you are using the form to provide notice of your stock issuance under the California limited offering exemption.

4 **Item 1:** Type the name of your corporation exactly as it appears in your articles of incorporation.

5 **Item 2:** Type the address of the principal executive office of your corporation (this is the address specified in the principal executive office resolution of your minutes prepared in Step 6, above). Make sure to provide a full street address (no P.O. boxes), including the city, state, and Zip code. If you use a mailing address different from your principal executive office, show this address on the second line of this item.

6 **Item 3:** Type the telephone number of the corporation, including the area code.

7 **Item 4:** Type "California" in this blank to indicate California as the state of your incorporation.

8 **Item 5:** Type "Common Stock" in this blank to indicate that you are issuing only one class of common shares. The articles of incorporation included with this book provide for one class of common shares.

9 **Item 6(a):** In these blanks, show the value of the shares that you will sell to your shareholders. For most small, closely held corporations, the value of the corporation's initial shares is the same as the value of the cash or noncash payments that will be made for the shares (see "The Value of Your Shares," below).

You have already prepared a list of the fair value of the payments to be made by your shareholders in the Stock Issuance Resolution in your minutes. Simply add up the cash payment and noncash payment amounts from the Fair Value column of your stock issuance resolution and place these totals in the blanks here. (We assume that the fair value figures in your stock issuance resolution do, in fact, reflect the actual value of any nonmonetary consideration to be received for your shares.)

Here's how to fill in each of the blanks in this section of the form:

- Indicate the total amount of all cash payments to be made by your California shareholders in the California column of Blank 6(a)(i).
- Indicate the total value of all noncash payments to be made by your California shareholders in the California column of Blank 6(a)(ii)—again, the actual value of any noncash payments made by your shareholders is shown in the stock issuance resolution in your minutes.
- Total the above amounts and place the result in the California column of Blank 6(a)(iii).
- If all your initial shareholders will be California shareholders, simply carry over the three California amounts to the corresponding row of the Total Offering column in Item 6(a). If you will sell

shares outside of California, add the out-of-state cash and noncash figures to the California figures and place these totals in the corresponding rows in the "Total Offering" column. Then provide a new overall total in the Blank 6(a)(iii) of the Total Offering column.

The calculations here are really quite easy and are best demonstrated with an example or two.

EXAMPLE 1: You plan to issue a total of 30,000 initial shares for cash and property totalling $30,000: $10,000 in cash, $20,000 as the fair value of all the property to be transferred for shares. All your prospective shareholders are California residents. You would fill out this item in the notice form as follows:

	California	Total Offering
(a) (i) in money	$ 10,000	$ 10,000
(ii) in consideration other than money	20,000	20,000
(iii) total of (i) and (ii)	$ 30,000	$ 30,000

EXAMPLE 2: Assume the same facts as the previous example except that 5,000 shares will also be issued to an out-of-state shareholder in return for $5,000 cash. In this case, the Total Offering column figures will be changed to reflect this out-of-state amount as follows:

	California	Total Offering
(a) (i) in money	$ 10,000	$ 15,000
(ii) in consideration other than money	20,000	20,000
(iii) total of (i) and (ii)	$ 30,000	$ 35,000

10 **Item 6(b):** Ignore this box ("Change in rights, preferences, privileges or restrictions of or on outstanding securities"). It applies to types of transactions we don't discuss here.

The Value of Your Shares

The total value figure of all of the securities (shares) you are issuing under the limited offering exemption is used to compute the filing fee for your notice form (as explained in Step 8, "Your Notice Form Filing Fee," below). As you might guess, there are legal guidelines for determining the fair value of your shares. The value of your initial shares is: (1) the price to be paid for the shares (money) or the actual value of any consideration other than money to be received for the shares; or (2) the value of the shares when issued; whichever is greater. In our instructions on filling in these blanks on your notice form, we assume that the value of your shares is (1) the actual price to be paid for the shares (if the shares are purchased for cash), or (2) the actual value of any consideration other than money (such as property) to be received for the shares. Most, if not all, privately held corporations can follow this rule to determine the fair value of their shares. However, if the value of your shares when issued is greater than the actual cash price or value of the noncash received for the shares, then this higher figure should be used when filling in these blanks on the notice form.

But don't worry—it is very unlikely that this alternative rule will apply to you. Your corporation's initial shares should have no value in and of themselves—there's no market for such shares. In other words, in the absence of outside market pressures driving up share values or outside investors vying for your initial shares, these shares should only be worth the actual amount your shareholders pay for them.

(11) **Item 7:** In answer to the "Type of filing under Securities Act of 1933, if applicable," type "None." This question relates to the federal securities laws. If you are actually registering your stock offering or filing a notice with the SEC (with the help of a lawyer), the attorney who is helping you with your federal filing will indicate "Registered" or show the number of the rule under which the federal filing was made on the separate notice form he is preparing for you. (See Chapter 3 for a discussion of the federal securities laws.)

(12) **Item 8:** If you are completing a paper notice because you qualify under the a hardship exception, you must check the applicable box and state your reasons for qualifying in the space provided.

(13) **Item 9:** Leave this item blank. As stated in the instructions, California corporations don't need to file a consent to service with the Department of Corporations.

(14) **Item 10:** Type the name of a corporate officer or director who will sign your notice form (on the line marked "Print name and title of signatory"); and this person's name, address, and phone number as the contact person for your corporation in the blanks indicated in the sample notice form. The contact person is the person the department will notify in the event there are any questions concerning your notice form.

Make sure to complete the date and signature lines in this part of the form on all copies of your notice form; these are the lines marked "Date" and "Authorized Signature on behalf of issuer."

Your Notice Form Filing Fee

Below is the latest fee schedule for filing the notice form. The filing fee is based upon the total value of the securities to be sold, as shown on Line 6(a)(iii) of your printed form in the "Total Offering" column.

Value of Securities Proposed to Be Sold (from "Total Offering" column, Line 6(a)(iii))	Filing Fee
$25,000 or less	$25
$25,001 to $100,000	$35
$100,001 to $500,000	$50
$500,001 to $1,000,000	$150
Over $1,000,000	$300

As you might guess, the fee for smaller corporations normally will be $25 or $35. Make sure you have the correct fee amount indicated at the top of the notice.

Filing Your Notice Form

After you submit the notice form and filing fee electronically to the Department of Corporations, you will have completed your filing. Be sure to print out, sign, and date a copy of your notice when you are done. Keep this signed copy in your corporate records book. The Department of Corporations can ask you to produce this paper copy later to prove you filed your notice form on time.

If you requested a hardship exception and are filing a paper copy, send two signed copies of the final form and a stamped, self-addressed envelope to the Department of Corporations at its main Sacramento address (the Department of Corporations addresses are listed in Appendix B). (You can mail the notice to any branch office address, but it will be forwarded to the Sacramento address.) Include a check payable to the "California Department of Corporations" for the amount of your filing fee. In a brief cover letter, ask the department to send you a file-stamped copy of the notice in your enclosed return envelope. You can also file your notice in person at any of the branch offices of the department (assuming you qualify to file a paper notice under the hardship exception). See Appendix B for these addresses.

Step 9. Issue Shares of Stock

The final step in your incorporation process is to issue stock to your shareholders. Issuing shares of stock is an essential step—as a general rule, you should not begin doing business as a corporation until you have issued your stock. (See "Piercing the Corporate Veil" in Chapter 2.)

Ten blank, ready-to-use stock certificates are included in Appendix B at the back of this book. They are specifically designed for use by corporations issuing their initial shares under the California limited offering exemption. If you want to order specially printed certificates for your corporation, you can do so by ordering through a legal stationery store. (For a further discussion on choosing the right certificates, see Step 3, above.)

A Few Reminders When You Issue Shares

- All of your initial shares should be sold for the same price per share. For example, if someone pays the corporation $1,000 cash for ten shares, then another person selling the corporation a machine worth $10,000 should receive 100 shares.
- Your corporation cannot issue more shares than you have authorized in your articles of incorporation. (As explained in Step 2, above, it's common for corporations to authorize more shares in their articles than they will actually issue here.)
- You must issue your initial shares under the California limited offering exemption when following the procedure contained in this book. (See "The Limited Offering Exemption" in Chapter 3 to refresh yourself on these rules.)

Comply With California's Bulk Sales Law

Before getting to the details of your stock issuance, we must make a slight detour to mention a preliminary formality that may apply to some readers—complying with California's bulk sales law. (See Division 6 of the California Commercial Code, starting with Section 6101.)

Generally, this law applies to you only if you meet all of these conditions:

- You are transferring more than half the value of the inventory and equipment of an unincorporated business located in California to your new corporation (if you are incorporating an existing sole proprietorship or partnership).
- The value of the business assets being transferred is at least $10,000 but no more than $5 million.

- The business being incorporated is a restaurant or is engaged in the principal business of selling inventory from stock (such as a retail or wholesale business, including a business that manufactures what it sells).

SKIP AHEAD

If each of the above conditions doesn't apply to your incorporation, you can ignore this section and skip ahead to "Taking Title to Stock," below.

Even if you do meet all three conditions, you may still be exempt from most of the provisions of California's bulk sales law. The exemption most often available to incorporators of small businesses applies if your corporation:

- assumes the debts of the unincorporated business
- is not insolvent after the assumption of these debts, and
- publishes and files a notice to creditors within 30 days of the transfer of assets (normally, the assets are transferred when shares are issued to the initial shareholders).

To comply with this exemption to the bulk sales law, call a local legal newspaper. The paper will send you a notice of bulk transfer form to prepare and will publish and file this form with the county recorder's and tax collector's offices for a fee.

Other exemptions also exist. (See Division 6 of the California Commercial Code for specifics.) If your corporation is not eligible for an exemption from the bulk sales provisions, the publication and filing procedures must be accomplished at least 12 business days *prior* to the transfer of business assets.

There are various notice forms that fit specific provisions of the bulk sales law. To rely on the exemption described above, prepare and have the newspaper publish and file a Notice to Creditors under Section 6013(c)(10) of the Uniform Commercial Code. This notice will usually include a heading indicating that it is a Bulk Sale and Assumption form. In any case, it must include a clause to the effect that "the buyer has assumed or will assume in full the debts that were incurred in the seller's business before the date of the bulk sale."

What Are the Bulk Sales Provisions?

The purpose of the bulk sales provisions in California (and other states) is to prevent business owners from secretly transferring the "bulk" of the assets of their business to another person or entity in an attempt to avoid creditors, and to prevent schemes whereby the prior business owners sell out (usually to a relative at bargain prices) and come back into the business through a back door later on. Of course, we assume you are simply changing the form of your unincorporated business, not trying to convince others that you are disassociated from their prior business (and its debts). In other words, if the bulk sales law applies to you, you should be complying with its notice and filing procedures only as formalities. If, on the other hand, your unincorporated business will have debts outstanding at the time of its incorporation and your corporation does not plan, or may not be able, to assume and promptly pay these debts as they become due, then compliance with the bulk sales procedures is more than a mere formality and you should see a lawyer.

Below is a sample Notice to Creditors under Section 6103(c)(10) of the bulk sales law.

If you don't comply with the requirements of the bulk sales law, a claimant against the prior business can collect the amount owed from the

RECORDING REQUESTED BY:
AND WHEN RECORDED MAIL TO:
Name
Address
City, State, Zip

Space Above This Line for Recorder's Use

NOTICE TO CREDITORS OF BULK SALE

[SECS. 6103(c)(10), (11), 6105 U.C.C.]

Escrow No. ______________________

Notice is hereby given to creditors of the within-named seller that a sale that may constitute a bulk sale has been or will be made.

The individual, partnership, or corporate names and the business addresses of the seller are:

As listed by the seller, all other business names and addresses used by the seller within three years before the date such list was sent or delivered to the buyer are: (if "none," so state)

The address to which inquiries about the sale may be made, if different from the seller's address: (if "same," so state)

The individual, partnership, or corporate names and the business addresses of the buyer are:

The assets sold or to be sold are described in general as:

and are located at:

The date or prospective date of the bulk sale was/is ______________________________,
at ____.

The buyer has assumed or will assume in full the debts that were incurred in the seller's business before the date of the bulk sale.

Dated: ______________________, 20 ____

____
(Signature of Buyer)

____
(Type or Print Name)

This form is provided at no charge as an accommodation to our customers. Any questions concerning its use should be referred to an attorney.

California Newspaper Service Bureau, Inc.

corporation. Of course, if the unincorporated business does not owe any money or have potential liabilities, or if you are sure that your corporation will pay any outstanding debts and claims as they become due, you may not be concerned with this penalty. Even so, we recommend that incorporators to whom the bulk sales law applies attend to these simple publication and filing formalities. Besides helping you avoid claims in the future, compliance with the bulk sales law is additional proof that you have perfected the separate legal existence of your corporation.

Taking Title to Stock

In the next section, you will actually fill out your stock certificates. Before you do, however, you need to know how your shareholders will take title to their stock—that is, whose name or names, and what additional descriptive language, if any, should be put on the stock certificates. If all shareholders will take title to stock in their own names, individually, you can skip most of this section. However, if joint ownership is involved, read this section carefully.

Taking title to stock, essentially, means putting the owner's name on the ownership line of the stock certificate. Often a married person will take title to stock in his or her name alone. This is perfectly legal, even if community property is used to buy the shares. The other (nonlisted) spouse has a half interest in the stock even if the spouse's name doesn't appear, and can enforce this interest against the named spouse if necessary (at death or divorce). The names that appear on the certificates are of concern primarily to the shareholders, not the corporation.

Sole ownership. Type the owner's name on the ownership line. That's all there is to it.

People sometimes wish to hold shares of stock jointly with another person. There are several common ways to do this, including co-owning shares in joint tenancy, as community property, or as tenancy in common. Here are the basics about each of these forms of joint ownership.

Joint tenancy. This form of ownership is often used by family members wishing to co-own property. On the death of one joint owner (joint tenant), the survivor takes full title to the shares automatically, without the property going through probate. When one person dies, the property legally belongs to the other co-owner. During life each joint tenant (assuming there are two) is viewed as owning half of the stock. Although joint tenancy property cannot be willed to a third party, it can be sold or transferred during the life of a co-owner (such a sale terminates the joint tenancy and turns the co-ownership into a tenancy in common—see the discussion below). The fact that a joint tenancy can be ended unilaterally by a joint tenant means that there is no guarantee that the surviving joint tenant(s) will end up owning all the property.

Joint tenancy ownership is created by using the word "as joint tenants" or "in joint tenancy" on the ownership line (for example, "Carolyn Kimura and Sally Sullivan, as joint tenants"). It is also common, but not legally necessary in California, to add the words "with right of survivorship" (for example, "Carolyn Kimura and Sally Sullivan, as joint tenants with right of survivorship").

TIP

As an estate planning measure, consider using a living trust. This allows the beneficiary of the trust to receive title to the shares upon the death of the shareholder, without the necessity of probate. Some shareholders may wish to transfer their shares to this type of trust for the benefit of another person rather than taking title to their shares in joint tenancy with the other person (married shareholders may also wish to transfer shares held as community property to this type of trust). If you do transfer your shares to a trust, you will need to make out new share certificates showing the trust as the owner of the transferred shares. For more details on this and other estate planning techniques, see *Plan Your Estate*, by Denis Clifford (Nolo).

Community property. Community property ownership can only be used by a husband and wife. Although spouses can use other joint ownership forms (such as joint tenancy), community property ownership is sometimes preferred when the stock is in fact purchased with community property—that is, money or property earned by either spouse during a marriage. Under federal and state tax rules, community property may gain some tax advantages when it is transferred after the death of the shareholders. Please check with your tax adviser before taking title to your shares to see if community property ownership may offer some tax advantages.

To signify this type of stock co-ownership, the spouses should use the phrase "as community property" after their names (for example, "Mai Chang and Lee Chang, as community property").

TIP

Understand basic probate rules. In the past, people routinely placed property in joint tenancy to avoid probate. This is no longer usually necessary for spouses, as probate law has been simplified to the point that community property can be transferred to a surviving spouse easily and quickly. However, if one spouse leaves his or her half share of community property to someone other than their surviving spouse, probate will normally be required. Again, check with a tax consultant or tax lawyer for the latest estate and probate rules and practices.

Tenancy in common. The third common category of co-ownership is tenancy in common. Each tenant in common holds an equal interest in the property and can sell, transfer, or will his or her interest to a third person at any time. This form of co-ownership does not have the special probate or income tax benefits associated with joint tenancy property or community property (mentioned above). Typically, unrelated people who wish to purchase property together take title in this fashion. However, it is unlikely that two unrelated persons will wish to co-own shares of your stock. More likely, each unrelated person will wish to separately purchase and hold title to his or her own shares. However, if, for some reason, shareholders do wish to jointly own stocks as tenants in common, the co-owners should use the phrase "as tenants in common" after their names (for example, "Reuben Ruiz and Herman Grizwold, as tenants in common").

CAUTION

Gifts are taxable. Adding another person's name to your shares without receiving money or property of fair value in exchange constitutes a gift, on which gift taxes may have to be paid. For example, if one spouse uses separate property to purchase shares that will be held as the community property of both spouses, or if a person buys shares with his own money but decides to take title to the shares in joint tenancy with another person, a gift has occurred.

Fill Out Your Stock Certificates and Stubs

Fill in the blanks on the tear-out stock certificates and stubs contained in Appendix B at the back of the book (or on the specially printed certificates you have ordered (see Step 3)). Simply follow the directions on the sample stock certificate which we provide below. The circled numbers in the blanks on the sample certificate refer to the instructions that follow.

Certificate Number ___(1)___
For (number of shares) ___ Shares

Issued To:
(name of shareholder)
(address of shareholder)
Dated (date of issuance) 20___

From Whom Transferred
___
Dates ___(8)___ 20___

No. Original Shares	No. Original Certificate	No. of Shares Transferred

Received Certificate Number ___(1)___
For (number of shares) ___ Shares
Dated (date of issuance) 20___

___
SIGNATURE

NUMBER ___(1)___ SHARES ___(2)___

INCORPORATED UNDER THE LAWS OF CALIFORNIA
Common Shares

(name of corporation) (3)

THE SHARES REPRESENTED BY THIS CERTIFICATE HAVE NOT BEEN REGISTERED OR QUALIFIED UNDER ANY FEDERAL OR STATE SECURITIES LAW. THEY HAVE BEEN ACQUIRED FOR INVESTMENT PURPOSES AND NOT WITH A VIEW TOWARD RESALE AND MAY NOT BE OFFERED FOR SALE, SOLD, TRANSFERRED, OR PLEDGED WITHOUT REGISTRATION AND QUALIFICATION PURSUANT TO SUCH LAWS OR AN OPINION OF LEGAL COUNSEL SATISFACTORY TO THE CORPORATION THAT SUCH REGISTRATION AND QUALIFICATION IS NOT REQUIRED.

This Certifies that (name of shareholder) (4) *is the owner of* (number of shares) (5) *fully paid and nonassessable Shares of the above Corporation transferable only on the books of the Corporation by the holder hereof in person or by duly authorized Attorney upon surrender of this Certificate properly endorsed.*

In Witness Whereof, the Corporation has caused this Certificate to be signed by its duly authorized officers and to be sealed with the Seal of the Corporation.

(7)

Dated (date of issuance) (6)

(signature of president) (6)
, President

(signature of secretary) (6)
, Secretary

Each stock certificate should represent the total number of shares the corporation is issuing to a particular shareholder (or, if issuing joint shares, to the joint owners of the shares). If shares are owned jointly, fill out one stock certificate for both joint owners, showing both names and the manner of taking title to the shares on the ownership line.

Instructions

1 Complete the left and right portions of the stub as indicated on the sample. The date of issuance and shareholder signature lines on the stubs will be filled out when you actually distribute your stock certificates. If you've ordered a corporate kit, fill out each separate stub page in your kit in the same manner.

Number each certificate and its associated stub. Each shareholder gets one certificate no matter how many shares she purchases (joint owners of shares get just one certificate for their jointly owned shares). The stock certificates issued by the corporation should be consecutively numbered and issued in order. This is important, since it helps the corporation keep track of who owns its shares.

> **EXAMPLE:** If you plan to issue stock at $50 per share to four people (no matter how many shares each person will receive), first number the certificates 1 through 4. If Jack pays $10,000, Sam $5,000, and Julie $2,500 and Ted transfers a computer with a fair market value of $1,000 for their shares, Jack should receive a certificate for 200 shares, Sam for 100 shares, Julie for 50 shares, and Ted for 20 shares. Despite the differences in the amount of shares purchased, each should get only one certificate.

Fixing a share price amount is arbitrary. In the above example it would be just as easy and sensible to establish a price per share of $25, with each shareholder receiving a stock certificate representing twice as many shares. But avoid a share price that would result in fractional shares—$15 per share in the example above. Although it is permissible, this is an unnecessarily complex method of issuing your shares.

2 Type in the number of shares that each certificate represents. The number of shares each person is entitled to receive is indicated in the stock issuance resolution of your minutes.

3 Type the name of the corporation exactly as it appears in your articles of incorporation.

4 Type the name of the shareholder. If the stock certificate will be held by two persons, indicate both persons' names and the form of co-ownership here (for example, "Mai Chang and Lee Chang, as community property" or "Carolyn Kimura and Sally Sullivan, as joint tenants").

5 Again, show the number of shares represented by each stock certificate. Simply type or spell out a number here. The number shown here should be the same number indicated in Special Instruction 2, above.

6 You will type in the date of issuance and obtain the signature of your president and secretary on each certificate when you distribute your shares.

7 Impress the corporate seal at the bottom of each stock certificate.

8 The transfer sections (both here on the stub, and on the back of each certificate) should be left blank. Use them only if, and when, the stock certificates are later transferred by the original shareholders.

After filling out the stock certificates and stubs, place the completed stubs in consecutive order in the stock certificate section of your corporate records book. These stubs represent your corporation's share register.

You'll need to neatly cut the stub away from the top of the stock certificate (along the dotted line) if you are using the certificates provided in Appendix B at the back of this book. It's easier to do this if you first tear out the entire page.

If you've ordered a corporate kit, keep the completed separate stub pages in the stock records book.

Prepare a Bill of Sale and/or Receipts for Your Shareholders

After filling out your stock certificates, you may wish to prepare receipts and, if incorporating a prior business, a bill of sale for your shareholders, before actually distributing your stock certificates. You are not legally required to prepare these forms, but we think it's a sensible precaution to avoid later confusion over who paid what for shares in your corporation.

A bill of sale and separate receipts are contained in Appendix B to this book and on the Nolo website (use the link provided in Appendix A). Make copies of the appropriate forms and prepare them according to the sample forms and instructions below.

Your method of transferring assets or interests in an existing business to a new corporation can have significant tax consequences. For a general overview, see the author's blog article "Converting an LLC to a Corporation—It's Not as Simple as It Seems," at LLC and Corporation Small Talk (www.llccorporationblog.com). Talk to your tax adviser before you choose a method or use this bill of sale.

Prepare a Bill of Sale for Assets of a Business

If you are transferring the assets of an unincorporated business to your corporation in return for the issuance of shares to the prior owners, you may wish to prepare a bill of sale. If not, skip to the next section below, "Prepare Receipts for Your Shareholders."

Below is a sample of the bill of sale form with instructions.

As indicated in the form, you should attach an inventory of the assets of the prior business that will be transferred to the corporation. If you have any questions, your tax adviser can help you prepare this inventory and choose among the options offered in this form.

Instructions

(1) Type (or print) the names of the prior business owners.

(2) Insert the name of your corporation.

(3) Enter the total number of shares to be issued to all prior owners of the business in return for the transfer of the business to the corporation.

> EXAMPLE: If Patricia and Kathleen will each receive 2,000 shares in return for their respective half interests in their preexisting partnership (which they are now incorporating), they would indicate 4,000 shares here.

(4) Use this line to show any assets of the prior business that are not being transferred to the corporation (for example, you may wish to continue to personally own real property associated with your business and lease it to your new corporation). If, as is generally the case, all prior business assets will be transferred to the corporation, you should type "No Exceptions" here.

As indicated in this paragraph of the bill of sale, you should attach a current inventory showing the assets of the prior business transferred to the corporation.

Bill of Sale for Assets of a Business

This is an agreement between: *(name of prior business owner)* (1) ____________ herein called "transferor(s)," and *(name of corporation)* (2) ____________, a California corporation, herein called "the corporation."

In return for the issuance of *(number of shares)* (3) shares of stock of the corporation, transferor(s) hereby sell(s), assign(s), and transfer(s) to the corporation all right, title, and interest in the following property:

All the tangible assets listed on the inventory attached to this bill of sale and all stock in trade, goodwill, leasehold interests, trade names, and other intangible assets [except *(any nontransferred assets shown here)* (4) ____________] of *(name of prior business)* (5) ____________, located at *(address of prior business)* (6) ____________.

In return for the transfer of the above property to it, the corporation hereby agrees to assume, pay, and discharge all debts, duties, and obligations that appear on the date of this agreement on the books and owed on account of said business [except *(any unassumed liabilities shown here)* (7) ____________]. The corporation agrees to indemnify and hold the transferor(s) of said business and their property free from any liability for any such debt, duty, or obligation and from any suits, actions, or legal proceedings brought to enforce or collect any such debt, duty, or obligation.

(8) The transferor(s) hereby appoint(s) the corporation as representative to demand, receive, and collect for itself any and all debts and obligations now owing to said business. The transferor(s) further authorize(s) the corporation to do all things allowed by law to recover and collect any such debts and obligations and to use the transferor's(s') name(s) in such manner as it considers necessary for the collection and recovery of such debts and obligations, provided, however, without cost, expense, or damage to the transferor(s).

Dated: *(date)* (9) *(signature of prior business owner)* (9)
(typed name) , Transferor

(signature of prior business owner)
(typed name) , Transferor

(signature of prior business owner)
(typed name) , Transferor

Dated: *(date)* (9) *(name of corporation)* (9)
Name of Corporation

(signature president)
(typed name) , President

(signature of treasurer)
(typed name) , Treasurer

Extra Steps Are Required to Transfer Real Property or Leases

If you are transferring real property or a lease to your corporation, you will have to prepare and execute new corporate ownership papers, such as deeds, leases, assignments of leases, and so on. An excellent California guide to transferring property interests and preparing new deeds (with tear-out forms) is *Deeds for California Real Estate,* by Mary Randolph (Nolo).

For rental property, you should talk to the landlord about having a new lease prepared showing the corporation as the new tenant. Or you can have the prior tenants assign the lease to the corporation; however, read your lease carefully before trying to do this, as many leases are not assignable without the landlord's permission.

If the property being transferred is mortgaged, you will most likely need the permission of the lender to transfer the property. If your real property note agreement contains a "due on sale or transfer" clause, you may even be required to refinance your mortgage if rates have gone up substantially since the existing deed of trust was executed. This, of course, may be so undesirable that you decide not to transfer the real property to the corporation, preferring to keep it in the name of the original owner and lease it to the corporation. And, don't forget that the transfer of real property to your corporation may trigger a Proposition 13 reassessment of the property; check with your tax advisor before completing a real property transfer to your corporation.

Prepare and execute these new ownership papers, lease documents, and so on before you give the prior property owners their shares. (See "Distribute Your Stock Certificates," below.)

(5) Insert the name of the prior business being transferred to the corporation. For sole proprietorships and partnerships not operating under a fictitious business name, the name(s) of the prior owners may simply be given here (for example, "Heather Langsley and Chester Treacher").

(6) Show the full address of the prior business.

(7) This paragraph indicates that your corporation will assume the liabilities of the prior business. If your corporation will not assume any of the liabilities of the prior business (see Chapter 4 for a discussion of some of the issues here), then you will need to retype the bill of sale, omitting this paragraph.

In the blank in this paragraph, list any liabilities of the prior business that will not be assumed by the corporation. If your new corporation will assume all liabilities of the prior business, you should indicate "No Exceptions" here.

(8) This paragraph is included in the bill of sale to indicate that your corporation is appointed to collect for itself any debts and obligations (accounts receivable) owed to the prior business that are being transferred to the corporation.

(9) Type the name of the corporation on the line indicated. Don't fill out the other blanks yet. You should date the form and have the prior business owners (transferors) and the president and treasurer of the corporation sign the bill of sale when you distribute the stock certificates to the prior business owners, as explained in "Distribute Your Stock Certificates," below.

Prepare Receipts for Your Shareholders

You may wish to prepare one or more receipts for your shareholders. In Appendix B and on the Nolo website (see the link in Appendix A), we have included receipts for the following types of payment made by a shareholder:

- cash
- cancellation of indebtedness
- specific items of property, and
- services rendered the corporation.

We look at each of these transactions and the associated receipt form below. You will need to make copies of each receipt to be prepared for more than one shareholder (for example, you will want to make two additional copies of the cash receipt form if you will be issuing shares in return for cash payments to be made by three shareholders).

Dating and signing the receipts. Fill in the date and signature lines on your receipts when you distribute your stock certificates in return for the payments made by each of your shareholders (see "Distribute Your Stock Certificates," below).

If you will issue shares to joint owners, you may, if you wish, show the names of both joint owners on the signature line in the sample receipt forms below (although a receipt showing the name of just one of the joint owners is sufficient). If two shareholders jointly contribute an item of property in return for the issuance of two separate blocks of individually owned shares, then you should prepare a separate receipt for each of these shareholders. The particular details of each transaction will usually determine the most appropriate way to prepare the receipt form (normally, you will wish to make out the receipt in the name of the shareholder making the payment).

> EXAMPLE 1: Teresa and Vernon Miller will pay $1,000 for 1,000 shares, which they will take title to jointly as community property. You make out a receipt in the name of the shareholder who writes the check (if the funds are written from a joint checking account, you will make the receipt form in the name of both spouses).

> EXAMPLE 2: Mike and his brother, Burt, transfer a jointly owned lathe with a value of $5,000. Each will receive 250 shares. You make out a separate receipt for each brother, showing the transfer of a one-half interest in the lathe in return for the issuance of 250 shares.

Receipt for Cash Payment

If shares are issued for cash, the shareholder normally pays by check payable to the corporation. The shareholder's cancelled check can serve as additional proof of payment. Here is a sample of the tear-out cash receipt form.

Instructions

(1) Fill in the amount of cash being paid by the shareholder in this blank.

(2), (3), (5), and (7) Type the name of the shareholder, the number of shares that will be issued to this shareholder, the name of your corporation, and the name of your treasurer in the appropriate blank as shown on the sample form.

(4) and (6) After receiving payment from the shareholder, your treasurer should date and sign each cash receipt on the lines indicated.

Receipt for Cash Payment

Receipt of $ *(amount of cash payment)* (1) from *(name of shareholder)* (2) representing payment in full for *(number of shares)* (3) shares of the stock of this corporation is hereby acknowledged.

Dated: *(date of payment)* (4)

Name of corporation: *(name of corporation)* (5)

By: *(signature of treasurer)* (6) ______________

(typed name), ______________ Treasurer (7)

Receipt for Cancellation of Indebtedness

If you issue shares in return for cancelling a debt owed by the corporation to a shareholder, you can prepare the receipt form shown below to document this type of stock issuance transaction. Attach a photocopy of the cancelled debt instrument if you have one, such as a promissory note or written loan agreement, to the receipt.

Instructions

(1) and (2) Insert the number of shares being issued and the name of the shareholder in these blanks.

(3) Indicate the date of the original loan made by the shareholder to the corporation.

(4) Show the total of the outstanding principal amount and accrued and unpaid interest (if any) owed on the loan in this blank.

(5) and (6) Indicate the date of cancellation of the note in the date line on the receipt—this will be the date you actually distribute the shares. Provide this date and have the shareholder sign the receipt (see "Distribute Your Stock Certificates," below).

> **Form for Cancellation of Indebtedness**
>
> The receipt of *(number of shares)* (1) shares of this corporation to *(name of shareholder)* (2) for the cancellation by *(name of shareholder)* (2) of a current loan outstanding to this corporation, dated *(date of loan)* (3), with a remaining unpaid principal amount and unpaid accrued interest, if any, totalling $*(loan balance)* (4) is hereby acknowledged.
>
> Dated: *(date of cancellation of loan)* (5)
>
> By: *(signature of shareholder)* (6) ______________
>
> *(typed name of shareholder)* (2)

Receipt for Specific Items of Property

If a shareholder is transferring specific items of property to the corporation in exchange for shares (other than the assets of an existing business; in this case, see "Prepare a Bill of Sale for Assets of a Business," above), you may wish to prepare a receipt (bill of sale) for the property before issuing shares to the shareholder. Make sure that the property has first been delivered to the corporation and that any ownership papers—such as the pink slip for a vehicle—have been signed over to the corporation. If you are transferring real property interests to your corporation, see "Prepare a Bill of Sale for Assets of a Business," above.

Below is a sample receipt (bill of sale) to document this type of stock transaction for one or more of your shareholders.

Instructions

(1), (2), and (3) Show the number of shares being issued, the name of the corporation, and the name of the shareholder in these blanks.

(4) Provide a short description of the property the shareholder is transferring to the corporation. This description should be brief but specific (for example, include the make, model, and serial numbers of the property or vehicle ID and registration number for vehicles).

(5) and (6) The date of the sale will be the date you distribute the stock certificate in return for the delivery of the property to the corporation. Complete this date line and have the shareholder (the transferor of the property) sign the receipt when you distribute your shares as part of the procedures described in "Distribute Your Stock Certificates," below.

Bill of Sale for Items of Property

In consideration of the issuance of *(number of shares)* (1) shares of stock in and by *(name of corporation)* (2) , *(name of shareholder)* (3) hereby sells, assigns, conveys, transfers, and delivers to the corporation all right, title, and interest in and to the following property:

(description of property) (4)

Dated: *(date of sale)* (5)

Name of corporation: *(name of corporation)* (5)

By: *(signature of shareholder)* (6)

(name of shareholder), Transferor (7)

Receipt for Services Rendered to the Corporation

If you are transferring shares in return for past services performed by a shareholder for the corporation, prepare the receipt form as explained below. Have the shareholder date and sign a bill for these services as "Paid in Full" showing the date of payment (the date you distribute the shares in return for these services—see "Distribute Your Stock Certificates," below). Remember, you cannot issue shares in return for services that will be performed in the future by a shareholder (see "Selling Stock," in Chapter 2).

This is not a common type of stock issuance transaction for newly formed corporations, since (1) most work done for the corporation will occur after your stock issuance, and (2) most contractors or other professionals who have performed services will want cash (not shares of stock) as payment for their services. However, if one of the principals of your closely held corporation has performed services for the corporation prior to your stock issuance, this type of stock issuance transaction may make sense. Of, course, to avoid unfairness to your other stockholders, you will want to make sure that the shareholder charges no more than the prevailing rate for the services performed. For a further discussion of this type of payment for shares, see the "Authorization of Issuance of Shares" section in Step 6 of this chapter. And don't forget, issuing stock for services can result in an immediate tax liability for the person receiving the shares—see "Issuing Shares in Return for the Performance of Services" in Chapter 4.

Instructions

(1), (2), and (3) Show the name of the corporation, the name of the shareholder, and the number of shares this person will receive in the blanks.

(4) Provide a short description in this space of the past services performed by the shareholder (for example, the date(s), description, and value of (amount billed for) past services performed by the shareholder).

(5) and (6) When you distribute the shares in return for the past services (see "Distribute Your Stock Certificates," below), provide the date of issuance of the shares and have the shareholder sign the receipt on the lines indicated above.

Receipt for Services Rendered

In consideration of the performance of the following services actually rendered to, or labor done for, *(name of corporation)* (1) ________, *(name of shareholder)* (2), the provider of such services or labor done, hereby acknowledges the receipt of *(number of shares)* (3) shares of stock in *(name of corporation)* (1) as payment in full for these services:

(description of past services) (4)

Dated: *(date of issuance)* (5)

By: *(signature of shareholder)* (6) ________
(name of shareholder) (3)

Distribute Your Stock Certificates

Now that you've filled in your stock certificates and prepared receipts for your shareholders (and a bill of sale if you are incorporating a prior business), it's time to distribute your stock certificates to your shareholders. Distribute your shares after receiving payment from each shareholder. To complete this step, do the following:

- Have each shareholder (or both shareholders, for jointly issued shares) sign his or her stock certificate stub. Indicate the date of stock issuance on each stub.
- Date each stock certificate and have your president and secretary sign each one, and impress your corporate seal in the circular space at the bottom of each certificate.
- Complete the date and signature lines on your receipts (and bill of sale for the assets of a business if you have prepared this form) as explained above. Give each shareholder a copy of his or her receipt(s) and/or a copy of the bill of sale.
- Make sure to place all your completed stock stubs and completed copies of all receipts, bills of sale, and any attachments (inventory of assets of the prior business, cancelled notes, paid-in-full bills for services, and the like) in your corporate records book.
- If you have not already done so, prepare and file your Notice of Stock transaction with the California Department of Corporations (see Step 8 of this chapter). Remember, you are required to file this notice form within 15 calendar days of your sale of stock.

Signing Corporate Documents

From now on, whenever you sign a document on behalf of the corporation, be certain to do so in the following manner:

(name of corporation), a California corporation

By: *(signature of corporate officer)*
(typed name), (corporate title, for example, president)

If you fail to sign documents this way (on behalf of the corporation in your capacity as a corporate officer or director), you may be leaving yourself open to personal liability for corporate obligations. This is but one example designed to illustrate a basic premise of corporate life: From now on, it is extremely important for you to maintain the distinction between the corporation and those of you who are principals of the corporation. As we've said, the corporation is a separate legal person, and you want to make sure that other people, businesses, the IRS, and the courts respect this distinction (see "Piercing the Corporate Veil" in Chapter 2 for a further discussion).

TIP

Throw out extra certificates. If you have stock certificates left over after filling out and distributing the certificates for your initial limited offering stock issuance, we suggest you tear them up and throw them away. Remember, future stock issuances or transfers may require a permit from the California Commissioner of Corporations, and you will need to consult a lawyer to ensure compliance with state and federal securities laws.

CONGRATULATIONS!

You have completed your last incorporation step! Please read through the postincorporation procedures in Chapter 6 to see how they may apply to your new corporation.

CHAPTER

6

After You Incorporate

At this point, you have formed your corporation. But as you know, operating any business, regardless of its size, involves ongoing attention to paperwork. In this chapter, we briefly cover some important steps you should take after organizing your corporation. We discuss how to comply with the various ongoing state and federal tax requirements that may apply to your corporation. We also recommend adopting a shareholder buy-sell agreement that helps control what happens to your small corporation when an owner dies or decides to leave. And we discuss other formalities related to hiring employees and conducting corporate business.

Postincorporation Paperwork and Tasks

There are a few formalities you should take care of shortly after you organize your corporation. Some of these apply to all incorporators; others apply only to those who have incorporated an existing business.

File Annual Statement of Information

Shortly after you file your articles of incorporation, you will receive an *Initial Statement of Information (Domestic Stock Corporation)* from the California Secretary of State's office. This form (Form SI-200 C) must be filled out and sent back to the secretary with a small filing fee within 90 days after your articles were filed. The purpose of this form is to provide the public with current information about the corporation, including the location of its principal executive office and the identities of its directors and officers.

Every year, you will receive a new *Statement of Information* (Form SI-200 C), which you must return by the date indicated. If there has been no change since the last statement, the corporation may file a simplified form, Form SI-200 N/C.

ONLINE RESOURCE

You can file your Statement of Information online. Go to the secretary of state's website (see Appendix B). Click "Business Entities," then "Annual/Biennial Statements," and go to the "E-File Statements" link and you can fill in and file Form SI-200C or SI-200N/C online.

In addition to filing a statement every year, the corporation may file a new statement any time the information contained in the last annual statement becomes inaccurate (for example, if new directors or officers are selected). You must file a new statement whenever the name or address of the corporation's agent for service of process changes. (Use Form SI-200 C for this.)

If the corporation fails to file the initial or annual statements on time, it is subject to a fine and a possible suspension of corporate powers. So make sure to follow this simple formality.

CAUTION

Watch out for corporate compliance scams. After you form your corporation, you may receive bogus corporate service solicitations that can easily be confused for official letters. They often come from "agencies" with names like the State Bureau of Corporations or the Corporate Minutes Compliance Counsel. They claim to provide services related to your domestic corporation statement or annual corporate minutes forms that you must pay for or risk losing your corporate status. These letters, which appear at first glance to be official state documents and forms, are bogus. Read the small print or check with the secretary of state's office before you pay any money for so-called state-mandated compliance services. The California Secretary of State's website has information about these on a "Customer Alert" page.

File and Publish Fictitious Business Name Statement (If Appropriate)

If your corporation will do business under a name other than the exact corporate name given in your articles of incorporation, you must file and publish a fictitious business name statement in the county of the corporation's principal place of business. For instance, if the name stated in your articles is "Acme Business Computers, Inc.," and you plan to do business under the acronym "ABC, Inc.," you should file and publish a fictitious business name statement. Remember, if you are the first to file this statement for a particular name in a particular county and if you actually engage in business in this county under this name, you are presumed to have the exclusive right to use this name in connection with your business in this county. Although another business can overcome this presumption if it was using the same or a similar name first, it doesn't hurt to stake your claim by getting your name on file.

You must file this statement within 40 days after you start doing business under your fictitious name. Also, you can be barred from using the courts to sue another business or person involving a transaction or contract in which you used your fictitious name unless you first file and publish this statement.

To file and publish your fictitious business name statement, do the following:

1. Obtain a fictitious business name statement and instructions from a legal newspaper or from your local county clerk's office. You can get to the website of each county clerk's office from a link on the Name Availability page of the corporation division's website—see Appendix B. If you haven't already done so (see Chapter 5, Step 1), you should check the county clerk's files to make sure that another business is not already using your fictitious name in the county.
2. Prepare the statement following the instructions for corporations. If your fictitious business name includes a corporate designator such as "Incorporated," "Inc.," "Corporation," or "Corp.," you may have to provide proof that you are a corporation (by showing the county clerk a certified copy of your articles).
3. File the original statement with the county clerk of the county in which the principal executive office of the corporation is located, along with the current filing fee. Obtain a file-endorsed copy of the statement from the county clerk.
4. Mail a copy of the statement to a qualified legal newspaper of general circulation in the county where the corporation's principal place of business is located. Ask the paper to publish your fictitious name statement and file an affidavit of publication with the county clerk (you will have to pay the newspaper's fee for this service). The newspaper will publish the statement once a week for four successive weeks, and should be willing to file an affidavit of publication with the county clerk for you. If you wish to make this filing yourself, follow the instructions accompanying the statement.
5. Place a copy of the endorsed-filed fictitious business name statement and endorsed-filed affidavit of publication in your corporate records book.
6. Make a note in your corporate records book to file another statement five years after your original filing (as explained in the instructions). The county clerk will not notify you of this renewal date.
7. Make similar filings (and publications of the statement), if you wish, in other counties in which you plan to use this name.

File Final Papers on Prior Business

If you have incorporated a preexisting business (transferred the assets of a business to the corporation in return for shares), the prior business owners should file all papers needed to terminate their prior business, including final sales tax and employment tax returns, if appropriate. Of course, you should close your previous business bank accounts and open the corporate bank accounts indicated in the bank account resolution of your minutes. In addition, if the old business holds any licenses or permits, you may need to cancel them and take out new licenses or permits in the name of the corporation.

Don't Forget to Hold Your Annual Meetings

Article II, Section 1, of the Bylaws provides for an annual meeting of shareholders for the election (and reelection) of directors for a one-year term. Article II, Section 7, of the Bylaws schedules an annual meeting of directors immediately after the shareholders' meeting at which the directors accept office for the new one-year term and transact other appropriate business.

For ready-to-use minute forms to document your corporation's annual (and special) shareholder and director meetings, see *The Corporate Records Handbook*, by Anthony Mancuso (Nolo).

We recommend you hold and document these meetings each year, even if you are only doing so as a formality to reelect your current directors and show their acceptance to serve another one-year term. These minutes are an important part of your corporation's "paper trail" and help show others—such as the courts and the IRS—that you take the separate legal existence of your corporation seriously. This will help ensure that they do the same.

Notify Creditors and Others of Dissolution of Prior Business

If you have incorporated a prior business, you should notify the creditors of the prior business and other interested parties (for example, suppliers, vendors, and others with whom you have open-book accounts or lines of credit), in writing, that the prior business is now a corporation.

If the prior business was a partnership, use the following notification procedure. Non-partnership businesses can simply send out a notification letter as discussed in Paragraph 4, below.

1. Obtain at least two copies of a Notice of Dissolution of a Partnership form from a legal newspaper.
2. Fill out the notice following the instructions on the form.
3. Send the completed notice to a legal newspaper circulated in the place or places where the partnership regularly did business, with the request that it publish the notice and file an affidavit of publication with the county clerk within 30 days afterwards. Include publication and filing fees with your request. Place copies of the notice form and the endorsed-filed affidavit of publication in your corporate records book.
4. Notify creditors (and other interested parties) by mail of the dissolution of the partnership or other type of prior business. This notice should be in letter form, addressed and sent to each creditor, and should contain the same information included in the published notice. However, you will want to modify the information in the letter to show that it is directed to a particular individual or business, rather than the general public. Indicate that your prior business has been dissolved and that you are now doing

business as a corporation under your new corporate name. Indicate your new corporate address if you have changed the location of your principal place of business. Place a copy of each letter in your corporate records book.

Adopt a Shareholders' Buy-Sell Agreement

By now you're surely tired of incorporation paperwork, and are ready to get down to business. Not so fast—there is one post-incorporation formality we want you to seriously consider: adopting a shareholder buy-sell agreement to control who can own shares in your corporation in the future and how much they must pay for them.

Some Shareholders Don't Need to Adopt a Buy-Sell Agreement

If you and your longtime spouse own 100% of corporate shares and you agree there is virtually no possibility that you will divorce, there normally is little reason to go to the trouble of creating a buy-sell agreement. After all, if one of you dies while you still own the business, chances are excellent that the other person will inherit the deceased spouse's shares—or that they will be left to a child or children according to a mutually agreed-upon estate plan.

A buy-sell agreement may also be unnecessary if shares are all owned by parents and their compatible children in a situation where all agree that the children will eventually be given or inherit the parents' interests.

You may be wondering, why deal with these issues while our corporation is still in the start-up phase? The answer is as simple as it is scary (potentially, at least): If all shareholders don't sign a buy-sell agreement when they begin corporate life, you could end up in a nasty dispute when a shareholder departs, dies, or divorces and his or her shares are transferred to an outsider the rest of you can't stand.

Here's the problem: When a shareholder in a closely held corporation dies, sells his or her shares, gives them away, or (in some cases) gets a divorce, this brings an outsider into the shareholder ranks. Think about it: Do you really want to have to deal with another shareholder's spoiled child, or hostile ex-spouse? Remember, a shareholder in a small corporation not only gets to vote at annual meetings for the election of the board, he or she also has a say in all major decisions brought before the shareholders for a vote. These decisions may include major structural changes to the corporation, such as amending the articles of incorporation or the corporate bylaws. But that isn't the worst part. A shareholder in a small corporation also may be able to elect him- or herself to a board position. This is true because, in most smaller corporations, a plurality—not a majority—shareholder vote is all that is needed to elect a person to the board. An outsider who gets elected to the board is given a management vote equal to all other board members (each board member has one vote), and thereby gets to participate in all major corporate decisions (and even if outvoted, will have to be heard).

A good shareholder buy-sell agreement deals with these and other issues in advance, when everyone is in a good mood. The agreement usually allows the corporation and remaining shareholders to buy shares offered to an outsider for sale. It also spells out whether the corporation and/or remaining shareholders get a chance, or are required, to buy the shares of a shareholder who stops working for the corporation, dies, divorces, or, under provisions in some agreements, becomes disabled. And it handles the important issue of setting a

Issues Covered in Shareholder Buy-Sell Agreements

Here are some of the basic issues most corporate buy-sell agreements cover, and typical ways they are handled:

- **Shareholder tries to sell to an outside buyer.** Agreements often provide that either the corporation or the other shareholders have a right to buy the shares before an outside shareholder gets a chance.
- **Shareholder wants to give or transfer shares to relatives.** Some agreements restrict all gifts or other transfers of shares. Others allow gifts to family members, as long as certain conditions are met (less than one-half of a shareholder's stock may be gifted to relatives).
- **Shareholder dies.** Some agreements give the corporation or remaining shareholders a right to purchase the shares from a deceased shareholder's estate within a specified number of days from the date of the shareholder's death. Other agreements require the corporation, if financially able, to buy back the shares from the estate or heirs of a deceased shareholder upon request by the representative of the estate or an heir.
- **Shareholder leaves the corporation.** Many agreements adopted by closely held corporations require a shareholder who quits the corporation to sell the shares back to the corporation. Other agreements simply give the corporation a right to require such a buyback, or let the ex-shareholder-employee demand a buyback if he or she wishes to sell the shares.
- **Current shareholder asks to be cashed out.** Some agreements let a shareholder request a buyout of his or her shares, even if he or she remains an employee of the corporation. The corporation has the choice whether to do so or not (and the approval of the other shareholders also may be required).
- **Shareholder divorces.** Agreements often provide that if a shareholder divorces, and shares are transferred to the shareholder's ex-spouse by court order as part of a marital settlement agreement, the corporation can demand a buyback of the shares from the ex-spouse. Typically, spouses of shareholders also sign the shareholder buy-sell agreements.
- **Shareholder becomes disabled.** Some agreements say nothing specific about the disability of a shareholder; the provisions of the agreement that deal with an employee who stops working for the corporation (whether due to quitting, firing, disability, or any other cause) handle the buyback. Other agreements require or permit the corporation to buy out the shares of a disabled shareholder, if a written statement of disability is submitted by one or two doctors.
- **Shareholder has debt problems.** If a shareholder files for personal bankruptcy, many agreements require the corporation, if financially able, to buy the shares back from the bankruptcy trustee. Some agreements prohibit a shareholder from pledging shares as collateral for a personal loan, and require a buyback from the creditor if shares have been pledged contrary to the agreement and the creditor gets possession of the shares due to the shareholder's default on the loan.
- **Buyback price or formula.** All agreements specify a default price or procedure that will be used to value shares for purposes of any buyout covered in the agreement. Typically, this provision only applies if a buyback price or procedure is not specified for a particular type of buyout covered elsewhere in the agreement (for example, it is common for agreements to allow the buyback of shares offered for sale by a shareholder to an outsider at the price the outsider is willing to pay). Different formulas are used,

Issues Covered in Shareholder Buy-Sell Agreements (continued)

depending on the type of business and the profit history of the corporation. Agreements adopted at the beginning of corporate life typically value shares at book value (the depreciated value of assets on the balance sheet of your corporation, minus liabilities). Later, after several years of continuing profits, corporations typically switch to a share valuation method based upon a multiple of the corporation's earnings (for example, the shares of a successful corporation may be valued at five times average annual earnings in the corporation's buy-sell agreement). Other valuation methods used in agreements include a share valuation made at the time of buyback by an independent appraiser or a price agreed to by the shareholders and specified in the agreement.

- **Different buyback prices.** Some agreements specify different buyback prices and terms for different buyback scenarios. For example, if a shareholder leaves the corporation within one year of its formation, the shareholder may get a discounted buyback price, such as 80% of the standard buyback price specified elsewhere in the agreement.
- **Buyback payment method.** Agreements also set out the terms for payment of the buyback price. All cash up front may be specified if the shareholders know the corporation will be able to afford it. More often, agreements provide for the payment of the buyout price in stages, with part cash paid at the time of buyback and the balance, plus interest, payable by the corporation in monthly installments.
- **Life insurance funding of buyback.** Often the corporation and/or shareholders are required to take out and pay for life insurance policies on each shareholder. If a shareholder dies, the cash proceeds from these policies are used to purchase the deceased shareholder's shares.

price, or a procedure to price, shares when the corporation and shareholders decide to buy shares under the buy-sell agreement. This is crucial, since one of the most potentially contentious issues involved in any buyback is how much the shares are worth. Without an advance agreement, arriving at a fair value can be murky—after all, with no ready market for the shares of a privately held corporation, their value is in the eye of the beholder (the holder of shares). And can't you just imagine how much an angry ex-spouse who receives shares as part of a divorce may claim they are worth?

Fortunately, armed with good information and forms, you can prepare a sound buy-sell agreement for your corporation. But to do so, you'll need more material than we have space to include here. One source, designed for use by self-help incorporators who want a basic buy-sell agreement to handle future buyback problems, is Nolo's publication *Business Buyout Agreements: A Step-by-Step Guide for Co-Owners,* by Anthony Mancuso and Bethany K. Laurence. This book takes you step by step through the process of adopting buy-sell provisions for your small corporation, limited liability company, or partnership, with particular attention paid to the concerns and issues of the small, closely held business. Ready-to-use agreements are included as tear-outs or downloads to help you accomplish this task efficiently.

Of course, you may find other sources for a buy-sell agreement, including other business or legal titles in bookstores or business or law libraries. But no matter how you prepare your agreement, the range of technical legal and tax considerations that may apply to your agreement and to any buy-sell transaction that later occurs under it makes it sensible to check with your legal or tax adviser before adopting your agreement. This will help ensure that the practical procedure you have agreed upon will not have any unwanted tax or legal effects later.

TIP

Don't wait too long to adopt a buy-sell agreement. Many incorporators are tempted to avoid discussing and deciding on buy-sell issues, particularly at this early stage of corporate operations. One bit of advice is in order: Don't give in to the temptation. Once your corporation begins to make money, the questions of who owns its shares and how much they are worth will quickly become loaded, and not just to your fellow shareholders. Spouses, children, and other eventual transferees or successors to the shares may also get agitated. In other words, trying to settle the basic questions of who can own shares and how much they are worth at the time of a buyout may be fraught with controversy, requiring the hiring of expensive lawyers (and accountants) to sort them out. Much better to agree, ahead of time, on a reasonable procedure to handle these possibilities.

Tax Forms—Federal

Another basic corporate formality is reporting and paying taxes. Here, we discuss the basic federal tax issues and forms that a corporation might need to handle. Because each corporation is different, we can't anticipate every tax your business might have to pay. Instead, this section is intended as a general guide to the routine tax questions corporations face.

You can get most of the tax forms discussed below from the IRS.

Tax and Business Resources

An excellent source of legal information on starting a small business, generally, is *Legal Guide for Starting & Running a Small Business*, by Fred S. Steingold (Nolo). Another excellent sourcebook of practical information, including financial ledgers and worksheets, is *Small Time Operator*, by Bernard Kamoroff (Bell Springs Publishing).

Federal tax forms and information are available over the Internet at www.irs.gov. California tax forms and information are available from www.ftb.ca.gov.

We suggest all incorporators obtain IRS Publication 509, *Tax Calendars*, prior to the beginning of each year. This pamphlet contains tax calendars showing the dates for corporate and employer filings during the year.

Information on withholding, depositing, reporting, and paying federal employment taxes can be found in IRS Publication 15, *Circular E, Employer's Tax Guide*, and the Publication 15-A and 15-B Supplements. Further federal tax information can be found in IRS Publication 542, *Corporations*, and Publication 334, *Tax Guide for Small Business*.

Helpful information on accounting methods and bookkeeping procedures is contained in IRS Publication 538, *Accounting Periods and Methods*, and Publication 583, *Starting a Business and Keeping Records*.

For information on withholding, contributing, paying, and reporting California employment taxes, go to the Employment Development Department (EDD) website at www.edd.ca.gov. See the "Forms & Publications" page.

S Corporation Tax Election

If you have decided to elect federal S corporation tax status, and have included an authorizing resolution in your minutes, you must make a timely election by filing IRS Form 2553 and the consents of your shareholders. (See "S Corporation Tax Status" in Chapter 4.) If you haven't made your election yet (and haven't consulted a tax adviser as to the timing of the election), call your adviser now and make sure the S corporation election form is sent in on time—you don't want to miss the deadline for this election.

TIP

Make tax year elections, too. Remember, S corporations must generally select a calendar tax year unless they are eligible to elect a fiscal tax year under IRS rules and regulations. (See "Corporate Accounting Periods and Tax Years" in Chapter 4.) Check with your tax advisor when you make your S corporation tax election to figure out whether you can, and should, elect a fiscal tax year.

Federal Employer Identification Number

As soon as possible after your articles are filed, your corporation must apply for a federal Employer Identification Number (EIN) by filling out IRS Form SS-4 and sending it to the nearest IRS center. The IRS should call back within a day or two with your assigned number. Form SS-4 is available online at the IRS website at www.irs.gov. You can fill in and file an SS-4 form online in a few minutes—just type "online SS-4" in the top search box on the main IRS Web page, then select the "Apply for an EIN online" link. If you are incorporating a preexisting sole proprietorship or partnership, you will need to apply for a new EIN for your corporation. You need this number for the employment tax returns and deposits discussed below. You will also need this number before you do your Notice of Transactions Pursuant to Corporation Code Section 25102(f) online (see Step 8 in Chapter 5).

Employee's Withholding Certificate

Each employee of the corporation must fill out and give the corporation an *Employee's Withholding Exemption Certificate* (IRS Form W-4) on or before starting work. This form is used in determining the amount of income taxes to be withheld from the employee's wages.

Generally, any individual who receives compensation for services rendered the corporation and who is subject to the control of the corporation, both as to what shall be done and how it should be done, is considered an employee. All shareholders of the corporation who receive salaries or wages for services as directors, officers, or nontitled personnel are considered employees of the corporation and must furnish a W-4.

TIP

Directors are not considered employees if they are paid only for attending board meetings. However, if they are paid for other services or are salaried employees of the corporation, they will be considered employees whose wages are subject to the employment taxes discussed below—check with the IRS and your local state employment tax district office for more information.

Income and Social Security Tax Withholding

The corporation must withhold federal income tax and Social Security tax (FICA) from wages paid to each employee. These, as well as other employment taxes, are withheld and reported on a calendar year basis, regardless of the tax year of the corporation, and returns and deposits must be submitted on a quarterly or more frequent basis.

The amount of federal income tax withheld is based upon the employee's wage level and marital status and the number of allowances claimed on the employee's W-4.

Social Security taxes are withheld at a specific rate on an employee's wage base (the rate and wage base figures change constantly). The corporation is required to make matching Social Security tax contributions for each employee.

Quarterly Withholding Returns and Deposits

The corporation is required to prepare and file a *Withholding Return* (IRS Form 941) for each quarter of the calendar year, showing all income and Social Security taxes withheld from employees' wages as well as matching corporation Social Security tax contributions.

The corporation is required to deposit federal income and Social Security taxes on a monthly (or more frequent) basis in an authorized commercial or federal reserve bank. You must submit payment for undeposited taxes owed at the end of a calendar quarter with the quarterly return. Consult IRS Publication 15 for specifics.

Annual Wage and Tax Statement

The corporation is required to furnish two copies of the *Wage and Tax Statement* (IRS Form W-2) to each employee if income tax has been withheld from this person's wages or would have been withheld if the employee had claimed no more than one withholding exemption on his or her W-4. This form must show total wages paid and amounts deducted for income and Social Security taxes. A special six-part W-2 should be used in California to show state income tax and disability insurance contributions in addition to the required federal withholding information. W-2 forms must be furnished to employees no later than January 31 following the close of the calendar year.

The corporation must submit the original of each employee's previous year's W-2 form and an annual *Transmittal of Income and Tax Statement* (Form W-3) to the Social Security Administration on or before the last day of February following the close of the calendar year.

Federal Unemployment Tax

Most corporations are subject to the federal unemployment tax provisions. Under the tax statutes, your corporation is subject to paying Federal Unemployment Tax (FUTA) if, during the current or preceding calendar year, the corporation:

- paid wages of $1,500 or more during any calendar quarter, or
- had one or more employees for some portion of at least one day during each of 20 different calendar weeks. These 20 weeks do not have to be consecutive.

FUTA taxes are paid by the corporation and are not deducted from employees' wages. The FUTA tax is determined by the employee wage base and is paid by the corporation (as usual, rates and wage base figures are subject to change). The corporation receives a credit for a percentage of this tax for California unemployment taxes paid or for receiving a favorable experience rating by the state.

Generally, the corporation must deposit the tax in an authorized commercial or federal reserve bank within one month following the close of the quarter. For help in computing your quarterly FUTA tax liability, see the instructions in IRS Publication 15. An annual FUTA return (IRS Form 940) must be filed by the corporation with the nearest IRS center by January 31 following the close of the calendar year for which the tax is due. Any tax still due is payable with the return.

Corporate Income Tax Return

A regular business corporation must file an annual *Corporation Income Tax Return* (IRS Form 1120) on or before the 15th day of the third month following the close of its tax year. The corporation's tax year must correspond with the corporation's accounting period (the period for which corporate books are kept as specified in your minutes). The tax year is established by the first income tax return filed by the corporation.

Your first corporate tax year may be a short year—that is, a year of less than 12 months. For example, if the corporate accounting period selected in the minutes is the calendar year, January 1 to December 31, and the corporate existence began on March 13 (the date the articles were filed), the corporation would establish its calendar tax year and report income for its first tax year by filing its first annual return on or before March 15 of the following year.

Note that this first return would be for the short year, March 13 to December 31. If the minutes select a fiscal tax year, say from July 1 to June 30, and the corporate existence begins on May 1, the first return would be filed on or before August 15 for the first short year of May 1 to June 30.

S Corporation Income Tax Return

Even though federal S corporations are, for the most part, not subject to the payment of corporate income taxes, such corporations must file an annual *U.S. Small Business Corporation Income Tax Return* (IRS Form 1120-S) on or before the 15th day of the third month following the close of the tax year for which the S corporation election is effective.

Corporate Employee and Shareholder Returns

Corporate employees and shareholders report employment and dividend income on their annual individual income tax returns (IRS Form 1040). S corporation shareholders report their pro rata share of undistributed corporate taxable income on Form 1040, Schedule E. (As noted in "S Corporation Tax Status" in Chapter 4, S corporation shareholders may be required to estimate and pay taxes on this undistributed taxable income during the year—check with your tax adviser.)

Estimated Corporate Income Tax Payments

Corporations that expect to owe federal corporate income taxes at the end of their tax year (and most will) are required to make estimated tax payments. Estimated tax payments must be deposited in an authorized commercial or federal reserve bank. The due date and amount of each installment are computed by a formula based upon the corporation's income tax liability.

To determine corporate estimated tax liability and the date and amount of deposits, obtain IRS Form 1120-W. This form is to be used for computational purposes only and should not be filed with the IRS.

Tax Forms—State

These are the basic state tax forms you will have to use in forming and running your corporation. You can get copies of these forms from the Franchise Tax Board.

Corporate Estimated Tax Return

A California profit corporation is required to pay an annual California franchise tax based on its annual net taxable income. It usually also must pay the minimum annual franchise tax each year. For all tax years, the corporation is required to estimate its franchise tax liability at the beginning of the tax year and make advance franchise tax payments each quarter. At least the minimum $800 annual amount must be submitted with the corporation's first-quarter estimated tax payment each year. Newly formed corporations are exempt from this requirement during their first tax year.

Annual Corporate Franchise Tax Return

Your corporation must submit an annual *California Corporate Franchise Tax Return* (Form 100) on or before the 15th day of the third month following the close of its tax year. With the return, you must submit payment for any portion of the tax due that wasn't estimated and paid during the year, as explained above.

Employer Registration Forms

All California corporations that have employees must register with the California Employment Development Department within 15 days of becoming subject to the California personal income tax withholding provisions and the California Unemployment Insurance Code (most are subject to these provisions immediately). If you have employees, register right now if you haven't done so. Registration forms can be obtained by calling the nearest California employment tax district office. If you are incorporating a preexisting business, you'll need to reregister with the Employment Development Department (even though you may be given the same account number). See the *Employer's Guide* mentioned in "Tax and Business Resources," above, and contact your local employment tax district office for more information—you can visit their website at www.edd.ca.gov.

CAUTION

Be sure to comply with unemployment insurance code provisions. Be careful about classifying people who perform services for your corporation as independent contractors. The EDD is particularly aggressive when it comes to collecting state unemployment taxes from businesses. The office routinely investigates employee complaints and conducts field audits to monitor compliance with California's Unemployment Insurance Code provisions. This includes making sure that employers are paying unemployment taxes for all of their workers who are really employees, regardless of how the employer has classified them.

State Withholding Allowance Certificate

Although the corporation can use the information contained in the federal W-4 form to compute the amount of state personal income taxes to be withheld from employees' wages, it is required to make a special *California Withholding Allowance Certificate* (DE-4) available to all its employees. Use of this form by the employee is optional. If not used, the corporation withholds state personal income tax from an employee's wages in accordance with the allowances on his or her federal W-4.

Personal Income Tax Withholding

The amount the corporation withholds from employee wages for state personal income tax is based on tax tables that take into account the marital status, claimed allowances, and wages of the employee. These tables automatically allow for applicable exemptions and the standard deduction.

California Unemployment and Disability Insurance

California unemployment insurance contributions are paid by the corporation at its employer contribution rate shown on the *Quarterly Withholding Return* (DE-3), discussed below. Employer contributions are payable on the current employee wage base amount.

The employer contribution rates vary and, except for new businesses, are based upon the employer's experience rating for each year. Experience ratings vary, depending upon the extent of unemployment benefits paid to former employees of the corporation.

While officers are employees for purposes of unemployment insurance contributions, unemployment benefits may be denied to them if they are laid off or terminated by the corporation and the corporation pays them any fringes while they are not working (such as profit-sharing or pension benefits). Also, if the officers and directors are the only shareholders of the corporation, they won't be eligible for benefits unless the corporation has to pay federal unemployment taxes. Check with your local employment tax district office about this when you first contact them.

Disability insurance contributions are paid by the employee—the employer has to withhold a certain amount from the employee's paycheck to make these payments.

Withholding Returns

Most corporations are required to file *Monthly Withholding Returns* (Form DE-3M) with the state, indicating California personal income tax withholding and disability and unemployment tax contributions for each employee.

The corporation must file a *Quarterly Withholding Return* (Form DE-3) reporting personal income tax withholding and disability and unemployment insurance contributions for the previous quarter and pay any balance not already paid with monthly returns. For more specific information, consult the *California Employer's Tax Guide* available from your local employment tax district office, mentioned in "Tax and Business Resources," above.

Annual Wage and Tax Statement

The corporation should prepare a six-part combined federal/state *Annual Wage and Tax Statement*, Form W-2, as discussed in "California Unemployment and Disability Insurance," above. One copy must be filed with the state.

Annual Reconciliation of Income Tax Withholding

The corporation must file a completed *Reconciliation of Income Tax Withheld Form* (Form DE-43 or DE-43A) together with one copy of each employee's W-2 form, copies of California unemployment insurance filings, and a total listing of all personal income tax withheld, with the California Employment Development Department on or before February 28 following the close of each calendar year.

Sales Tax Permits and Returns

Subject to a few exceptions, every corporation that has gross receipts from the sale of personal property in California (that is, merchandise sold to customers) must apply for a seller's permit by filing an application (Form BT-400) with the nearest office of the California Board of Equalization. This form also registers you as an employer with the Employment Development Department. No fee is required.

Some applicants may be required to post a bond or other security for payment of future sales taxes, although this amount may be waived if you indicate that you plan to do very little resale business. A separate permit is required for each place of business where transactions generating sales tax are customarily entered into with customers. You must add sales tax to the price of certain goods and collect them from the purchaser.

Wholesalers, as well as retailers, must obtain a permit. A wholesaler, however, is not required to collect sales tax from a retailer who holds a valid seller's permit and who buys items for resale to customers, provided a resale certificate is completed in connection with the transaction.

Sellers must file periodic sales and use tax returns to report and pay sales tax collected from customers. A seller must keep complete records of all business transactions, including sales, receipts, purchases, and other expenditures, and have them available for inspection by the board at all times.

The State Board of Equalization also collects an annual environmental fee from corporations with 50 or more employees doing business in California. Corporations with 50 to 100 employees pay $100 per year. Call the excise tax division of the Board of Equalization in Sacramento for more information or visit its website at www.boe.ca.gov.

Licenses and Permits

Many businesses, whether operating as corporations or not, are required to obtain state licenses or permits before commencing business. To get a license or permit, you generally have to meet one or more requirements relating to registration, experience, education, examination scores, and adequate bonding.

Your corporation should obtain all proper licenses before commencing corporate operations. Even if you are incorporating an already licensed business, you must comply with any corporate license requirement in your field. Some businesses must obtain licenses in the name of the corporation, while others must obtain them in the name of supervisory corporate personnel. For specific information relating to corporate licensing requirements, check with a local Department of Consumer Affairs office. They will either refer you to one of their boards or to an appropriate outside agency.

Workers' Compensation Insurance

With some exceptions, all employees of a corporation, whether officers or otherwise, must be covered by workers' compensation insurance. Rates vary depending on the salary level and risk associated with an employee's job. Generally, if all of the officers are the only shareholders of the corporation, they do not have to be covered by workers' compensation. Also, if directors are only paid travel expenses for attending meetings, they may be exempt from coverage (although flat per-meeting payments will generally make them subject to coverage). This is a blurry area, so check with your local state compensation insurance commission office for names of carriers, rates, and extent of required coverage in all cases.

For online workers' compensation information, go to the California Department of Insurance website at www.insurance.ca.gov.

Private Insurance Coverage

Corporations, like other businesses, should carry the usual kinds of insurance to prevent undue loss in the event of an accident, fire, theft, and so on. Although the corporate form may insulate shareholders from personal loss, it won't prevent corporate assets from being jeopardized by such hazards. You can obtain basic commercial coverage, which often includes coverage for autos, inventory, and personal injuries on premises. Additional coverage for product liability and directors' and officers' liability, and other specialized types of insurance, may also be appropriate (of course, these policies may be more costly for a closely held corporation to obtain). Many smaller companies elect to have a large deductible to keep premium payments down. Obviously, there are a number of options to consider when putting together your corporate insurance package. Talk to a few experienced commercial insurance brokers and compare rates, areas, and extent of coverage before deciding. Look for someone who suggests ways to get essential coverage for an amount you can live with—not someone who wants to sell you a policy that will protect you from all possible risks. This type of policy really doesn't exist—and even if it did, you probably wouldn't want to pay the price.

CHAPTER

7

Lawyers and Accountants

Lawyers

It often makes sense to consult an experienced attorney to review your incorporation papers and suggest any specific modifications you might want to consider before you file your incorporation papers. Reviewing your incorporation papers with an attorney is a sensible way to ensure that all of your papers are up to date and meet your specialized needs.

But remember: Asking a lawyer to review the forms and organizational aspects of your incorporation is quite different from having him or her do, or redo, all the work for you. The lawyer should have experience in small business incorporations, should be prepared to answer your specific, informed questions, and should review, not rewrite (unless absolutely necessary), the forms you have prepared.

Throughout this book, we have flagged areas of potential complexity that may require a lawyer's help. If any of these issues come up for you, go over them with an experienced lawyer before filing your articles of incorporation. For example, the following areas will require a lawyer's (or other professional's) services:

- One of your proposed shareholders needs (or wishes) to designate and rely on the advice of a lawyer, accountant, or other professional advisor in order to be eligible as a suitable shareholder under Category 5 of the California limited offering exemption—see Chapter 5, Step 7, and "The Limited Offering Exemption" in Chapter 3.
- You wish to have a lawyer prepare or review a shareholders' buy-sell agreement for the repurchase of shares in your corporation—see "Adopt a Shareholders' Buy-Sell Agreement" in Chapter 6.
- You wish to form a California statutory close corporation, in which case you will need a lawyer's help in preparing a special close corporation shareholders' agreement and adding the required close corporation provisions to your articles of incorporation and stock certificates—see Chapter 5, Step 2, and "The Close Corporation" in Chapter 2.

If you decide to consult a lawyer, you may well ask, "What type of lawyer should I consult?" The best lawyer to choose is someone whom you personally know and trust and who has lots of experience advising small businesses. The next best is usually a small business expert whom a friend (with his or her own business experience) recommends. If you make some calls, you can almost always find someone via this reliable word-of-mouth approach. You can try to find an attorney through a lawyer referral service, but make sure the service is certified by the State Bar of California. For more information on certified lawyer referral services, call the state bar or check their website at www.calbar.ca.gov. You can also check Nolo's online Lawyer Directory at www.nolo.com for information on lawyers in your area.

When you call a prospective lawyer (not just his or her law office), you can probably get a good idea of how the person operates by paying close attention to the way your call is handled. Is the lawyer available? Is your call returned promptly? Is the lawyer willing to spend at least a few minutes talking to you to determine if he or she is really the best person for the job? Do you get a good personal feeling from your conversation? Oh, and one more thing: Be sure to get the hourly rate the lawyer will charge set in advance.

Rules of the state bar require a lawyer to provide you with a written fee agreement in advance if the fee for services will exceed a certain amount (or in contingency fee cases).

If you are using this book, you will probably not be impressed by—or need—someone who charges $350 per hour to support an office at the top of the tallest building in town.

RESOURCE

Look up the law yourself. Some incorporators may wish to research legal information not covered in this book. County law libraries are open to the public and are not difficult to use once you understand how the information is categorized and stored. They are an invaluable source of corporate and general business forms, corporate tax procedures, and information. Research librarians will usually go out of their way to help you find the right statute, form, or background reading on any corporate or tax issue. If you are interested in doing self-help legal research, an excellent source on how to break the code of the law libraries is *Legal Research: How to Find & Understand the Law,* by Stephen Elias and the Editors of Nolo (Nolo).

ONLINE RESOURCE

Check the California Corporations Code online. If you want to browse the Corporations Code, go to the following Internet website: www.leginfo.ca.gov, click "California Law," then select "Corporations Code" and click on "Search." The General Corporation law, which applies to California business corporations, is contained in Title 1, Division 1.

Accountants and Tax Advisers

As you already know, organizing and operating a corporation involves a significant amount of financial and tax work and decisions. Again, we have flagged tricky areas involving financial planning and corporate tax issues throughout this book, including:

- Does it make more sense to form an LLC for your California unlicensed business (and possibly elect corporate tax treatment for your LLC) instead of incorporating?—see "The Limited Liability Company" in Chapter 1.
- Should you elect federal S corporation tax status?—see "S Corporation Tax Status" in Chapter 4.
- Are you eligible for Section 351 tax-free exchange treatment?—see "Tax Treatment When an Existing Business Is Incorporated" in Chapter 4.
- Do you need help in selecting your corporate tax year?—see Chapter 5, Step 6.
- Do you wish to set up IRS-qualified fringe benefit packages for yourself and other employees?—see "Tax Treatment of Employee Compensation and Benefits" in Chapter 4.
- Will you rely on an accountant or other professional in setting up your corporate books (double-entry journals and general ledger) and in making ongoing corporate and employment tax filings?—see the discussion below and "Tax Forms–Federal" and "Tax Forms–State" in Chapter 6.
- Do you need to obtain a valuation of the assets before transferring a prior business to your corporation in return for shares?—see Chapter 5, Step 9.

Although we tend to use the terms tax adviser, financial consultant, and accountant interchangeably, you may want to refer these initial incorporation considerations to a certified public accountant with corporate experience. For general assistance and advice, a qualified financial planner may also be very helpful.

Once your initial incorporation questions have been answered, your corporation is set up, and your books established, you may want to have routine tax filings and bookkeeping tasks performed by corporate personnel or independent contractors who have been trained in bookkeeping and tax matters (in many instances trained or recommended by the accountant you have previously consulted).

Most corporations will have at least their annual corporate returns handled by their accountant or other tax return preparer.

For future financial advice, you may wish to contact an officer in the corporate department of the bank where you keep your corporate account(s). Banks are an excellent source of financial advice, particularly if they will be corporate creditors—after all, they will have a stake in the success of your corporation. Further, the Small Business Administration can be an ideal source of financial and tax information and resources (as well as financing, in some cases).

Whatever your arrangement for financial or tax advice and assistance, you may wish to order the IRS publications listed in "Tax and Business Resources" in Chapter 6 to familiarize yourself with some of the tax and bookkeeping aspects of operating a corporation.

When you select an accountant, bookkeeper, or financial adviser, the same considerations apply as when selecting a lawyer. Choose someone you know or whom a friend with business experience recommends. Be as specific as you can regarding the services you wish performed, and find someone with experience in corporate taxation and corporate and employee tax returns and requirements. And find out ahead of time how much you will have to pay.

APPENDIX

Using the Interactive Forms

This book comes with interactive files that you can access online at **www.nolo.com/back-of-book/CCOR.html**. To use the files, your computer must have specific software programs installed. Here is a list of types of files provided by this book, as well as the software programs you'll need to access them:

- **RTF.** You can open, edit, print, and save these form files with most word processing programs such as Microsoft *Word*, Windows *WordPad*, and recent versions of *WordPerfect*.
- **PDF.** You can view these files with Adobe *Reader*, free software from www.adobe.com. Government PDFs are sometimes fillable using your computer, but most PDFs are designed to be printed out and completed by hand.

TIP

Note to Macintosh Users. These forms were designed for use with Windows. They should also work on Macintosh computers; however Nolo cannot provide technical support for non-Windows users.

Editing RTFs

Here are some general instructions about editing RTF forms in your word processing program. Refer to the book's instructions and sample agreements for help about what should go in each blank.

- **Underlines.** Underlines indicate where to enter information. After filling in the needed text, delete the underline. In most word processing programs you can do this by highlighting the underlined portion and typing CTRL-U.
- **Bracketed and italicized text.** Bracketed and italicized text indicates instructions. Be sure to remove all instructional text before you finalize your document.
- **Signature lines.** Signature lines should appear on a page with at least some text from the document itself.

Every word processing program uses different commands to open, format, save, and print documents, so refer to your software's help documents for help using your program. Nolo cannot provide technical support for questions about how to use your computer or your software.

CAUTION

In accordance with U.S. copyright laws, the forms provided by this book are for your personal use only.

List of Forms

The following files are in rich text format (RTF): You can download these forms at **www.nolo.com/back-of-book/CCOR.html.**

Document Title	File Name
Articles of Incorporation	Articles.rtf*
Cover Letter for Filing Articles	Coverlet.rtf
Bylaws	Bylaws.rtf
Waiver of Notice and Consent to Holding of First Meeting of Board of Directors	Waiver.rtf
Minutes of First Meeting of the Board of Directors	Minutes.rtf
Shareholder Representation Letter	Sharelet.rtf
Bill of Sale for Assets of a Business	SaleBusiness.rtf
Receipt for Cash Payment	Receipts.rtf
Form for Cancellation of Indebtedness	Cancel.rtf
Bill of Sale for Items of Property	SaleProperty.rtf
Receipt for Services Rendered	Services.rtf
Incorporator's Statement	Statement.rtf

***If you reformat the articles:** If you reformat the ARTICLES.RTF file, make sure to leave a 3-inch-square space in the upper right-hand corner of the first page of this form for the California Secretary of State's file stamp. We have inserted hard carriage returns at the top of the first page of the articles form to leave space for this stamp.

The following files are in portable document format (PDF): You can download these forms at **www.nolo.com/back-of-book/CCOR.html.**

Document Title	File Name
Name Availability Inquiry Letter	NameInquiry.pdf
Name Reservation Request Form	NameReserve.pdf
Notice of Transaction Pursuant to Corporations Code Section 25102(f)	25102F.pdf**

****Using the stock notice form:** Before filing this form, we suggest you go to www.corp.ca.gov, to see if the version of this form included in this book ("Notice of Stock Transaction Under Section 25102(f)/01/02 version") is the latest. If not, use the form provided on the website. As an alternative, you can prepare and file your Notice online instead of preparing and filing a paper form (see Chapter 5, Step 7).

Contact Information and Incorporation Forms (included as Tear-Outs)

California Secretary of State Contact Information

California Department of Corporations Contact Information

* **Using the Stock Notice Form:** You must prepare and file this notice online unless you qualify for a hardship exemption. For more information, see Chapter 5, Step 8. If you qualify for the exemption and are filing a paper copy, we suggest you go to www.corp.ca.gov, to see if the version of this form included in this book is the latest. If not, use the form provided on the website.

California Secretary of State Contact Information

www.sos.ca.gov/business/business.htm

Office Hours

Monday through Friday
8:00 a.m. to 5:00 p.m.
(excluding state holidays)

Office Location

1500 11th Street
Sacramento, CA 95814

Phone Number

916-657-5448

Mailing Addresses

Information Requests
(*Copies, Status Reports, and Certificates*)
Certification and Records
P.O. Box 944260
Sacramento, CA 94244-2600

Name Availability and Name Reservation Requests
(*Corporation, Limited Liability Company, and Limited Partnership Names*)
Name Availability
1500 11th Street, 3rd Floor
Sacramento, CA 95814

Annual and Biennial Statement Filings
(*Corporations and Limited Liability Companies*)
Statement of Information
P.O. Box 944230
Sacramento, CA 94244-2300

Corporate Filings
Document Filing Support
P.O. Box 944260
Sacramento, CA 94244-2600

Limited Liability Company Filings
Document Filing Support
P.O. Box 944228
Sacramento, CA 94244-2280

Limited Partnership Filings
Document Filing Support
P.O. Box 944225
Sacramento, CA 94244-2250

General Partnership Filings
Document Filing Support
P.O. Box 944225
Sacramento, CA 94244-2250

Limited Liability Partnership Filings
Document Filing Support
P.O. Box 944228
Sacramento, CA 94244-2280

Other Business Filings
(*Unincorporated Associations, Foreign Lending Institutions, and Foreign Partnerships*)
Document Filing Support
P.O. Box 944225
Sacramento, CA 94244-2250

Substituted Service of Process
(*must be hand-delivered*)
1500 11th Street, 3rd Floor, Room 390
Sacramento, CA 95814

Regional Office
The regional office, located in Los Angeles, provides limited services relating to corporations. Please refer to the Regional Office Web page for the office address and services available.

California Department of Corporations Contact Information

www.corp.ca.gov

Contact Information

The Department of Corporations has four offices. The hours of operation are Monday through Friday, 8:00 a.m. to 5:00 p.m., excluding state holidays:

320 West 4th Street, Suite 750
Los Angeles, CA 90013-2344
213-576-7500 or 866-275-2677
(866-ASK-CORP)

1515 K Street, Suite 200
Sacramento, CA 95814-4052
916-445-7205 or 866-275-2677
(866-ASK-CORP)

1350 Front Street, Room 2034
San Diego, CA 92101-3697
619-525-4233 or 866-275-2677
(866-ASK-CORP)

One Sansome Street, Suite 600
San Francisco, CA 94104-4428
415-972-8565 or 866-275-2677
(866-ASK-CORP)

Name Availability Inquiry Letter

(Corporation, Limited Liability Company and Limited Partnership Names)

To check on the availability of a corporation, limited liability company or limited partnership name in California, complete the form below, and submit the completed form by mail, along with a self-addressed envelope, to Secretary of State, Name Availability Unit, 1500 11th Street, 3rd Floor, Sacramento, CA 95814.

Note: Checking the availability of a corporation, limited liability company or limited partnership name does not reserve the name and has no binding effect on the Secretary of State, nor does it confer any rights to a name. Please refer to our Name Availability webpage at www.sos.ca.gov/business/be/name-availability.htm for information about reserving a name.

Email and/or online inquiries regarding name availability cannot be accepted at this time.

Requestor's Information

Your name: ______________________________

Firm name, if any: ______________________________

Address: ______________________________

City / State / Zip: ______________________________

Phone #: ______________ FAX #: ______________

Entity Type (Select the applicable entity type. **CHECK ONLY ONE BOX.**)

☐ Corporation ☐ Limited Liability Company ☐ Limited Partnership

Name(s) To Be Checked (You may list up to three names to be checked.)

1st Choice: ______________________________

( ) is available. ( ) is not available. We have:

____

2nd Choice: ______________________________

( ) is available. ( ) is not available. We have:

____

3rd Choice: ______________________________

( ) is available. ( ) is not available. We have:

____

The space below is reserved for office use only.

Date:	I #	**By:**

Secretary of State
Business Programs Division

1500 11th Street, 3rd Floor
Sacramento, CA 95814

Business Entities
(916) 657-5448

Name Reservation Request

(Corporation, Limited Liability Company, or Limited Partnership Names)

To request the reservation of a corporation, limited liability company or limited partnership name, complete the Name Reservation Request Form on the following page, attach a check in the amount of $10 (made payable to the Secretary of State) and submit the request:

- **By mail**, along with a self-addressed envelope, to Secretary of State, Name Availability Unit, 1500 11th Street, 3rd Floor, Sacramento, CA 95814.
- **In person (drop off)** at the Secretary of State's office in Sacramento. A request to reserve a *corporation* name also can be dropped off in person at our Los Angeles regional office, 300 South Spring Street, Room 12513, Los Angeles, CA 90013. In addition to the $10 name reservation fee, each drop off request must include a separate, non-refundable special handling fee in the amount of $10. Note: The special handling fee is not applicable to requests submitted by mail.

Please go to www.sos.ca.gov/business/be/processing-times.htm for the current processing times at our Sacramento office.

Only one reservation will be made per request form. You may list up to three names, in order of preference, and the first available name will be reserved for a period of 60 days. The remaining names will not be researched.

A name reservation is made for a period of 60 days. The name reservation can be renewed to the same applicant or for the benefit of the same party, but not for consecutive periods.

E-mail and/or online requests for name reservations cannot be accepted at this time. Please complete the Name Reservation Request Form on the following page.

Note: The reservation of a proposed corporation, limited liability company or limited partnership name does not guarantee that the reserved name complies with all federal and state laws. At the time of filing the document containing the reserved name, it is your responsibility to ensure that you have complied with all federal and state laws, including specific name requirements. In some circumstances, the reserved name may require additional approval/consent pursuant to applicable law at the time of filing. Name styles for particular types of business entities and the need for consent/approval required by law are not considered at the time of the name reservation. Therefore, no financial commitment relating to the proposed name should be made based on the reservation, since the business entity record is not created/qualified/amended until the appropriate documents have been submitted to and filed by the Secretary of State.

Secretary of State
Business Programs Division

1500 11th Street, 3rd Floor
Sacramento, CA 95814

Business Entities
(916) 657-5448

Name Reservation Request Form

(Corporation, Limited Liability Company, or Limited Partnership Names)

The proposed name is being reserved for use by:

Your Name: ______________________ Phone #: ______________

Firm Name (if any): ______________________ Fax #: ______________

Address: ______________________

City/State/Zip: ______________________

Type of Entity (Select the applicable entity type. Only one type may be selected. **Note:** If the "Limited Partnership" type is selected, see page 2 of this Name Reservation Request Form for an additional requirement.)

☐ Corporation ☐ Limited Liability Company ☐ Limited Partnership

Name To Be Reserved (Enter the name to be reserved. Only one reservation will be made per Name Reservation Request Form. You may list up to three names, in order of preference, and the first available name will be reserved for a period of 60 days. The remaining names will not be researched.)

1st Choice: ______________________

____ *is available.* ____ *is available only with consent from:* ____ *is not available. We have:*

____

2nd Choice: ______________________

____ *is available.* ____ *is available only with consent from:* ____ *is not available. We have:*

____

3rd Choice: ______________________

____ *is available.* ____ *is available only with consent from:* ____ *is not available. We have:*

Suspended/Forfeited Entity

☐ If the proposed name is being reserved for the purpose of reviving a suspended or forfeited entity, check the box and include the entity number.

____
Entity Number

Mail Back Response

☐ If the Name Reservation Request Form is submitted in person **and** if you would like the reservation to be mailed back, check the box and include a self-addressed envelope.

Fees (Please make check(s) payable to the Secretary of State.)

Reservation Fee: The fee for reserving a corporation, limited liability company or limited partnership name is $10.00 (per reserved name).

Special Handling Fee:

- In addition to the reservation fee, a $10.00 special handling fee is applicable for processing each Name Reservation Request Form delivered in person (drop off) to the Secretary of State's office.
- The $10.00 special handling fee must be remitted by separate check and will be retained whether the proposed name is accepted or denied for reservation.
- The special handling fee does not apply to name reservation requests submitted by mail.

THE SPACE BELOW IS RESERVED FOR OFFICE USE ONLY

Date:	Amt Rec'd:	R #:	By:

- ☐ **Corporation Names:**

  A corporation name must not be a name that is "likely to mislead the public or the same as, or resembling so closely as to tend to deceive," the name of a California or foreign corporation that has registered with this office or a name that has been reserved by another party. Note: Names are considered deceptive if the only difference is a corporate ending. (California Corporations Code section 201(b) and 2106(b).) A Corporation name is reserved pursuant to California Corporations Code section 201(c).

- ☐ **Limited Liability Company (LLC) Names:**

  An LLC name: (1) must not be a name that is "likely to mislead the public or which is the same as, or resembles so closely as to tend to deceive," the name of a California or foreign LLC that has registered with this office or a name that has been reserved by another party. Note: Names are considered deceptive if the only difference is an LLC ending; (2) must end with the words “Limited Liability Company,” or the abbreviations “LLC” or “L.L.C.” The words “Limited” and “Company” may be abbreviated to “Ltd.” and “Co.,” respectively; (3) may not contain the words “bank,” “trust,” “trustee,” “incorporated,” “inc.,” “corporation,” or “corp.;” and (4) must not contain the words “insurer” or “insurance company” or any other words suggesting that it is in the business of issuing policies of insurance and assuming insurance risks. (California Corporations Code section 17052 and 17452.) An LLC name is reserved pursuant to California Corporations Code section 17053.

- ☐ **Limited Partnership (LP) Names:**

  An LP name: (1) must be distinguishable in the records of the Secretary of State from the name of an existing LP or an LP name that has been reserved by another party. Note: Names are not considered distinguishable if the only difference is a limited partnership ending; (2) must end with the phrase “Limited Partnership” or the abbreviation “LP” or “L.P.”; and (3) may not contain the words “bank,” “insurance,” “trust,” “trustee,” “incorporated,” “inc.,” “corporation,” or “corp.” Note: If entity is a foreign LP that is a foreign limited liability LP, the name must contain the phrase “limited liability limited partnership,” or the abbreviation “LLLP” or “L.L.L.P.” and may not contain the abbreviation “LP” or “L.P.” (California Corporations Code section 15901.08, 15909.05.) An LP name is reserved pursuant to California Corporations Code section 15901.09.

Additional Requirement - Limited Partnership Names

In addition to completing the information on page 1 of this Name Reservation Request Form, a request to reserve a limited partnership name also must state the eligibility for the reservation as required by California Corporations Code section 15901.09. **Please select the applicable statement below** and attach this page to page 1 of this request form. Note: Only one statement may be selected.

The exclusive right to the use of the proposed limited partnership name is being reserved by:

- ☐ a person intending to organize a limited partnership under Chapter 5.5 of the California Corporations Code and adopt the name.
- ☐ a domestic (California) limited partnership or a foreign (out-of-state or out-of-country) limited partnership authorized to transact business in California intending to adopt the name.
- ☐ a foreign limited partnership intending to obtain a certificate of registration to transact business in California and adopt the name.
- ☐ a person intending to organize a foreign limited partnership in the foreign jurisdiction and intending to have it obtain a certificate of registration to transact business in California and adopt the name.
- ☐ a foreign limited partnership formed in the foreign jurisdiction under the name.
- ☐ a foreign limited partnership formed in the foreign jurisdiction under a name that does not comply with the requirements of California Corporations Code section 15901.08(b) or 15901.08(c), but the name to be reserved may differ from the foreign limited partnership's actual name only to the extent necessary to comply with California Corporations Code section 15901.08(b) or 15901.08(c).

Cover Letter for Filing Articles

____

____

____

Secretary of State
Document Filing Support Unit
P.O. Box 944260
Sacramento, CA 94244-2600

Re: ______________________________________

Dear Secretary of State:

I enclose the proposed Articles of Incorporation of ________________________________
____.

["This corporate name was reserved with your office pursuant to Certificate of Reservation #(______________________________)."]

Also enclosed is a check/money order in payment of the following fees:

Filing Articles of Incorporation $100

Please file the Articles and return a copy to me at the above address.

Very truly yours,

____
, Incorporator

Bylaws

____

ARTICLE I
OFFICES

SECTION 1. PRINCIPAL EXECUTIVE OFFICE

The location of the principal executive office of the corporation shall be fixed by the board of directors. It may be located at any place within or outside the state of California. The secretary of this corporation shall keep the original or a copy of these bylaws, as amended to date, at the principal executive office of the corporation if this office is located in California. If this office is located outside California, the bylaws shall be kept at the principal business office of the corporation within California. The officers of this corporation shall cause the corporation to file an annual statement with the Secretary of State of California as required by Section 1502 of the California Corporations Code specifying the street address of the corporation's principal executive office.

SECTION 2. OTHER OFFICES

The corporation may also have offices at such other places as the board of directors may from time to time designate, or as the business of the corporation may require.

ARTICLE II
SHAREHOLDERS' MEETINGS

SECTION 1. PLACE OF MEETINGS

All meetings of the shareholders shall be held at the principal executive office of the corporation or at such other place as may be determined by the board of directors.

SECTION 2. ANNUAL MEETINGS

The annual meeting of the shareholders shall be held each year on ______________________________

____,

at which time the shareholders shall elect a board of directors and transact any other proper business. If this date falls on a legal holiday, then the meeting shall be held on the following business day at the same hour.

SECTION 3. SPECIAL MEETINGS

Special meetings of the shareholders may be called by the board of directors, the chairperson of the board of directors, the president, or by one or more shareholders holding at least 10 percent of the voting power of the corporation.

SECTION 4. NOTICES OF MEETINGS

Notices of meetings, annual or special, shall be given in writing to shareholders entitled to vote at the meeting by the secretary or an assistant secretary or, if there be no such officer, or in the case of his or her neglect or refusal, by any director or shareholder.

Such notices shall be given either personally or by first-class mail or other means of written communication, addressed to the shareholder at the address of such shareholder appearing on the stock transfer books of the corporation or given by the shareholder to the corporation for the purpose of notice. Notice shall be given not less than ten (10) nor more than sixty (60) days before the date of the meeting.

Such notice shall state the place, date, and hour of the meeting and (1) in the case of a special meeting, the general nature of the business to be transacted, and that no other business may be transacted, or (2) in the case of an annual meeting, those matters which the board at the time of the mailing of the notice, intends to present for action by the shareholders, but, subject to the provisions of Section 6 of this Article, any proper matter may be presented at the annual meeting for such action. The notice of any meeting at which directors are to be elected shall include the names of the nominees which, at the time of the notice, the board of directors intends to present for election. Notice of any adjourned meeting need not be given unless a meeting is adjourned for forty-five (45) days or more from the date set for the original meeting.

SECTION 5. WAIVER OF NOTICE

The transactions of any meeting of shareholders, however called and noticed, and wherever held, are as valid as though had at a meeting duly held after regular call and notice, if a quorum is present, whether in person or by proxy, and if, either before or after the meeting, each of the persons entitled to vote, not present in person or by proxy, signs a written waiver of notice or a consent to the holding of the meeting or an approval of the minutes thereof. All such waivers or consents shall be filed with the corporate records or made part of the minutes of the meeting. Neither the business to be transacted at the meeting, nor the purpose of any annual or special meeting of shareholders, need be specified in any written waiver of notice, except as provided in Section 6 of this Article.

SECTION 6. SPECIAL NOTICE AND WAIVER OF NOTICE REQUIREMENTS

Except as provided below, any shareholder approval at a meeting, with respect to the following proposals, shall be valid only if the general nature of the proposal so approved was stated in the notice of meeting, or in any written waiver of notice:

a. Approval of a contract or other transaction between the corporation and one or more of its directors or between the corporation and any corporation, firm, or association in which one or more of the directors has a material financial interest, pursuant to Section 310 of the California Corporations Code;

b. Amendment of the articles of incorporation after any shares have been issued pursuant to Section 902 of the California Corporations Code;

c. Approval of the principal terms of a reorganization pursuant to Section 1201 of the California Corporations Code;

d. Election to voluntarily wind up and dissolve the corporation pursuant to Section 1900 of the California Corporations Code;

e. Approval of a plan of distribution of shares as part of the winding up of the corporation pursuant to Section 2007 of the California Corporations Code.

Approval of the above proposals at a meeting shall be valid with or without such notice, if it is by the unanimous approval of those entitled to vote at the meeting.

SECTION 7. ACTION WITHOUT MEETING

Any action that may be taken at any annual or special meeting of shareholders may be taken without a meeting and without prior notice if a consent, in writing, setting forth the action so taken, shall be signed by the holders of outstanding shares having not less than the minimum number of votes that would be necessary to authorize or take such action at a meeting at which all shares entitled to vote thereon were present and voted.

Unless the consents of all shareholders entitled to vote have been solicited in writing, notice of any shareholders' approval, with respect to any one of the following proposals, without a meeting, by less than unanimous written consent shall be given at least ten (10) days before the consummation of the action authorized by such approval:

a. Approval of a contract or other transaction between the corporation and one or more of its directors or another corporation, firm, or association in which one or more of its directors has a material financial interest, pursuant to Section 310 of the California Corporations Code;

b. To indemnify an agent of the corporation pursuant to Section 317 of the California Corporations Code;

c. To approve the principal terms of a reorganization, pursuant to Section 1201 of the California Corporations Code; or

d. Approval of a plan of distribution as part of the winding up of the corporation pursuant to Section 2007 of the California Corporations Code.

Prompt notice shall be given of the taking of any other corporate action approved by shareholders without a meeting by less than a unanimous written consent to those shareholders entitled to vote who have not consented in writing.

Notwithstanding any of the foregoing provisions of this section, and except as provided in Article III, Section 4, of these bylaws, directors may not be elected by written consent except by the unanimous written consent of all shares entitled to vote for the election of directors.

A written consent may be revoked by a writing received by the corporation prior to the time that written consents of the number of shares required to authorize the proposed action have been filed with the secretary of the corporation, but may not be revoked thereafter. Such revocation is effective upon its receipt by the secretary of the corporation.

SECTION 8. QUORUM AND SHAREHOLDER ACTION

A majority of the shares entitled to vote, represented in person or by proxy, shall constitute a quorum at a meeting of shareholders. If a quorum is present, the affirmative vote of the majority of shareholders represented at the meeting and entitled to vote on any matter shall be the act of the shareholders, unless the vote of a greater number is required by law and except as provided in the following paragraphs of this section.

The shareholders present at a duly called or held meeting at which a quorum is present may continue to transact business until adjournment notwithstanding the withdrawal of enough shareholders to leave less than a quorum, if any action is approved by at least a majority of the shares required to constitute a quorum.

In the absence of a quorum, any meeting of shareholders may be adjourned from time to time by the vote of a majority of the shares represented either in person or by proxy, but no other business may be transacted except as provided in the foregoing provisions of this section.

SECTION 9. VOTING

Only shareholders of record on the record date fixed for voting purposes by the board of directors pursuant to Article VIII, Section 3, of these bylaws or, if there be no such date fixed, on the record dates given below, shall be entitled to vote at a meeting.

If no record date is fixed:

a. The record date for determining shareholders entitled to notice of, or to vote, at a meeting of shareholders, shall be at the close of business on the business day next preceding the day on which notice is given or, if notice is waived, at the close of business on the business day next preceding the day on which the meeting is held.

b. The record date for determining the shareholders entitled to give consent to corporate actions in writing without a meeting, when no prior action by the board is necessary, shall be the day on which the first written consent is given.

c. The record date for determining shareholders for any other purpose shall be at the close of business on the day on which the board adopts the resolution relating thereto, or the 60th day prior to the date of such other action, whichever is later.

Every shareholder entitled to vote shall be entitled to one vote for each share held, except as otherwise provided by law, by the articles of incorporation, or by other provisions of these bylaws. Except with respect to elections of directors, any shareholder entitled to vote may vote part of his or her shares in favor of a proposal and refrain from voting the remaining shares or vote them against the proposal. If a shareholder fails to specify the number of shares he or she is affirmatively voting, it will be conclusively presumed that the shareholder's approving vote is with respect to all shares the shareholder is entitled to vote.

At each election of directors, shareholders shall not be entitled to cumulate votes unless the candidates' names have been placed in nomination before the commencement of the voting and a shareholder has given notice at the meeting, and before the voting has begun, of his or her intention to cumulate votes. If any shareholder has given such notice, then all shareholders entitled to vote may cumulate their votes by giving one candidate a number of votes equal to the number of directors to be elected multiplied by the number of his or her shares or by distributing such votes on the same principle among any number of candidates as he or she thinks fit. The candidates receiving the highest number of votes, up to the number of directors to be elected, shall be elected. Votes cast against a candidate or which are withheld shall have no effect. Upon the demand of any shareholder made before the voting begins, the election of directors shall be by ballot rather than by voice vote.

SECTION 10. PROXIES

Every person entitled to vote shares may authorize another person or persons to act by proxy with respect to such shares by filing a proxy with the secretary of the corporation. For purposes of these bylaws, a "proxy" means a written authorization signed or an electronic transmission authorized by a shareholder or the shareholder's attorney in fact giving another person or persons power to vote with respect to the shares of the shareholder. "Signed" for the purpose of these bylaws means the placing of the shareholder's name or other authorization on the proxy (whether by manual signature, typewriting, telegraphic or electronic transmission, or otherwise) by the shareholder or the shareholder's attorney in fact. A proxy may be transmitted by an oral telephonic transmission if it is submitted with information from which it may be determined that the proxy was authorized by the shareholder, or his or her attorney in fact.

A proxy shall not be valid after the expiration of eleven (11) months from the date thereof unless otherwise provided in the proxy. Every proxy shall continue in full force and effect until revoked by the person executing it prior to the vote pursuant thereto, except as otherwise provided in Section 705 of the California Corporations Code.

ARTICLE III
DIRECTORS

SECTION 1. POWERS

Subject to any limitations in the articles of incorporation and to the provisions of the California Corporations Code, the business and affairs of the corporation shall be managed and all corporate powers shall be exercised by, or under the direction of, the board of directors.

SECTION 2. NUMBER

The authorized number of directors shall be ______________________________.

After issuance of shares, this bylaw may only be amended by approval of a majority of the outstanding shares entitled to vote; provided, moreover, that a bylaw reducing the fixed number of directors to a number less than five (5) cannot be adopted unless in accordance with the additional requirements of Article IX of these bylaws.

SECTION 3. ELECTION AND TENURE OF OFFICE

The directors shall be elected at the annual meeting of the shareholders and hold office until the next annual meeting and until their successors have been elected and qualified.

SECTION 4. VACANCIES

A vacancy on the board of directors shall exist in the case of death, resignation, or removal of any director or in case the authorized number of directors is increased, or in case the shareholders fail to elect the full authorized number of directors at any annual or special meeting of the shareholders at which any director is elected. The board of directors may declare vacant the office of a director who has been declared of unsound mind by an order of court or who has been convicted of a felony.

Except for a vacancy created by the removal of a director, vacancies on the board of directors may be filled by approval of the board or, if the number of directors then in office is less than a quorum, by (1) the unanimous written consent of the directors then in office, (2) the affirmative vote of a majority of the directors then in office at a meeting held pursuant to notice or waivers of notice complying with this article of these bylaws, or (3) a sole remaining director. Vacancies occurring on the board by reason of the removal of directors may be filled only by approval of the shareholders. Each director so elected shall hold office until the next annual meeting of the shareholders and until his or her successor has been elected and qualified.

The shareholders may elect a director at any time to fill a vacancy not filled by the directors. Any such election by written consent other than to fill a vacancy created by the removal of a director requires the consent of a majority of the outstanding shares entitled to vote.

Any director may resign effective upon giving written notice to the chairperson of the board of directors, the president, the secretary, or the board of directors, unless the notice specifies a later time for the effectiveness of the resignation. If the resignation is effective at a later time, a successor may be elected to take office when the resignation becomes effective. Any reduction of the authorized number of directors does not remove any director prior to the expiration of such director's term in office.

SECTION 5. REMOVAL

Any or all of the directors may be removed without cause if the removal is approved by a majority of the outstanding shares entitled to vote, subject to the provisions of Section 303 of the California Corporations Code. Except as provided in Sections 302, 303, and 304 of the California Corporations Code, a director may not be removed prior to the expiration of the director's term of office.

The superior court of the proper county may, on the suit of shareholders holding at least 10 percent of the number of outstanding shares of any class, remove from office any director in case of fraudulent or dishonest acts or gross abuse of authority or discretion with reference to the corporation and may bar from reelection any director so removed for a period prescribed by the court. The corporation shall be made a party to such action.

SECTION 6. PLACE OF MEETINGS

Meetings of the board of directors shall be held at any place, within or without the state of California, which has been designated in the notice of the meeting or, if not stated in the notice or if there is no notice, at the principal executive office of the corporation or as may be designated from time to time by resolution of the board of directors. Meetings of the board may be held through use of conference telephone, electronic video screen communication, or electronic transmission by or to the corporation (see Article X). Participation in a meeting through use of conference telephone or electronic video screen communication constitutes presence in person at that meeting as long as all members participating in the meeting are able to hear one another. Participation in a meeting through electronic transmission by and to the corporation (other than conference telephone and electronic video screen communication) constitutes presence in person at that meeting if both of the following apply:

(a) Each member participating in the meeting can communicate with all of the other members concurrently.

(b) Each member is provided the means of participating in all matters before the board, including, without limitation, the capacity to propose, or to interpose an objection to, a specific action to be taken by the corporation.

SECTION 7. ANNUAL, REGULAR, AND SPECIAL DIRECTORS' MEETINGS

An annual meeting of the board of directors shall be held without notice immediately after and at the same place as the annual meeting of the shareholders.

Other regular meetings of the board of directors shall be held at such times and places as may be fixed from time to time by the board of directors. Call and notice of these regular meetings shall not be required.

Special meetings of the board of directors may be called by the chairperson of the board, president, vice president, secretary, or any two directors. Special meetings of the board of directors shall be held upon four (4) days' notice by mail, or forty-eight (48) hours' notice delivered personally or by telephone or telegraph or by other electronic means including facsimile or electronic mail message. Mailed notice shall be sent by first-class mail to the director's address that appears on the records of the corporation, or the address given by the director for the purpose of mailing such notice. Notice by voice or facsimile telephone shall be to the telephone number given by a director for such notice. Notice to an electronic mail message system shall be sent to the electronic mail address designated by the director for such mail. A notice or waiver of notice need not specify the purpose of any special meeting of the board of directors.

If any meeting is adjourned for more than 24 hours, notice of the adjournment to another time or place shall be given before the time of the resumed meeting to all directors who were not present at the time of adjournment of the original meeting.

SECTION 8. QUORUM AND BOARD ACTION

A quorum for all meetings of the board of directors shall consist of ________________ of the authorized number of directors until changed by amendment to this article of these bylaws.

Every act or decision done or made by a majority of the directors present at a meeting duly held at which a quorum is present is the act of the board, subject to the provisions of Section 310 (relating to the approval of contracts and transactions in which a director has a material financial interest); the provisions of Section 311 (designation of committees); and Section 317(e) (indemnification of directors) of the California Corporations Code. A meeting at which a quorum is initially present may continue to transact business notwithstanding the withdrawal of directors, if any action taken is approved by at least a majority of the required quorum for such meeting.

A majority of the directors present at a meeting may adjourn any meeting to another time and place, whether or not a quorum is present at the meeting.

SECTION 9. WAIVER OF NOTICE

The transactions of any meeting of the board, however called and noticed or wherever held, are as valid as though undertaken at a meeting duly held after regular call and notice if a quorum is present and if, either before or after the meeting, each of the directors not present signs a written waiver of notice, a consent to holding the meeting, or an approval of the minutes thereof. All such waivers, consents, and approvals shall be filed with the corporate records or made a part of the minutes of the meeting. Waivers of notice or consents need not specify the purpose of the meeting.

SECTION 10. ACTION WITHOUT MEETING

Any action required or permitted to be taken by the board may be taken without a meeting, if all members of the board shall individually or collectively consent in writing to such action. Such written consent or consents shall be filed with the minutes of the proceedings of the board. Such action by written consent shall have the same force and effect as a unanimous vote of the directors.

For purposes of this section of the bylaws only, "all members of the board" shall include an "interested director" as described in Subdivision (a) of Section 310 of the California Corporations Code or a "common director" as described in Subdivision (b) of said Section 310 who abstains in writing from providing consent, where (1) the disclosures required by said Section 310 have been made to the noninterested or noncommon directors, as applicable, prior to their execution of the written consent or consents, (2) the specified disclosures are conspicuously included in the written consent or consents executed by the noninterested or noncommon directors, and (3) the noninterested or noncommon directors, as applicable, approve the action by a vote that is sufficient without counting the votes of the interested or common directors. If written consent is provided by the directors in accordance with the immediately preceding sentence and the disclosures made regarding the action that is the subject of the consent do not comply with the requirements of said Section 310, the action that is the subject of the consent shall be deemed approved, but in any suit brought to challenge the action, the party asserting the validity of the action shall have the burden of proof in establishing that the action was just and reasonable to the corporation at the time it was approved.

SECTION 11. COMPENSATION

No salary shall be paid directors, as such, for their services but, by resolution, the board of directors may allow a reasonable fixed sum and expenses to be paid for attendance at regular or special meetings. Nothing contained herein shall prevent a director from serving the corporation in any other capacity and receiving compensation therefor. Members of special or standing committees may be allowed like compensation for attendance at meetings.

ARTICLE IV
OFFICERS

SECTION 1. OFFICERS

The officers of the corporation shall be a president, a vice president, a secretary, and a treasurer who shall be the chief financial officer of the corporation. The corporation also may have such other officers with such titles and duties as shall be determined by the board of directors. Any number of offices may be held by the same person.

SECTION 2. ELECTION

All officers of the corporation shall be chosen by, and serve at the pleasure of, the board of directors.

SECTION 3. REMOVAL AND RESIGNATION

An officer may be removed at any time, either with or without cause, by the board. An officer may resign at any time upon written notice to the corporation given to the board, the president, or the secretary of the corporation. Any such resignation shall take effect at the date of receipt of such notice or at any other time specified therein. The removal or resignation of an officer shall be without prejudice to the rights, if any, of the officer or the corporation under any contract of employment to which the officer is a party.

SECTION 4. PRESIDENT

The president shall be the chief executive officer and general manager of the corporation and shall, subject to the direction and control of the board of directors, have general supervision, direction, and control of the business and affairs of the corporation. He or she shall preside at all meetings of the shareholders and directors and be an ex-officio member of all the standing committees, including the executive committee, if any, and shall have the general powers and duties of management usually vested in the office of president of a corporation and shall have such other powers and duties as may from time to time be prescribed by the board of directors or these bylaws.

SECTION 5. VICE PRESIDENT

In the absence or disability of the president, the vice presidents, in order of their rank as fixed by the board of directors (or if not ranked, the vice president designated by the board) shall perform all the duties of the president and, when so acting, shall have all the powers of, and be subject to all the restrictions upon, the president. Each vice president shall have such other powers and perform such other duties as may from time to time be prescribed by the board of directors or these bylaws.

SECTION 6. SECRETARY

The secretary shall keep, or cause to be kept, at the principal executive office of the corporation, a book of minutes of all meetings of directors and shareholders. The minutes shall state the time and place of holding of all meetings; whether regular or special, and if special, how called or authorized; the notice thereof given or the waivers of notice received; the names of those present at directors' meetings; the number of shares present or represented at shareholders' meetings; and an account of the proceedings thereof.

The secretary shall keep, or cause to be kept, at the principal executive office of the corporation, or at the office of the corporation's transfer agent, a share register, showing the names of the shareholders and their addresses, the number and classes of shares held by each, the number and date of certificates issued for shares, and the number and date of cancellation of every certificate surrendered for cancellation.

The secretary shall keep, or cause to be kept, at the principal executive office of the corporation, the original or a copy of the bylaws of the corporation, as amended or otherwise altered to date, certified by him or her.

The secretary shall give, or cause to be given, notice of all meetings of shareholders and directors required to be given by law or by the provisions of these bylaws.

The secretary shall have charge of the seal of the corporation and have such other powers and perform such other duties as may from time to time be prescribed by the board or these bylaws.

In the absence or disability of the secretary, the assistant secretaries if any, in order of their rank as fixed by the board of directors (or if not ranked, the assistant secretary designated by the board of directors), shall have all the powers of, and be subject to all the restrictions upon, the secretary. The assistant secretaries, if any, shall have such other powers and perform such other duties as may from time to time be prescribed by the board of directors or these bylaws.

SECTION 7. TREASURER

The treasurer shall be the chief financial officer of the corporation and shall keep and maintain, or cause to be kept and maintained, adequate and correct books and records of accounts of the properties and business transactions of the corporation.

The treasurer shall deposit monies and other valuables in the name and to the credit of the corporation with such depositories as may be designated by the board of directors. He or she shall disburse the funds of the corporation in payment of the just demands against the corporation as authorized by the board of directors; shall render to the president and directors, whenever they request it, an account of all his or her transactions as treasurer and of the financial condition of the corporation; and shall have such other powers and perform such other duties as may from time to time be prescribed by the board of directors or the bylaws.

In the absence or disability of the treasurer, the assistant treasurers, if any, in order of their rank as fixed by the board of directors (or if not ranked, the assistant treasurer designated by the board of directors), shall perform all the duties of the treasurer and, when so acting, shall have all the powers of and be subject to all the restrictions upon the treasurer. The assistant treasurers, if any, shall have such other powers and perform such other duties as may from time to time be prescribed by the board of directors or these bylaws.

SECTION 8. COMPENSATION

The officers of this corporation shall receive such compensation for their services as may be fixed by resolution of the board of directors.

ARTICLE V
EXECUTIVE COMMITTEES

SECTION 1

The board may, by resolution adopted by a majority of the authorized number of directors, designate one or more committees, each consisting of two or more directors, to serve at the pleasure of the board. Any such committee, to the extent provided in the resolution of the board, shall have all the authority of the board, except with respect to:

a. The approval of any action for which the approval of the shareholders or approval of the outstanding shares is also required.

b. The filling of vacancies on the board or in any committee.

c. The fixing of compensation of the directors for serving on the board or on any committee.

d. The amendment or repeal of bylaws or the adoption of new bylaws.

e. The amendment or repeal of any resolution of the board which by its express terms is not so amendable or repealable.

f. A distribution to the shareholders of the corporation, except at a rate or in a periodic amount or within a price range determined by the board.

g. The appointment of other committees of the board or the members thereof.

ARTICLE VI
CORPORATE RECORDS AND REPORTS

SECTION 1. INSPECTION BY SHAREHOLDERS

The share register shall be open to inspection and copying by any shareholder or holder of a voting trust certificate at any time during usual business hours upon written demand on the corporation, for a purpose reasonably related to such holder's interest as a shareholder or holder of a voting trust certificate. Such inspection and copying under this section may be made in person or by agent or attorney.

The accounting books and records of the corporation and the minutes of proceedings of the shareholders and the board and committees of the board shall be open to inspection upon the written demand of the corporation by any shareholder or holder of a voting trust certificate at any reasonable time during usual business hours, for any proper purpose reasonably related to such holder's interests as a shareholder or as the holder of such voting trust certificate. Such inspection by a shareholder or holder of voting trust certificate may be made in person or by agent or attorney, and the right of inspection includes the right to copy and make extracts.

Shareholders shall also have the right to inspect the original or copy of these bylaws, as amended to date and kept at the corporation's principal executive office, at all reasonable times during business hours.

SECTION 2. INSPECTION BY DIRECTORS

Every director shall have the absolute right at any reasonable time to inspect and copy all books, records, and documents of every kind and to inspect the physical properties of the corporation, domestic or foreign. Such inspection by a director may be made in person or by agent or attorney. The right of inspection includes the right to copy and make extracts.

SECTION 3. RIGHT TO INSPECT WRITTEN RECORDS

If any record subject to inspection pursuant to the California Corporations Code is not maintained in written form, a request for inspection is not complied with unless and until the corporation at its expense makes such record available in written form.

SECTION 4. WAIVER OF ANNUAL REPORT

The annual report to shareholders, described in Section 1501 of the California Corporations Code, is hereby expressly waived, as long as this corporation has less than 100 holders of record of its shares. This waiver shall be subject to any provision of law, including Section 1501(c) of the California Corporations Code, allowing shareholders to request the corporation to furnish financial statements.

SECTION 5. CONTRACTS, ETC.

The board of directors, except as otherwise provided in the bylaws, may authorize any officer or officers, agent or agents, to enter into any contract or execute any instrument in the name and on behalf of the corporation. Such authority may be general or confined to specific instances. Unless so authorized by the board of directors, no officer, agent, or employee shall have any power or authority to bind the corporation by any contract, or to pledge its credit, or to render it liable for any purpose or to any amount.

ARTICLE VII
INDEMNIFICATION AND INSURANCE OF CORPORATE AGENTS

SECTION 1. INDEMNIFICATION

The directors and officers of the corporation shall be indemnified by the corporation to the fullest extent not prohibited by the California Corporations Code.

SECTION 2. INSURANCE

The corporation shall have the power to purchase and maintain insurance on behalf of any agent (as defined in Section 317 of the California Corporations Code) against any liability asserted against or incurred by the agent in such capacity or arising out of the agent's status as such, whether or not the corporation would have the power to indemnify the agent against such liability under the provisions of Section 317 of the California Corporations Code.

ARTICLE VIII
SHARES

SECTION 1. CERTIFICATES

The corporation shall issue certificates for its shares when fully paid. Certificates of stock shall be issued in numerical order, and shall state the name of the recordholder of the shares represented thereby; the number, designation, if any, and the class or series of shares represented thereby; and contain any statement or summary required by any applicable provision of the California Corporations Code.

Every certificate for shares shall be signed in the name of the corporation by (1) the chairperson or vice chairperson of the board or the president or a vice president and (2) by the treasurer or the secretary or an assistant secretary.

SECTION 2. TRANSFER OF SHARES

Upon surrender to the secretary or transfer agent of the corporation of a certificate for shares duly endorsed or accompanied by proper evidence of succession, assignment, or authority to transfer, it shall be the duty of the secretary of the corporation to issue a new certificate to the person entitled thereto, to cancel the old certificate, and to record the transaction upon the share register of the corporation.

SECTION 3. RECORD DATE

The board of directors may fix a time in the future as a record date for the determination of the shareholders entitled to notice of and to vote at any meeting of shareholders or entitled to receive payment of any dividend or distribution, or any allotment of rights, or to exercise rights in respect to any other lawful action. The record date so fixed shall not be more than sixty (60) days nor less than ten (10) days prior to the date of the meeting nor more than sixty (60) days prior to any other action. When a record date is so fixed, only shareholders of record on that date are entitled to notice of and to vote at the meeting or to receive the dividend, distribution, or allotment of rights, or to exercise the rights as the case may be, notwithstanding any transfer of any shares on the books of the corporation after the record date.

ARTICLE IX
AMENDMENT OF BYLAWS

SECTION 1. BY SHAREHOLDERS

Bylaws may be adopted, amended, or repealed by the affirmative vote or by the written consent of holders of a majority of the outstanding shares of the corporation entitled to vote. However, a bylaw amendment which reduces the fixed number of directors to a number less than five (5) shall not be effective if the votes cast against the amendment or the shares not consenting to its adoption are equal to more than 16-2/3 percent of the outstanding shares entitled to vote.

SECTION 2. BY DIRECTORS

Subject to the right of shareholders to adopt, amend, or repeal bylaws, the directors may adopt, amend, or repeal any bylaw, except that a bylaw amendment changing the authorized number of directors may be adopted by the board of directors only if prior to the issuance of shares.

ARTICLE X
ELECTRONIC TRANSMISSIONS

SECTION 1. ELECTRONIC TRANSMISSION BY THE CORPORATION

For the purposes of these Bylaws "electronic transmission by the corporation" means a communication

a. delivered by

   (1) facsimile telecommunication or electronic mail when directed to the facsimile number or electronic mail address, respectively, for that recipient on record with the corporation,

   (2) posting on an electronic message board or network which the corporation has designated for those communications, together with a separate notice to the recipient of the posting, which transmission shall be validly delivered upon the later of the posting or delivery of the separate notice thereof, or

   (3) other means of electronic communication,

b. to a recipient who has provided an unrevoked consent to the use of those means of transmission for communications under or pursuant to this code, and

c. that creates a record that is capable of retention, retrieval, and review, and that may thereafter be rendered into clearly legible tangible form. However, an electronic transmission under the California Corporations Code by a corporation to an individual shareholder or member of the corporation who is a natural person, and if an officer or director of the corporation, only if communicated to the recipient in that person's capacity as a shareholder or member, is not authorized unless, in addition to satisfying the requirements of this article, the consent to the transmission has been preceded by or includes a clear written statement to the recipient as to:

   (1) any right of the recipient to have the record provided or made available on paper or in nonelectronic form,

(2) whether the consent applies only to that transmission, to specified categories of communications, or to all communications from the corporation, and

(3) the procedures the recipient must use to withdraw consent.

SECTION 2. ELECTRONIC TRANSMISSION TO THE CORPORATION

For the purposes of these Bylaws "electronic transmission to the corporation" means a communication

a. delivered by

(1) facsimile telecommunication or electronic mail when directed to the facsimile number or electronic mail address, respectively, which the corporation has provided from time to time to shareholders or members and directors for sending communications to the corporation,

(2) posting on an electronic message board or network which the corporation has designated for those communications, and which transmission shall be validly delivered upon the posting, or

(3) other means of electronic communication,

b. as to which the corporation has placed in effect reasonable measures to verify that the sender is the shareholder or member (in person or by proxy) or director purporting to send the transmission, and

c. that creates a record that is capable of retention, retrieval, and review, and that may thereafter be rendered into clearly legible tangible form.

CERTIFICATE

This is to certify that the foregoing is a true and correct copy of the bylaws of the corporation named in the title thereto and that such bylaws were duly adopted by the board of directors of the corporation on the date set forth below.

Dated:____________________ ______________________________

, Secretary

Incorporator's Statement

The undersigned, the incorporator of ______________________________

____,

who signed and filed its Articles of Incorporation with the California Secretary of State, appoints the following individuals to serve as the initial directors of the corporation, who shall serve as directors until the first meeting of shareholders for the election of directors and until their successors are elected and agree to serve on the board:

Initial Directors' Names and Addresses:

____

____

____

____

____

____

____

____

____

____

Date: ______________________________

Signature: ____, Incorporator

Typed Name of Incorporator: ______________________________

Waiver of Notice and Consent to Holding of First Meeting of Board of Directors

of

____

We, the undersigned, being all the directors of ____________________________

____,

a California corporation, hereby waive notice of the first meeting of the board of directors of the corporation and consent to the holding of said meeting at ____________________

____,

on ______________________________, at __________, and consent to the transaction of any and all business by the directors at the meeting including, without limitation, the adoption of bylaws, the election of officers, the selection of the corporation's accounting period, the designation of the principal executive office of the corporation, the selection of the place where the corporation's bank account will be maintained, and the authorization of the sale and issuance of the initial shares of stock of the corporation.

Dated: __________________ ___________________________________

, Director

____

, Director

____

, Director

Minutes of First Meeting of the Board of Directors

of

____

The board of directors of ______________________________
held its first meeting at ______________________________,
on ______________, at __________.

The following directors, marked as present next to their names, were in attendance at the meeting and constituted a quorum of the full board:

______________________________ ☐ Present ☐ Absent
______________________________ ☐ Present ☐ Absent
______________________________ ☐ Present ☐ Absent

On motion and by unanimous vote, ______________________________
was elected temporary chairperson and then presided over the meeting. ______________
______________________________ was elected temporary secretary of the meeting.

The chairperson announced that the meeting was held pursuant to written waiver of notice and consent to holding of the meeting signed by each of the directors. Upon a motion duly made, seconded, and unanimously carried, it was resolved that the written waiver of notice and consent to holding of the meeting be made a part of the minutes of the meeting and placed in the corporation's minute book.

ARTICLES OF INCORPORATION

The chairperson announced that the articles of incorporation of the corporation had been filed with the California Secretary of State's office on ______________. The chairperson then presented to the meeting a certified copy of the articles showing such filing, and the secretary was instructed to insert this copy in the corporation's minute book.

BYLAWS

A proposed set of bylaws of the corporation was then presented to the meeting for adoption. The bylaws were considered and discussed and, upon motion duly made and seconded, it was unanimously

RESOLVED, that the bylaws presented to this meeting be and hereby are adopted as the bylaws of this corporation;

RESOLVED FURTHER, that the secretary of this corporation be and hereby is directed to execute a certificate of adoption of the bylaws, to insert the bylaws as so certified in the corporation's minute book, and to see that a copy of the bylaws, similarly certified, is kept at the corporation's principal executive office, as required by law.

ELECTION OF OFFICERS

The chairperson then announced that the next item of business was the election of officers. Upon motion, the following persons were unanimously elected to the following offices, at the annual salaries, if any as determined at the meeting, shown to the right of their names:

	Name	Salary
President:	______________________________	$ ____________
Vice President:	______________________________	$ ____________
Secretary:	______________________________	$ ____________
Treasurer: (Chief Financial Officer)	______________________________	$ ____________

Each officer who was present accepted his or her office. Thereafter, the president presided at the meeting as chairperson, and the secretary acted as secretary.

CORPORATE SEAL

The secretary presented to the meeting for adoption a proposed form of seal of the corporation. Upon motion duly made and seconded, it was

RESOLVED, that the form of the corporate seal presented to this meeting be and hereby is adopted as the corporate seal of this corporation, and the secretary of this corporation is directed to place an impression thereof in the space directly next to this resolution.

STOCK CERTIFICATE

The secretary then presented to the meeting for adoption a proposed form of stock certificate for the corporation. Upon motion duly made and seconded, it was

RESOLVED, that the form of stock certificate presented to this meeting be and hereby is adopted for use by this corporation, and the secretary of this corporation is directed to annex a copy thereof to the minutes of this meeting.

ACCOUNTING PERIOD

The chairperson informed the board that the next order of business was the selection of the accounting period of the corporation. After discussion and upon motion duly made and seconded, it was

RESOLVED, that the accounting period of this corporation shall end on ____________________________ ____________________________ of each year.

PRINCIPAL EXECUTIVE OFFICE

After discussion as to the exact location of the corporation's principal executive office, upon motion duly made and seconded, it was

RESOLVED, that the principal executive office of this corporation shall be located at ________________ ____.

BANK ACCOUNT

The chairperson recommended that the corporation open a bank account with ____________________ ____. Upon motion duly made and seconded, it was

RESOLVED, that the funds of this corporation shall be deposited with the bank and branch office indicated just above.

RESOLVED FURTHER, that the treasurer of this corporation is hereby authorized and directed to establish an account with said bank and to deposit the funds of this corporation therein.

RESOLVED FURTHER, that any officer, employee, or agent of this corporation is hereby authorized to endorse checks, drafts, or other evidences of indebtedness made payable to this corporation, but only for the purpose of deposit.

RESOLVED FURTHER, that all checks, drafts, and other instruments obligating this corporation to pay money shall be signed on behalf of this corporation by any ______________________ of the following:

____

____

____

RESOLVED FURTHER, that said bank is hereby authorized to honor and pay any and all checks and drafts of this corporation signed as provided herein.

RESOLVED FURTHER, that the authority hereby conferred shall remain in force until revoked by the board of directors of this corporation and until written notice of such revocation shall have been received by said bank.

RESOLVED FURTHER, that the secretary of this corporation be and is hereby authorized to certify as to the continuing authority of these resolutions, the persons authorized to sign on behalf of this corporation, and the adoption of said bank's standard form of resolution, provided that said form does not vary materially from the terms of the foregoing resolutions.

PAYMENT, DEDUCTION, AND AMORTIZATION OF ORGANIZATIONAL EXPENSES

The board next considered the question of paying the expenses incurred in the formation of this corporation. A motion was made, seconded, and unanimously approved, and it was

RESOLVED, that the president and the treasurer of this corporation are authorized and empowered to pay all reasonable and proper expenses incurred in connection with the organization of the corporation, including, among others, filing, licensing, and attorney's and accountant's fees, and to reimburse any persons making any such disbursements for the corporation, and it was

FURTHER RESOLVED, that the treasurer is authorized to elect to deduct and amortize the foregoing expenditures pursuant to, and as permitted by, Section 248 of the Internal Revenue Code of 1986, as amended.

FEDERAL S CORPORATION TAX TREATMENT

The board of directors next considered the advantages of electing to be taxed under the provisions of Subchapter S of the Internal Revenue Code of 1986, as amended. After discussion, upon motion duly made and seconded, it was unanimously

RESOLVED, that this corporation hereby elects to be treated as a Small Business Corporation for federal income tax purposes under Subchapter S of the Internal Revenue Code of 1986, as amended.

RESOLVED FURTHER, that the officers of this corporation take all actions necessary and proper to effectuate the foregoing resolution, including, among other things, obtaining the requisite consents from the shareholders of this corporation and executing and filing the appropriate forms with the Internal Revenue Service within the time limits specified by law.

QUALIFICATION OF STOCK AS SECTION 1244 STOCK

The board next considered the advisability of qualifying the stock of this corporation as Section 1244 Stock as defined in Section 1244 of the Internal Revenue Code of 1986, as amended, and of organizing and managing the corporation so that it is a Small Business Corporation as defined in that section. Upon motion duly made and seconded, it was unanimously

RESOLVED, that the proper officers of the corporation are, subject to the requirements and restrictions of federal, California, and any other applicable securities laws, authorized to sell and issue shares of stock in return for the receipt of an aggregate amount of money and other property, as a contribution to capital and as paid-in surplus, which does not exceed $1,000,000.

RESOLVED FURTHER, that the sale and issuance of shares shall be conducted in compliance with Section 1244 so that the corporation and its shareholders may obtain the benefits of that section.

RESOLVED FURTHER, that the proper officers of the corporation are directed to maintain such records as are necessary pursuant to Section 1244 so that any shareholder who experiences a loss on the transfer of shares of stock of the corporation may determine whether he or she qualifies for ordinary loss deduction treatment on his or her individual income tax return.

AUTHORIZATION OF ISSUANCE OF SHARES

The board of directors next took up the matter of the sale and issuance of stock to provide capital for the corporation. Upon motion duly made and seconded, it was unanimously

RESOLVED, that the corporation sell and issue the following number of its authorized common shares to the following persons, in the amounts and for the consideration set forth under their names below. The board also hereby determines that the fair value to the corporation of any consideration for such shares issued other than for money is as set forth below:

Name	Number of Shares	Consideration	Fair Value
______________________	______	______________	$ __________
______________________	______	______________	$ __________
______________________	______	______________	$ __________
______________________	______	______________	$ __________
______________________	______	______________	$ __________
______________________	______	______________	$ __________
______________________	______	______________	$ __________

RESOLVED FURTHER, that these shares shall be sold and issued by this corporation strictly in accordance with the terms of the exemption from qualification of these shares as provided for in Section 25102(f) of the California Corporations Code.

RESOLVED FURTHER, that the appropriate officers of this corporation are hereby authorized and directed to take such actions and execute such documents as they may deem necessary or appropriate to effectuate the sale and issuance of such shares for such consideration.

Since there was no further business to come before the meeting, upon motion duly made and seconded, the meeting was adjourned.

____
, Secretary

Shareholder Representation Letter

To: ____

____

____

I, ____ ,

an connection with my purchase of a/an ______________________________________

interest in ____________________ common shares of the corporation named above, hereby make the following representations:

A. I am a suitable purchaser of these shares under the California limited offering exemption because:

Category 1. Inside Shareholder:

☐ 1. I am a director, officer, or promoter of the corporation, or because I occupy a position with the corporation with duties and authority substantially similar to those of an executive officer of the corporation.

Category 2. Existing Relationship:

☐ 2. I have a preexisting personal and/or business relationship with the corporation, or one or more of its directors, officers, or controlling persons, consisting of personal or business contacts of a nature and duration which enables me to be aware of the character, business acumen, and general business and financial circumstances of the person (including the corporation) with whom such relationship exists.

Category 3. Sophisticated Shareholder:

☐ 3. I have the capacity to protect my own interests in connection with my purchase of the above shares by reason of my own business and/or financial experience.

Category 4. Major Shareholders:

(Check box 4(a) or box 4(b) below: check both if both apply)

☐ 4(a). Pursuant to Section 260.102.13(e) of Title 10 of the California Code of Regulations, I am purchasing $150,000 or more of the corporation's shares, and either (1) my investment (including mandatory assessments) does not exceed 10% of my net worth or joint net worth with my spouse, or (2) by reason of my own business and/or financial experience, or the business and/or financial experience of my professional adviser (who is unaffiliated with and not compensated

by the corporation or any of its affiliates or selling agents), I have, or my professional adviser has, the capacity to protect my own interests in connection with the purchase of these shares.

☐ 4(b). Pursuant to Section 260.102.13(g) of Title 10 of the California Code of Regulations, I am an "accredited investor" under Rule 501(a) of Regulation D adopted by the Securities and Exchange Commission under the Securities Act of 1933. This means either (1) my individual net worth, or joint net worth with my spouse, at the time of the purchase of these shares, exceeds $1,000,000; (2) my individual income is in excess of $200,000 in each of the two most recent years or my joint income with my spouse is in excess of $300,000 in each of those years, and I have a reasonable expectation of reaching the same income level in the current year; or (3) I qualify under one of the other accredited investor categories of Rule 501(a) of SEC Regulation D.

Category 5. Reliance on Professional Adviser:

☐ 5(a). I have the capacity to protect my own interests in connection with my purchase of the above shares by reason of the business and/or financial experience of ______________________

____,

whom I have engaged and hereby designate as my professional adviser in connection with my purchase of the above shares.

☐ 5(b). REPRESENTATION OF PROFESSIONAL ADVISER

____

____ hereby represents:

(1) I have been engaged as the professional adviser of ______________________

______________ and have provided him or her with investment advice in connection with the purchase of __________ common shares in ______________________.

(2) As a regular part of my business as a/an ______________________________,
I am customarily relied upon by others for investment recommendations or decisions and I am customarily compensated for such services, either specifically or by way of compensation for related professional services.

(3) I am unaffiliated with and am not compensated by the corporation or any affiliate or selling agent of the corporation, directly or indirectly. I do not have, nor will I have (a) a relationship of employment with the corporation, either as an employee, employer, independent contractor, or principal; (b) the beneficial ownership of securities of the corporation, its affiliates, or selling agents, in excess of 1% of its securities; or (c) a relationship with the corporation such that I control, am controlled by, or am under common control with the corporation, and, more specifically, a relationship by which I possess, directly or indirectly, the power to direct, or cause the direction, of the management, policies, or actions of the corporation.

Dated: ______________________ ______________________________

, Professional Adviser

Category 6. Relative of Another Suitable Shareholder:

☐ I am the spouse, relative, or relative of the spouse of another purchaser of shares and I have the same principal residence as this purchaser.

B. I represent that I am purchasing these shares for investment for my own account and not with a view to, or for, sale in connection with any distribution of the shares. I understand that these shares have not been qualified or registered under any state or federal securities law and that they may not be transferred or otherwise disposed of without such qualification or registration pursuant to such laws or an opinion of legal counsel satisfactory to the corporation that such qualification or registration is not required.

C. I have not received any advertisement or general solicitation with respect to the sale of the shares of the above-named corporation.

D. I represent that, before signing this document, I have been provided access to, or been given, all material facts relevant to the purchase of my shares, including all financial and written information about the corporation and the terms and conditions of the stock offering and that I have been given the opportunity to ask questions and receive answers concerning any additional terms and conditions of the stock offering or other information which I, or my professional adviser if I have designated one, felt necessary to protect my interests in connection with the stock purchase transaction.

Dated: ______________________ ______________________________

(Department of Corporations Use Only)
Fee paid $_______________

____

Receipt No. _______________

DEPARTMENT OF CORPORATIONS FILE NO., if any:

____

____

Insert File number(s) of Previous Filings Before the Department, if any.

Fee: $25.00 $35.00 $50.00 $150.00 $300.00
(Circle the appropriate amount of fee. See Corporations Code Section 25608(c))

COMMISSIONER OF CORPORATIONS
STATE OF CALIFORNIA

NOTICE OF TRANSACTION PURSUANT TO CORPORATIONS CODE SECTION 25102(f)
A. Check one: Transaction under ( ) Section 25102(f) ( ) Rule 260.103.

ELECTRONIC FILING REQUIREMENT AND HARDSHIP EXCEPTION:
This notice must be filed electronically through the Internet process made available by the Department of Corporations on www.corp.ca.gov, unless the issuer claims the hardship exception as described in Number 8 below.

1. Name of Issuer:

____

2. Address of Issuer:

____

Street City State Zip

Mailing Address:

____

Street City State Zip

3. Area Code and Telephone Number: _______________________________________

4. Issuer's state (or other jurisdiction) of incorporation or organization:

____

5. Title of class or classes of securities sold in transaction:

____

____

6. The value of the securities sold or proposed to be sold in the transaction, determined in accordance with Corporations Code Sec. 25608(g) in connection with the fee required upon filing this notice, is (fee based on amount shown in line (iii) under "Total Offering"):

	California	*Total Offering*
(a)(i) in money	$__________	$__________
(ii) in consideration other than money	$__________	$__________
(iii) total of (i) and (ii)	$__________	$__________

(b) ( ) Change in rights, preferences, privileges or restrictions of or on outstanding securities ($25.00 fee.) (See Rule 260.103.)

260.102.14(c) (8-05)

7. Type of filing under Securities Act of 1933, if applicable: ______________________________

____

8. **Hardship Exception for electronic filing.** An issuer may file this paper notice in person or by mail only if either of the following exceptions apply. The issuer shall check applicable box and include the reason(s) and description(s) for the hardship exception in the space provided.

☐ Computer equipment including hardware and software is unavailable to the issuer without unreasonable burden or expense. If this is the case, describe below both of the following; the reason(s) that the computer equipment including hardware and software is unavailable without unreasonable burden or expense, and the description(s) of the unreasonable burden or expense.

☐ The issuer cannot obtain and provide information (including credit card or other identifying information) requested on the Department's electronic notice or through the Internet filing process. If this is the case, describe below both of the following: the reason(s) that the issuer cannot obtain and provide the requested information on the electronic notice or through the Internet filing process without unreasonable burden or expense, and the description(s) of the unreasonable burden or expense to the issuer to make the electronic filing.

After checking the applicable hardship exception above, the issuer shall describe below the reason(s) and description(s) for that hardship exception. (If additional space is needed, attach a separate sheet to this notice.)

____

____

____

____

____

____

9. ( ) Check if issuer already has a consent to service of process on file with the Commissioner. (Instruction: Each issuer (other than a California Corporation) filing a notice under Section 25102(f) must file a consent to service of process (Form 260.165), unless it already has a consent to service on file with the Commissioner. If no consent to service of process is on file with the Commissioner, attach the consent to this notice.)

10. ______________________________

Authorized Signature on behalf of issuer

____

Print name and title of signatory

____

Date

Name, Address and Phone number of contact person:

____

____

____

Bill of Sale for Assets of a Business

This is an agreement between: ____

____ herein called "transferor(s)," and

____,

a California corporation, herein called "the corporation."

In return for the issuance of ______________ shares of stock of the corporation, transferor(s) hereby sell(s), assign(s), and transfer(s) to the corporation all right, title, and interest in the following property:

All the tangible assets listed on the inventory attached to this bill of sale and all stock in trade, goodwill, leasehold interests, trade names, and other intangible assets except ______________________

____

____

____

____

____

____

____

____

of ____, located at

____.

In return for the transfer of the above property to it, the corporation hereby agrees to assume, pay, and discharge all debts, duties, and obligations that appear on the date of this agreement on the books and owed on account of said business except ____________________________________

____

____

____

____

____

____

____

____

____.

The corporation agrees to indemnify and hold the transferor(s) of said business and their property free from any liability for any such debt, duty, or obligation and from any suits, actions, or legal proceedings brought to enforce or collect any such debt, duty, or obligation.

The transferor(s) hereby appoint(s) the corporation as representative to demand, receive, and collect for itself any and all debts and obligations now owing to said business. The transferor(s) further authorize(s) the corporation to do all things allowed by law to recover and collect any such debts and obligations and to use the transferor's(s') name(s) in such manner as it considers necessary for the collection and recovery of such debts and obligations, provided, however, without cost, expense, or damage to the transferor(s).

Dated: ____________________ ______________________________________

, Transferor

____

, Transferor

____

, Transferor

Dated: ____________________ ______________________________________

Name of Corporation

____

, President

____

, Treasurer

Receipt for Cash Payment

Receipt of $ ______________________ from ____

____ representing payment in full for

______________________________ shares of the stock of this corporation is hereby acknowledged.

Dated: ______________________________

Name of corporation: ____

By: ____

, Treasurer

Form for Cancellation of Indebtedness

The receipt of ______________________ shares of this corporation to ______________________

____

for the cancellation by ____

of a current loan outstanding to this corporation, dated ____________________, with a remaining unpaid principal amount and unpaid accrued interest, if any, totalling $________________, is hereby acknowledged.

Dated: ____________________ ____

Signature

Bill of Sale for Items of Property

In consideration of the issuance of ______________________ shares of stock in and by

____,

____

hereby sells, assigns, conveys, transfers, and delivers to the corporation all right, title, and interest in and to the following property:

Dated: ____________________ ______________________________________

, Transferor

Receipt for Services Rendered

In consideration of the performance of the following services actually rendered to, or labor done for,

____,

the provider of such services or labor done, hereby acknowledges the receipt of ________________

shares of stock in ____

______________________________ as payment in full for these services:

Dated: ________________ ______________________________

Signature

Share Register

Certificate Number	Number	Date of Issue			Shareholder's Name and Address	Amount Paid
		No.	Day	Year		

Share Register

Certificate Number	Number	Date of Issue			Shareholder's Name and Address	Amount Paid
		No.	Day	Year		

Transfer Ledger

Transfer Date			Transferee's Name and Address	Certificate Reissued		Certificate Surrendered	
No.	Day	Year		No.	No. of Shares	No.	No. of Shares

Transfer Ledger

Transfer Date			Transferee's Name and Address	Certificate Reissued		Certificate Surrendered	
No.	Day	Year		No.	No. of Shares	No.	No. of Shares

Certificate Number ____________

For ____________ Shares

Issued To:

____

____

Dated ____________ 20____

From Whom Transferred

____

Dates ____________ 20____

No. Original Shares	No. Original Certificate	No. of Shares Transferred

Received Certificate Number ____________

For ____________ Shares

Dated ____________ 20____

____

SIGNATURE

NUMBER ____________ SHARES ____________

INCORPORATED UNDER THE LAWS OF CALIFORNIA

Common Shares

____

THE SHARES REPRESENTED BY THIS CERTIFICATE HAVE NOT BEEN REGISTERED OR QUALIFIED UNDER ANY FEDERAL OR STATE SECURITIES LAW. THEY HAVE BEEN ACQUIRED FOR INVESTMENT PURPOSES AND NOT WITH A VIEW TOWARD RESALE AND MAY NOT BE OFFERED FOR SALE, SOLD, TRANSFERRED, OR PLEDGED WITHOUT REGISTRATION AND QUALIFICATION PURSUANT TO SUCH LAWS OR AN OPINION OF LEGAL COUNSEL SATISFACTORY TO THE CORPORATION THAT SUCH REGISTRATION AND QUALIFICATION IS NOT REQUIRED.

This Certifies that ____________ is the owner of ____________ fully paid and nonassessable Shares of the above Corporation transferable only on the books of the Corporation by the holder hereof in person or by duly authorized Attorney upon surrender of this Certificate properly endorsed.

In Witness Whereof, the Corporation has caused this Certificate to be signed by its duly authorized officers and to be sealed with the Seal of the Corporation.

Dated ____________

____________ *, President*

____________ *, Secretary*

For value received, the undersigned hereby sells, assigns, and transfers to

____

PRINT OR TYPE NAME AND ADDRESS OF ASSIGNEE

____

____ *Shares*

represented by the within Certificate, and does hereby irrevocably constitute and appoint ______________________________

Attorney to transfer the said shares on the books of the within-named Corporation with full power of substitution in the premises.

Dated: ______________________________

In presence of ______________________________

NOTICE: The signature to this assignment must correspond with the name as written upon the face of this certificate in every particular without alteration or enlargement, or any change whatever.

Certificate Number ____________

For ____________ Shares

Issued To:

____

____

Dated ____________ 20____

From Whom Transferred

____

Dates ____________ 20____

No. Original Shares	No. Original Certificate	No. of Shares Transferred

Received Certificate Number ____________

For ____________ Shares

Dated ____________ 20____

____

SIGNATURE

NUMBER ____________ SHARES ________

INCORPORATED UNDER THE LAWS OF CALIFORNIA

Common Shares

____

THE SHARES REPRESENTED BY THIS CERTIFICATE HAVE NOT BEEN REGISTERED OR QUALIFIED UNDER ANY FEDERAL OR STATE SECURITIES LAW. THEY HAVE BEEN ACQUIRED FOR INVESTMENT PURPOSES AND NOT WITH A VIEW TOWARD RESALE AND MAY NOT BE OFFERED FOR SALE, SOLD, TRANSFERRED, OR PLEDGED WITHOUT REGISTRATION AND QUALIFICATION PURSUANT TO SUCH LAWS OR AN OPINION OF LEGAL COUNSEL SATISFACTORY TO THE CORPORATION THAT SUCH REGISTRATION AND QUALIFICATION IS NOT REQUIRED.

This Certifies that ____________ is the owner of ____________ fully paid and nonassessable Shares of the above Corporation transferable only on the books of the Corporation by the holder hereof in person or by duly authorized Attorney upon surrender of this Certificate properly endorsed.

In Witness Whereof, the Corporation has caused this Certificate to be signed by its duly authorized officers and to be sealed with the Seal of the Corporation.

Dated ____________

____________ *, President*

____________ *, Secretary*

For value received, the undersigned hereby sells, assigns, and transfers to

____

PRINT OR TYPE NAME AND ADDRESS OF ASSIGNEE

____

____ *Shares*

represented by the within Certificate, and does hereby irrevocably constitute and appoint ____________________________________
Attorney to transfer the said shares on the books of the within-named Corporation with full power of substitution in the premises.

Dated: __________________________________

In presence of ____

NOTICE: The signature to this assignment must correspond with the name as written upon the face of this certificate in every particular without alteration or enlargement, or any change whatever.

Certificate Number ______________________

For ______________________ Shares

Issued To:

____

____

Dated ______________________ 20______

From Whom Transferred

____

Dates ______________________ 20______

No. Original Shares	No. Original Certificate	No. of Shares Transferred

Received Certificate Number ______________________

For ______________________ Shares

Dated ______________________ 20______

____

SIGNATURE

NUMBER ______________ SHARES ________

INCORPORATED UNDER THE LAWS OF CALIFORNIA

Common Shares

____

THE SHARES REPRESENTED BY THIS CERTIFICATE HAVE NOT BEEN REGISTERED OR QUALIFIED UNDER ANY FEDERAL OR STATE SECURITIES LAW. THEY HAVE BEEN ACQUIRED FOR INVESTMENT PURPOSES AND NOT WITH A VIEW TOWARD RESALE AND MAY NOT BE OFFERED FOR SALE, SOLD, TRANSFERRED, OR PLEDGED WITHOUT REGISTRATION AND QUALIFICATION PURSUANT TO SUCH LAWS OR AN OPINION OF LEGAL COUNSEL SATISFACTORY TO THE CORPORATION THAT SUCH REGISTRATION AND QUALIFICATION IS NOT REQUIRED.

This Certifies that ______________________ is the owner of ____________ fully paid and nonassessable Shares of the above Corporation transferable only on the books of the Corporation by the holder hereof in person or by duly authorized Attorney upon surrender of this Certificate properly endorsed.

In Witness Whereof, the Corporation has caused this Certificate to be signed by its duly authorized officers and to be sealed with the Seal of the Corporation.

Dated ______________________

______________________ *, President*

______________________ *, Secretary*

For value received, the undersigned hereby sells, assigns, and transfers to

____

PRINT OR TYPE NAME AND ADDRESS OF ASSIGNEE

____

____ *Shares*

represented by the within Certificate, and does hereby irrevocably constitute and appoint ______________________________

Attorney to transfer the said shares on the books of the within-named Corporation with full power of substitution in the premises.

Dated: ______________________________

In presence of ______________________________

NOTICE: The signature to this assignment must correspond with the name as written upon the face of this certificate in every particular without alteration or enlargement, or any change whatever.

Certificate Number ____________

For ____________ Shares

Issued To:

____

____

Dated ____________ 20______

From Whom Transferred

____

Dates ____________ 20______

No. Original Shares	No. Original Certificate	No. of Shares Transferred

Received Certificate Number ____________

For ____________ Shares

Dated ____________ 20______

____

SIGNATURE

NUMBER ____________ SHARES ______

INCORPORATED UNDER THE LAWS OF CALIFORNIA

Common Shares

____

THE SHARES REPRESENTED BY THIS CERTIFICATE HAVE NOT BEEN REGISTERED OR QUALIFIED UNDER ANY FEDERAL OR STATE SECURITIES LAW. THEY HAVE BEEN ACQUIRED FOR INVESTMENT PURPOSES AND NOT WITH A VIEW TOWARD RESALE AND MAY NOT BE OFFERED FOR SALE, SOLD, TRANSFERRED, OR PLEDGED WITHOUT REGISTRATION AND QUALIFICATION PURSUANT TO SUCH LAWS OR AN OPINION OF LEGAL COUNSEL SATISFACTORY TO THE CORPORATION THAT SUCH REGISTRATION AND QUALIFICATION IS NOT REQUIRED.

This Certifies that ____________ is the owner of ____________ fully paid and nonassessable Shares of the above Corporation transferable only on the books of the Corporation by the holder hereof in person or by duly authorized Attorney upon surrender of this Certificate properly endorsed.

In Witness Whereof, the Corporation has caused this Certificate to be signed by its duly authorized officers and to be sealed with the Seal of the Corporation.

Dated ____________

____________ *, President* ____________ *, Secretary*

For value received, the undersigned hereby sells, assigns, and transfers to

____

PRINT OR TYPE NAME AND ADDRESS OF ASSIGNEE

____

____ *Shares*

represented by the within Certificate, and does hereby irrevocably constitute and appoint ______________________________

Attorney to transfer the said shares on the books of the within-named Corporation with full power of substitution in the premises.

Dated: ______________________________

In presence of ______________________________

NOTICE: The signature to this assignment must correspond with the name as written upon the face of this certificate in every particular without alteration or enlargement, or any change whatever.

Certificate Number ______________________

For ______________________ Shares

Issued To:

____

____

Dated ______________________ 20______

From Whom Transferred

____

Dates ______________________ 20______

No. Original Shares	No. Original Certificate	No. of Shares Transferred

Received Certificate Number ______________________

For ______________________ Shares

Dated ______________________ 20______

____

SIGNATURE

NUMBER ______________ SHARES ________

INCORPORATED UNDER THE LAWS OF CALIFORNIA

Common Shares

____

THE SHARES REPRESENTED BY THIS CERTIFICATE HAVE NOT BEEN REGISTERED OR QUALIFIED UNDER ANY FEDERAL OR STATE SECURITIES LAW. THEY HAVE BEEN ACQUIRED FOR INVESTMENT PURPOSES AND NOT WITH A VIEW TOWARD RESALE AND MAY NOT BE OFFERED FOR SALE, SOLD, TRANSFERRED, OR PLEDGED WITHOUT REGISTRATION AND QUALIFICATION PURSUANT TO SUCH LAWS OR AN OPINION OF LEGAL COUNSEL SATISFACTORY TO THE CORPORATION THAT SUCH REGISTRATION AND QUALIFICATION IS NOT REQUIRED.

This Certifies that ______________________ is the owner of ____________ fully paid and nonassessable Shares of the above Corporation transferable only on the books of the Corporation by the holder hereof in person or by duly authorized Attorney upon surrender of this Certificate properly endorsed.

In Witness Whereof, the Corporation has caused this Certificate to be signed by its duly authorized officers and to be sealed with the Seal of the Corporation.

Dated ______________________

______________________ *, President*

______________________ *, Secretary*

For value received, the undersigned hereby sells, assigns, and transfers to

____

PRINT OR TYPE NAME AND ADDRESS OF ASSIGNEE

____

____ *Shares*

represented by the within Certificate, and does hereby irrevocably constitute and appoint ____
Attorney to transfer the said shares on the books of the within-named Corporation with full power of substitution in the premises.

Dated: ____________________________________

In presence of ____

NOTICE: The signature to this assignment must correspond with the name as written upon the face of this certificate in every particular without alteration or enlargement, or any change whatever.

Certificate Number ______________

For ______________ Shares

Issued To:

____

____

Dated ______________ 20______

From Whom Transferred

____

Dates ______________ 20______

No. Original Shares	No. Original Certificate	No. of Shares Transferred

Received Certificate Number ______________

For ______________ Shares

Dated ______________ 20______

____

SIGNATURE

NUMBER ______________ SHARES ______

INCORPORATED UNDER THE LAWS OF CALIFORNIA

Common Shares

____

THE SHARES REPRESENTED BY THIS CERTIFICATE HAVE NOT BEEN REGISTERED OR QUALIFIED UNDER ANY FEDERAL OR STATE SECURITIES LAW. THEY HAVE BEEN ACQUIRED FOR INVESTMENT PURPOSES AND NOT WITH A VIEW TOWARD RESALE AND MAY NOT BE OFFERED FOR SALE, SOLD, TRANSFERRED, OR PLEDGED WITHOUT REGISTRATION AND QUALIFICATION PURSUANT TO SUCH LAWS OR AN OPINION OF LEGAL COUNSEL SATISFACTORY TO THE CORPORATION THAT SUCH REGISTRATION AND QUALIFICATION IS NOT REQUIRED.

This Certifies that ______________ is the owner of ______________ fully paid and nonassessable Shares of the above Corporation transferable only on the books of the Corporation by the holder hereof in person or by duly authorized Attorney upon surrender of this Certificate properly endorsed.

In Witness Whereof, the Corporation has caused this Certificate to be signed by its duly authorized officers and to be sealed with the Seal of the Corporation.

Dated ______________

______________, *President*

______________, *Secretary*

For value received, the undersigned hereby sells, assigns, and transfers to

____

PRINT OR TYPE NAME AND ADDRESS OF ASSIGNEE

____

____ *Shares*

represented by the within Certificate, and does hereby irrevocably constitute and appoint ______________________________

Attorney to transfer the said shares on the books of the within-named Corporation with full power of substitution in the premises.

Dated: ______________________________

In presence of ______________________________

NOTICE: The signature to this assignment must correspond with the name as written upon the face of this certificate in every particular without alteration or enlargement, or any change whatever.

Certificate Number ____________________

For ____________________ Shares

Issued To:

____

____

Dated ____________________ 20______

From Whom Transferred

____

Dates ____________________ 20______

No. Original Shares	No. Original Certificate	No. of Shares Transferred

Received Certificate Number ____________________

For ____________________ Shares

Dated ____________________ 20______

____

SIGNATURE

NUMBER ____________ SHARES ________

INCORPORATED UNDER THE LAWS OF CALIFORNIA

Common Shares

____

THE SHARES REPRESENTED BY THIS CERTIFICATE HAVE NOT BEEN REGISTERED OR QUALIFIED UNDER ANY FEDERAL OR STATE SECURITIES LAW. THEY HAVE BEEN ACQUIRED FOR INVESTMENT PURPOSES AND NOT WITH A VIEW TOWARD RESALE AND MAY NOT BE OFFERED FOR SALE, SOLD, TRANSFERRED, OR PLEDGED WITHOUT REGISTRATION AND QUALIFICATION PURSUANT TO SUCH LAWS OR AN OPINION OF LEGAL COUNSEL SATISFACTORY TO THE CORPORATION THAT SUCH REGISTRATION AND QUALIFICATION IS NOT REQUIRED.

This Certifies that ____________________ *is the owner of* ____________ *fully paid and nonassessable Shares of the above Corporation transferable only on the books of the Corporation by the holder hereof in person or by duly authorized Attorney upon surrender of this Certificate properly endorsed.*

In Witness Whereof, the Corporation has caused this Certificate to be signed by its duly authorized officers and to be sealed with the Seal of the Corporation.

Dated ____________________

____________________ *, President*

____________________ *, Secretary*

For value received, the undersigned hereby sells, assigns, and transfers to

____

PRINT OR TYPE NAME AND ADDRESS OF ASSIGNEE

____

____ *Shares*

represented by the within Certificate, and does hereby irrevocably constitute and appoint ______________________________

Attorney to transfer the said shares on the books of the within-named Corporation with full power of substitution in the premises.

Dated: ______________________________

In presence of ______________________________

NOTICE: The signature to this assignment must correspond with the name as written upon the face of this certificate in every particular without alteration or enlargement, or any change whatever.

Certificate Number ____________

For ____________ Shares

Issued To:

____

____

Dated ____________ 20____

From Whom Transferred

____

Dates ____________ 20____

No. Original Shares	No. Original Certificate	No. of Shares Transferred

Received Certificate Number ____________

For ____________ Shares

Dated ____________ 20____

____

SIGNATURE

NUMBER ____________ SHARES ____________

INCORPORATED UNDER THE LAWS OF CALIFORNIA

Common Shares

____

THE SHARES REPRESENTED BY THIS CERTIFICATE HAVE NOT BEEN REGISTERED OR QUALIFIED UNDER ANY FEDERAL OR STATE SECURITIES LAW. THEY HAVE BEEN ACQUIRED FOR INVESTMENT PURPOSES AND NOT WITH A VIEW TOWARD RESALE AND MAY NOT BE OFFERED FOR SALE, SOLD, TRANSFERRED, OR PLEDGED WITHOUT REGISTRATION AND QUALIFICATION PURSUANT TO SUCH LAWS OR AN OPINION OF LEGAL COUNSEL SATISFACTORY TO THE CORPORATION THAT SUCH REGISTRATION AND QUALIFICATION IS NOT REQUIRED.

This Certifies that ____________ is the owner of ____________ fully paid and nonassessable Shares of the above Corporation transferable only on the books of the Corporation by the holder hereof in person or by duly authorized Attorney upon surrender of this Certificate properly endorsed.

In Witness Whereof, the Corporation has caused this Certificate to be signed by its duly authorized officers and to be sealed with the Seal of the Corporation.

Dated ____________

____________ *, President*

____________ *, Secretary*

For value received, the undersigned hereby sells, assigns, and transfers to

____

PRINT OR TYPE NAME AND ADDRESS OF ASSIGNEE

____

____ *Shares*

represented by the within Certificate, and does hereby irrevocably constitute and appoint ______________________________

Attorney to transfer the said shares on the books of the within-named Corporation with full power of substitution in the premises.

Dated: ______________________________

In presence of ______________________________

NOTICE: The signature to this assignment must correspond with the name as written upon the face of this certificate in every particular without alteration or enlargement, or any change whatever.

Certificate Number ____________

For ____________ Shares

Issued To:

____

____

Dated ____________ 20____

From Whom Transferred

____

Dates ____________ 20____

No. Original Shares	No. Original Certificate	No. of Shares Transferred

Received Certificate Number ____________

For ____________ Shares

Dated ____________ 20____

____

SIGNATURE

NUMBER ____________ SHARES ________

INCORPORATED UNDER THE LAWS OF CALIFORNIA

Common Shares

____

THE SHARES REPRESENTED BY THIS CERTIFICATE HAVE NOT BEEN REGISTERED OR QUALIFIED UNDER ANY FEDERAL OR STATE SECURITIES LAW. THEY HAVE BEEN ACQUIRED FOR INVESTMENT PURPOSES AND NOT WITH A VIEW TOWARD RESALE AND MAY NOT BE OFFERED FOR SALE, SOLD, TRANSFERRED, OR PLEDGED WITHOUT REGISTRATION AND QUALIFICATION PURSUANT TO SUCH LAWS OR AN OPINION OF LEGAL COUNSEL SATISFACTORY TO THE CORPORATION THAT SUCH REGISTRATION AND QUALIFICATION IS NOT REQUIRED.

This Certifies that ____________ is the owner of ____________ fully paid and nonassessable Shares of the above Corporation transferable only on the books of the Corporation by the holder hereof in person or by duly authorized Attorney upon surrender of this Certificate properly endorsed.

In Witness Whereof, the Corporation has caused this Certificate to be signed by its duly authorized officers and to be sealed with the Seal of the Corporation.

Dated ____________

____________ *, President*

____________ *, Secretary*

For value received, the undersigned hereby sells, assigns, and transfers to

____

PRINT OR TYPE NAME AND ADDRESS OF ASSIGNEE

____

____ *Shares*

represented by the within Certificate, and does hereby irrevocably constitute and appoint ________________________________
Attorney to transfer the said shares on the books of the within-named Corporation with full power of substitution in the premises.

Dated: ______________________________

In presence of ____

NOTICE: The signature to this assignment must correspond with the name as written upon the face of this certificate in every particular without alteration or enlargement, or any change whatever.

Certificate Number ______________

For ______________ Shares

Issued To:

____

____

Dated ______________ 20______

From Whom Transferred

____

Dates ______________ 20______

No. Original Shares	No. Original Certificate	No. of Shares Transferred

Received Certificate Number ______________

For ______________ Shares

Dated ______________ 20______

____

SIGNATURE

NUMBER ______________ SHARES ______

INCORPORATED UNDER THE LAWS OF CALIFORNIA

Common Shares

____

THE SHARES REPRESENTED BY THIS CERTIFICATE HAVE NOT BEEN REGISTERED OR QUALIFIED UNDER ANY FEDERAL OR STATE SECURITIES LAW. THEY HAVE BEEN ACQUIRED FOR INVESTMENT PURPOSES AND NOT WITH A VIEW TOWARD RESALE AND MAY NOT BE OFFERED FOR SALE, SOLD, TRANSFERRED, OR PLEDGED WITHOUT REGISTRATION AND QUALIFICATION PURSUANT TO SUCH LAWS OR AN OPINION OF LEGAL COUNSEL SATISFACTORY TO THE CORPORATION THAT SUCH REGISTRATION AND QUALIFICATION IS NOT REQUIRED.

This Certifies that ______________ is the owner of ______________ fully paid and nonassessable Shares of the above Corporation transferable only on the books of the Corporation by the holder hereof in person or by duly authorized Attorney upon surrender of this Certificate properly endorsed.

In Witness Whereof, the Corporation has caused this Certificate to be signed by its duly authorized officers and to be sealed with the Seal of the Corporation.

Dated ______________

______________ *, President*

______________ *, Secretary*

For value received, the undersigned hereby sells, assigns, and transfers to

____

PRINT OR TYPE NAME AND ADDRESS OF ASSIGNEE

____

____ *Shares*

represented by the within Certificate, and does hereby irrevocably constitute and appoint ____________________________________
Attorney to transfer the said shares on the books of the within-named Corporation with full power of substitution in the premises.

Dated: __________________________________

In presence of ____

NOTICE: The signature to this assignment must correspond with the name as written upon the face of this certificate in every particular without alteration or enlargement, or any change whatever.

Index

A

B

C

D

E

M

N

O

P

Q

R

S

NOLO

Keep Up to Date

Go to Nolo.com/newsletters to sign up for free newsletters and discounts on Nolo products.

- **Nolo's Special Offer.** A monthly newsletter with the biggest Nolo discounts around.
- **Landlord's Quarterly.** Deals and free tips for landlords and property managers.

2

Don't forget to check for updates. Find this book at Nolo.com and click "Legal Updates."

Let Us Hear From You

Register your Nolo product and give us your feedback at Nolo.com/customer-support/productregistration.

- Once you've registered, you qualify for technical support if you have any trouble with a download (though most folks don't).
- We'll send you a coupon for 15% off your next Nolo.com order!

CCOR15